The Human Cost of Food

The Human Cost of Food

Farmworkers' Lives, Labor, and Advocacy

Edited by Charles D. Thompson, Jr.,
and Melinda F. Wiggins

UNIVERSITY OF TEXAS PRESS
Austin

"Standing Idly By: 'Organized' Farmworkers in South Florida during the Depression and World War II" by Cindy Hahamovitch was reprinted in its entirety from *Southern Labor in Transition, 1940–1995* (Knoxville: University of Tennessee Press, 1997). Used with permission.

"*Bella Juventud*"/"Wonderful Youth" by Gloria Velásquez is reprinted with permission from the publisher of *I Used to Be a Superwoman* (Houston: Arte Público Press, University of Houston, 1997).

The lyrics of the song "El Otro México" written by Enrique Franco are reprinted with the permission of Los Tigres del Norte, San Jose, California.

Requests for permission to reproduce material from this work should be sent to Permissions, University of Texas Press, P.O. Box 7819, Austin, TX 78713-7819.

⊗ The paper used in this book meets the minimum requirements of ANSI/NISO Z39.48-1992 (R1997) (Permanence of Paper).

Every effort has been made to trace any copyright owners. The University of Texas Press will be happy to hear from any who proved impossible to contact.

Library of Congress Cataloging-in-Publication Data

The human cost of food : farmworkers' lives, labor, and advocacy / edited by Charles D. Thompson, Jr., and Melinda F. Wiggins.— 1st ed.
    p.   cm.
ISBN 0-292-78177-6 (cloth : alk. paper) — ISBN 0-292-78178-4 (pbk. : alk. paper)
1. Migrant agricultural laborers—Southern States. 2. Migrant agricultural laborers—Government policy—United States.   3. Social advocacy—Southern States.—I. Thompson, Charles Dillard. II. Wiggins, Melinda.
HD1527 .S85 H86   2002
331.5′44′0975—dc21   2002000859

*To all SAF interns, and in memory of 1994
SAF intern Oliver Townes (1942–1999).
As with too many of the farmworkers he
supported, Oliver's death was due, in part,
to having no health care insurance.*

Contents

List of Abbreviations

AEWR	Adverse Effect Wage Rate
AFDC	Aid to Families with Dependent Children
AHS	American Housing Survey
AWOC	Agricultural Workers Organizing Committee
AWPA	Migrant and Seasonal Agricultural Worker Protection Act
BWI	British West Indies
BWICLO	British West Indies Central Labour Organization
CAMP	College Assistance Migrant Program
CBO	Community-Based Organization
CDBG	Community Development Block Grant
CHIP	Children's Health Insurance Program
CIA	Central Intelligence Agency
CIW	Coalition of Immokalee Workers
CORE	Congress of Racial Equality
CSM	Chateau Ste. Michelle
CSO	Community Service Organization
DOL	Department of Labor
ECMHSP	East Coast Migrant Head Start Program
EPA	Environmental Protection Agency
ES	Employment Service
ESL	English as a Second Language
ETA	Department of Labor Employment and Training Administration
FBI	Federal Bureau of Investigation
FERA	Federal Emergency Relief Administration
FHSI	Farmworker Health and Safety Institute
FHSI	Farmworker Health Services, Inc.
FLCRA	Farm Labor Contractor Registration Act
FLOC	Farm Labor Organizing Committee

FLSA	Fair Labor Standards Act
FmHA	Farmer's Home Administration
FSA	Farm Security Administration
GAO	General Accounting Office
HAC	Housing Assistance Council
HEP	High School Equivalency Program
HHANES	Hispanic Health and Nutrition Examination Survey
HSED	High School Equivalency Diploma
HUD	Department of Housing and Urban Development
INS	Immigration and Naturalization Service
IRCA	Immigration Reform and Control Act
JTPA	Job Training Partnership Act
LEP	Limited English Proficient
LIHTC	Low-Income Housing Tax Credits
MCN	Migrant Clinicians Network
MEP	Migrant Education Program
MFLU	Mississippi Farm Labor Union
MSRTA	Migrant Student Record Transfer System
NAACP	National Association for the Advancement of Colored People
NAFTA	North America Free Trade Agreement
NASDME	National Association of State Directors of Migrant Education
NAWS	National Agricultural Workers Survey
NCALL	National Council on Agricultural Life and Labor Research, Inc.
NFWA	National Farm Workers Association
NIRA	National Industrial Recovery Act
NLRA	National Labor Relations Act
OBEMLA	Office of Bilingual Education and Minority Language Affairs
OSHA	Occupational Safety and Health Administration
PASS	Portable Assisted Study Sequence
PCUN	Pineros y Campesinos Unidos del Noroeste/Northwest Treeplanters and Farmworkers United
RHS	Rural Housing Service
SAF	Student Action with Farmworkers

SAW	Special Agricultural Worker Program
SNCC	Student Non-Violent Coordinating Committee
STFU	Southern Tenant Farmers Union
UFW	United Farm Workers
UFWOC	United Farm Workers Organizing Committee
UFWWS	United Farm Workers of Washington State
UNDRCA	National Union of Autonomous Regional Campesinos in Agriculture
USDA	United States Department of Agriculture
USES	United States Employment Service
WIA	Workforce Investment Act
WIC	Women and Infant Children
WICLO	West Indies Central Labour Organization

Preface

As a child I hated living the life of a farmworker. I was embarrassed by the fact that my family and I had to labor in the fields in order to make a living. I rarely let anyone know this fact about me. Those who did know were only my closest friends. When our family stopped working in the fields I felt relieved and promised myself to never mention this part of my life to anyone.

As the years passed and I entered college on a CAMP (College Assistance Migrant Program) scholarship, memories of my childhood came back to me. I felt I had to let others know what was going on in the fields and the conditions [under which] farmworkers work. In order to do this I wanted to see if things had changed since I was last in the fields. That is when I found out about Student Action with Farmworkers (SAF). SAF gave me the opportunity to go and experience the [conditions] of today's farmworkers. Sadly [not much] has changed . . . New laws have been passed but [are] poorly enforced.

[After] my internship at SAF I [became] president of the Mexican-Chicano Association [chapter] at Penn State. Our group [gave] various presentations on Mexican/Chicano culture and more importantly we . . . sponsor[ed] a Cesar Chavez presentation . . . about farmworker conditions. During my two summers

after SAF I went on to [become] a teacher's
aide at our migrant summer school program.
SAF breathed new life into me that I needed
so much.

LETTER FROM DAVID CRUZ, 1996 SAF INTERN

The impetus for this book began more than a quarter-century ago. In the spring of 1975, twelve Duke University students participated in a course on social problems in the rural South, with a special concentration on farmworkers. A central objective of the course was to go beyond academic study of agricultural laborers and to engage directly in the lives of farmworkers through advocacy and outreach in the Southeast, particularly in eastern North Carolina and southern Florida. Their firsthand experiences with farmworkers inspired the students to learn more about the realities of agricultural work, so they extended their work into the summer.

Through close work with established governmental agencies and community-based organizations, the students photographed and recorded documentary projects with farmworkers, conducted on-site health screenings and surveys with farmworkers about their needs, and participated in demonstrations and marches for better treatment for farmworkers. Gradually this work made a visible difference in farmworker lives, labor, and advocacy and a considerable difference in the lives of the participants themselves.

In 1990, fifteen years after the first students began the project, their successors collaborated with the Center for Documentary Studies to document the living conditions of farmworker children. In 1992 Student Action with Farmworkers was officially incorporated as a nonprofit organization under the leadership of former intern Carolyn Corrie. SAF has since expanded to five full-time staff members, thirty interns per year, and national campus outreach.

Since 1993, SAF's internship program known as Into the Fields has placed nearly three hundred college students in more than fifty affiliate farmworker agencies in the Carolinas. Each summer, approximately thirty interns from across the country participate in the Into the Fields program, both to learn more about farmworkers and to work alongside farmworkers as they struggle to improve their conditions. One of the most exciting components of the Into the Fields program is SAF's collaboration with College Assistance Migrant Programs (CAMP) to recruit student interns from farmworker families. Approximately one-half of the current interns are former farmworkers or children of farmworkers.

After completing internships with SAF, many students stay involved in farmworker advocacy. Former SAF interns carry their experience with them as they pursue careers as diverse as teaching, law, community organizing, primary health care, and ministry. For example, 1994 intern Juan Ramirez works for a nonprofit in California that teaches English as a Second Language and Citizenship classes to farmworkers, and 2000 intern Leo Peralez works at a legal aid organization in Texas. Eric Martin, who was an intern in the early nineties, recently wrote a novel called *Luck* about his summer internship experience.

Over the past twenty-five years, SAF has continued its early efforts of community-based experiential education and activism with farmworkers and young people and has expanded to many campuses throughout North Carolina, the Southeast, and the United States. SAF has accumulated expansive holdings of print and multimedia materials, thus becoming a national clearinghouse of information on farmworkers for students, advocates, and professors. Through these resources, workshops on various campuses, and numerous consultations, SAF staff members have provided the impetus for new programs, courses, and organizations linking universities with community groups supporting farmworkers.

SAF found significant gaps in academic materials related to farmworkers in the Southeast. Hence SAF commissioned this work to provide students, faculty, and advocates with an introduction to a broad spectrum of farmworker issues and advocacy. In this text we strive to emphasize action *with* farmworkers, rather than simply *for* farmworkers.

Acknowledgments

Just as SAF has relied on collective action in our advocacy work, we have relied on support to complete this book. We especially want to acknowledge Libby Manly, Laura Podolsky, Angeline Echeverría, Cynthia Wood, Theresa May, Rachel Chance, Allison Faust, Lynne Chapman, Sheila Payne, Tana Silva, Carolyn Christman, Jason Wagner, and Iris Tillman Hill for their editorial and production help. This work would not have been possible without the support of the staff, interns, and boards of directors of both Student Action with Farmworkers and the Center for Documentary Studies.

We also want to acknowledge the support from our families, particularly those members who taught us by example about agricultural work, including W. Clifford and Cloey Thompson, Ollie Lindsey, Hortense Wiggins Herring, Shirley Wiggins, and Thairdy Wiggins, Jr.

Special gratitude and love go to David Angelo DeVito, Hope J. Shand, and Marshall Thompson for their patience and support during this project.

The Human Cost of Food

**Sowing Seeds
for Change
symposium
address,
Gainesville,
Florida**

Lucas Benitez,
farmworker
and organizer

Sowing seeds for change. It seems so simple, so obvious, that we as farmworkers . . . are in desperate need of change: a decent wage, the right to organize without fear of retaliation, the right to earn overtime wages for overtime worked. These are simple ideas, simple changes made in most other industries over the first half of [the twentieth] century.

Introduction

Charles D. Thompson, Jr.

This book is about students, consumers, and advocates joining farmworkers in their struggle for justice. It introduces a variety of issues and challenges that farmworkers face in health care, housing, education, and other areas, including legal and political hurdles. And it provides guidance on what farmworker advocates can do about these challenges.

We have concentrated on the southeastern United States—the region that includes Alabama, Florida, Georgia, Kentucky, Louisiana, Mississippi, North Carolina, South Carolina, Tennessee, Virginia, and West Virginia—because this is where we live and work and a region that has received too little attention in farmworker literature, even though more than 40 percent of U.S. farmworkers labor in the region today. By some estimates, farmworkers in the Southeast may number nearly one and one-half million.

By targeting farmworkers in the Southeast, we locate them in a long history of mostly landless and underpaid people who have provided farm labor for centuries. The South, as the one-time bastion of slaveholding and later the Jim Crow laws of segregation, has long been known for its agricultural and labor inequities. This region, which once measured these differences in terms of black and white people, has become multiethnic as Latinos have moved into the Southeast in greater numbers.

According to the U.S. Census Bureau, the Latino population nearly doubled in the region during the 1990s alone. The Latino population of Georgia and North Carolina more than doubled from 1990 to 1998. No southeastern state is left unaffected by this Latino influx. Even West Virginia, with its relatively small agricultural economy, saw a 21 percent increase in its Latino population during the 1990s. Nationwide, the proportion of foreign-born farmworkers, most of them Mexican men under thirty-five years of age, rose from 10 percent in 1989 to 81 percent in 1998 (Mehta et al. 2000). Quite simply, inequities confronting agricultural workers, while centuries old, have new and often changing faces.

Along with explaining farmworker demographics and the particular challenges of various facets of farm work, we have endeavored to concentrate on farmworker lives. Challenging the notion that farmworkers are victims, we discuss farmworkers as human beings with rich cultural and religious lives well beyond their labor in the fields. Above all, we combine this information about farmworker lives and labor with a call to action among readers who want to do something to right the injustices farmworkers endure.

In this spirit, we invited contributors to this volume who are experts in their respective areas and who are advocates for farmworkers. Regardless of background or vocation, the authors share a common commitment to making a difference in the lives and working conditions of the people who provide the nation's food and to ending farmworker exploitation and injustices that persist today.

These injustices are not inherent to agriculture. Rather, they have become ingrained in its very structure because of discrimination and greed, due in large part to the control of agricultural power structures increasingly centered in large corporations. Injustices in farming in the United States continue because agribusiness resists changes to farm labor practices and labor laws that threaten its power. Yet this book came about because we know change is possible. We have witnessed reforms, although change historically has occurred incrementally and with a struggle.

Who Are Farmworkers?

Though definitions may vary somewhat, farmworkers are laborers who cultivate, harvest, and prepare a variety of seasonal crops for market or storage, including fruits and nuts (33 percent of workers), vegetables (28 percent), horticulture (14 percent), and field crops (16 percent). The remaining 9 percent of workers may work in several categories in a single year. There are three main groups of farmworkers, though we must be aware that any of these categories may shift and change for individual workers during a single season: migrant farmworkers, seasonal farmworkers, and guestworkers. Food animal workers, such as those who work in poultry and hog processing, often share similar migration histories and labor inequities and can be called farmworkers as well. Though obtaining exact numbers is next to impossible, the U.S. Department of Agriculture (USDA) estimates between two million and three million fieldworkers alone in the United States today.

Migrant farmworkers are individuals whose primary employment is seasonal agriculture, who live in temporary housing, and who travel more than seventy-five miles to obtain a job in U.S. agriculture. Fifty-six percent of all farmworkers must travel to secure employment. Nearly 40 percent of migrants are "shuttle migrants" who journey between two primary locations, such as Mexico and the Carolinas. Seventeen percent are "follow the crop" migrants who move year-round with crops. Migrant farmworkers in agriculture today number at least 900,000 adults along with 400,000 children (Mehta et al. 2000).

Seasonal farmworkers are those whose principal employment is agricultural labor but who reside permanently in a single community. Forty-four percent of farmworkers are seasonal workers, and most are U.S.-born (Mehta et al. 2000). These seasonal workers are often poor due to underemployment stemming from the seasonal nature of farm work.

Similar to the Bracero program created in the 1940s to replace the population drawn away from farms by World War II, the H-2 guestworker program, which came into widespread use by 1964, was created to allow foreign workers to enter the United States temporarily to perform agricultural labor. Though it represents a small percentage of the national farmworker population, the H-2A agricultural guestworker program is significant because it signals a trend in the agricultural industry toward importing immigrant labor instead of increasing wages and benefits for domestic workers. The H-2A program is noteworthy also because the numbers of H-2A workers have increased significantly since the late 1980s; more than ten thousand Mexican H-2A workers came to North Carolina alone in 2001, mostly to work the tobacco crop. Almost every year since the mid-1990s, the agricultural industry has lobbied Congress to ease the restrictions on bringing in more foreign workers. Guestworkers are isolated from other workers, have few means to settle into a community, and stay for too short a time to fight for any changes in the program or the agricultural system as a whole.

Flow of Migrant Farmworkers

Migrant farmworkers travel many streams through the United States, generally starting in California, Texas, and Florida in the early spring and heading northward as crops ripen in each succeeding area. In the Southeast, migrant workers who pick perishable food crops begin with citrus in the winter in Florida and move north to

FIGURE 0.1. *Farmworker loads tobacco, 1998. Photograph by Jesus Raya.*

harvest strawberries, tomatoes, beans, peppers, and other crops as they ripen in the Carolinas and spread out to other states in and outside the region. Travel patterns vary significantly. Some farmworkers remain in Florida for longer periods for melon and blueberry harvests, for example, while others begin their treks northward. Some workers end their northward movement in Maine or Michigan with early-fall blueberry harvests. After this northward trek, many return to Florida to begin the cycle again or head to other countries, often to Mexico, to continue the harvest season.

There are many diversions along their routes. Thousands of workers leave the stream to plant, prune, harvest, and pack Christmas trees in the North Carolina mountains for the entire year, for instance. Thousands more stop to work in tobacco and apples in the Carolinas, Tennessee, Kentucky, Virginia, Maryland, and Pennsylvania. In some areas, such as the apple- and peach-producing areas of Virginia, farmworkers have become semipermanent residents of particular areas, staying near the farms to do the pruning, spraying, planting, and packaging of crops in the off-season.

Because of the multiple routes and means by which farmworkers travel, it is best to avoid imagining single streams flowing south to north but rather more accurate to picture a series of small rivulets that diverge from several tributaries flowing in different directions, some of which never converge. We can picture part of the flow coming to a stop in particular places and other branches that deviate and reconnect at various points. Thus, farmworkers follow more than a few channels, with many streams running at once, overlapping, and even overflowing into non-farm work at times. Guestworkers form a separate stream as they are bused from their native countries directly to the states where they work for the duration of the season and are bused back at the end of their contracts.

Many farmworkers have been able to form mobile communities and remain in groups from the same town, sharing important information as they travel. However, even in small communities, it is common to find individuals who have come from many different places and who have arrived by different routes. Further divergences result when large extended families or groups that originate from a single community in Mexico or Central America split up for some of the year due to children's school schedules or special work arrangements such as temporary jobs in chicken plants. Often, unforeseen occurrences such as car troubles, investigations by the Immigration and Naturalization Service, illness, and death determine the paths of farmworkers on the move.

The flow of people within the network of agricultural labor streams is often transnational, with workers living part of the year outside the United States. In other cases, particularly among U.S. citizens, people may live during the winter in the U.S. community where they were born and enter a migrant stream for only the summer months. Sometimes a family may live in Mexico an entire year and travel as migrants for two years following. In short, idiosyncrasies occur in individual lives that complicate ascertaining the numbers and mapped routes of farmworkers.

In 1998 the National Agricultural Workers Survey (NAWS) revealed that 77 percent of all farmworkers were Mexican-born, up from 66 percent in 1995. Among the other groups, 9 percent in 1998 were U.S.-born Latino citizens, 1 percent were African American citizens, 7 percent were U.S.-born non-Latino whites, 1 percent were foreign-born Asian, and the remaining 5 percent were U.S.-born or non-U.S. citizens from the Caribbean and Latin American countries other than Mexico (Mehta et al. 2000).

Federal estimates show that at present approximately 22 percent of farmworkers are U.S. citizens, 24 percent are legal permanent residents who have "green cards," and 52 percent are undocumented. Though the Immigration Reform and Control Act (IRCA) of 1986 gave legal status to two and one-half million Mexican immigrants, including 33 percent of all estimated undocumented farmworkers, many of these farmworkers left farm work for other occupations. Thus, new immigrants from Mexico have replaced those who gained legal permanent residency status through IRCA.

Undocumented workers earn as little as half the wages earned by legal residents (Mehta et al. 2000). More than three-fifths of farmworkers are poor, and this number is increasing each year. Seventy-five percent of all farmworkers earn less than $10,000 annually. The purchasing power of farmworker wages has dropped more than 10 percent since 1989. The average wage of farmworkers in 1998 was $5.94 per hour, with 10 percent of farmworkers earning below minimum wage.

An estimated 84 percent of all farmworkers speak Spanish as their first language, while 12 percent are native English-speakers, and 4 percent speak other languages including indigenous languages from Latin America. The median highest schooling completed by farmworkers is sixth grade; 20 percent complete only three years, and 15 percent complete high school (Mehta et al. 2000).

Neat statistics, while extremely important, rarely tell the whole story. Some people, for example, shift from one category of worker to another in a single year, such as migrant workers who harvest crops in Florida but who then "settle out" to work in tobacco, Christmas trees, and meat processing because work is available for longer periods of time during the calendar year. Some agencies, such as the Migrant Education Program, count these semipermanent residents of rural communities as farmworkers. Counting animal processing workers along with fieldworkers is sometimes important for purposes related to housing, education, and other issues of advocacy, particularly when overall numbers of farmworkers are important.

Though definitions are crucial for federal and state services, ethically speaking there is little reason to differentiate between these groups of agricultural workers when thinking of U.S. society's obligations to them. In this regard, there is often little difference between a worker who lives year-round on a single dairy farm and one who works on a variety of vegetable farms in several states. Both types of workers often are underpaid, have no long-term job security, health care, or retirement plan, and subsist in the margins of society where services do not reach them. Indeed, some workers do more than one type of agricultural job in a single year and thus live in multiple worlds of farm labor, such as an individual who may pick tomatoes during the summer and process poultry during the winter. Therefore, some people are classified as migrant workers during the cropping season and meat packers during the rest of the year. These kinds of job changes are survival strategies that farmworkers employ, making any statistic on farmworkers a less than perfect gauge.

This much appears certain: the numbers of farmworkers in the Southeast will remain large and perhaps even grow in the future. While some agricultural representatives complain, usually falsely, of a shortage of laborers, some growers and producers increase their farm labor forces and allow their costly harvesting equipment to remain idle. This is because it is actually cheaper for some farmers to pay farmworker wages than to operate these machines. In other cases, though domestic farmworkers could be available for slightly higher wages, growers instead hire guestworkers.

Because of the diverse work patterns of agricultural workers, the multifarious flow of migrant workers toward a plethora of destinations, and the different means people use to put together livelihoods, we can only speak in generalities about farm labor demographics. Imprecision in counting farmworkers is a major problem of farmworker advocacy (Martin and Martin 1994, 7). Even so, farmworkers and advocates within particular communities can gather and share information with other advocates about the workers in their local areas and the patterns these workers follow in their routes to such locations. Farmworkers can provide essential knowledge to advocates about their peers.

Invisible Agriculture

Food corporations and grocery chains would rather not advertise how food is brought to consumers, thereby obscuring the presence of farmworkers in their communities and in the food system as a whole. In effect, farmworkers are invisible to many people. They remain a hidden underpinning of the system that brings us the food we enjoy without ever appearing on food labels.

Farmworker invisibility is not unlike the way U.S. consumers are sheltered from reminders of how animals are slaughtered and brought to market in packages or how pesticides are applied to the foods we eat. Labor injustices, as well as other types of unfairness within the food system, are disguised in such misleading slogans as "farm fresh" and "fresh picked" that say nothing about the real and often tragic stories of food production. Even organic foods can be harvested under abusive conditions for workers. "Natural" does not mean just, particularly as large food corporations enter the organic industry seeking their share of a lucrative market. Hence, the hands that feed us are often invisible hands, hands of people who work in the shadows of a multibillion-dollar industry without enjoying its rewards. Farmworkers receive too little pay and remain poor even as the U.S. food system outpaces in productivity and output every other system on the planet and as U.S. farms "feed the world."

Farmworker Treadmill

Farmworkers are the peasants in the modern U.S. agricultural system. They are unlike the stereotypical "hired hands" of agriculture who sometimes appear on television or in movies treated practically as family members or those who once commonly served as apprentices, "gaining skills and experience in hopes of one day becoming farmers themselves" (Schwartz 1945, quoted in Griffith and Kissam 1995, 13). Rather, they remain "unskilled" workers who rarely if ever graduate to landownership or to a position of respect in the agricultural community. Though farmworkers have farm knowledge and real skills that are invaluable on farms, skills learned from generations of ancestors in Mexico and elsewhere, these skills do not help them advance in the field of agriculture. Thus, farm work as it is organized today is a treadmill of labor that benefits agribusiness and entraps workers in cycles of travel and poverty.

Flight Rather Than Fight

It comes as no surprise that many farmworkers simply leave agricultural jobs whenever possible. This flight of farmworkers from fields creates what Phillip Martin and David Martin call the "endless quest" for workers, along with a seemingly endless search for reforms in farmworker policy (Martin and Martin 1994). Leaving farm work is often the only recourse for diminishing individual suffering, but it does nothing for the system as a whole. When a farmworker leaves the field permanently, another must replace him or her. As long as the labor supply seems endless, there is little incentive to change the agricultural system.

Philosophical Orientation

At its very foundation, the agricultural system in its present state depends on farmworkers. While the arrangement is not a holdover from the days of slavery, comparisons of present-day farm work to slavery are warranted. Contrary to myths regarding the lack of human involvement in a mechanized food system, farmworkers continue to work alongside machines. Though agriculture has experienced monumental changes over the past century—including the near-demise of the family farm—fruit, vegetable, tobacco, and nursery production, among other agricultural endeavors, have remained dependent upon farmworkers. Modern agriculture, even large-scale organic agriculture, could not function without migrant and seasonal laborers.

The presence of farmworkers in the United States is not just about "Mexicans" trying to get a piece of the American pie, as some might assume. Rather, while individuals from Latin America and elsewhere attempt to maximize their incomes by taking jobs as farmworkers in the United States, they also are pushed northward by failing local economies due in part to U.S. trade policies, such as structural adjustments and the North American Free Trade Agreement (NAFTA). In addition, farmworkers are pulled by forces of corporate agriculture that have, in turn, eliminated small-farming opportunities across the globe while maintaining large numbers of low-paying, seasonal, and often dangerous jobs in the United States or on U.S.-controlled farms in Mexico. Most of these jobs are exempt from labor standards common to other U.S. industries. People also come to the United States seeking opportunities for their children, to reunite with family already in the United States, and in search of the "American Dream." And labor recruiters hire young men in Mexico who fall prey to the dream's lure.

Because of poor conditions in farm work along with availability of job opportunities elsewhere for most U.S. citizens, few U.S. workers are now willing to do farm work. Though farmworkers may take pride in their work, as well they should, no one enjoys working for too little money and under inhumane conditions. Farmworkers want to work, that much is certain. But it is unfair to say that farmworkers are satisfied with what they make or with living in substandard housing while doing this work. Contrary to some popular myths, no ethnic groups are better suited to field work and poor living conditions than the rest of humanity. Rather, some people just have few, if any, other options.

Farm work could be valued and justly paid, but instead it is denigrated to standards unacceptable in any other U.S. economic sector. It comes as no surprise, then, that many people leave farm work as quickly as other opportunities arise and that many shifts in farmworker demographics have occurred over the past quarter-century. Most arresting is the fact that while 81 percent of full-time farm laborers in agriculture today were born outside the United States, more than one-fifth of them at any given time are in their first year of work (Mehta et al. 2000). New workers, most of them young men traveling without their families, continually enter agricultural fields and in many cases stay for as little time as they can while looking for other work. In addition, guestworkers have been brought into the country on a seasonal basis to fill ostensible labor gaps and thereby increase pressures on full-time farmworkers to accept poor conditions or be replaced.

Without question, the U.S. agricultural industry can afford to pay farmworkers a fair wage, provide them with benefits, and give them safer working conditions. Taking these steps could assure some permanency in the agricultural workforce while increasing food prices only minimally. Unfortunately, this is not the type of system that large-scale agribusiness wants because such improvements would certainly affect its profit margins.

Corporate profits notwithstanding, farmworkers should be entitled to fair labor practices and policies that will protect and reward them for their difficult work. This is true especially because farmworkers provide food for the richest consumers in the world, but also, of course, because they are human beings. At the very least, they are entitled to a living wage, adequate nutrition and health care, decent housing, education for their children, and the physical and ideological space for nurturing their cultural and religious identities.

As farmworkers and their advocates have long realized, turning ethical stances such as these into tangible realities is no easy task. The obstacles to justice in farm labor not only consist of the bureaucratic hurdles that make delivering services to people on the move difficult, though this is often the case. Farmworkers seldom receive any orientation to their rights in U.S. society and rarely receive even the basic services to which they are entitled. This lack of information stems from the fact that too many of the power-holders in agriculture and commerce— including agribusiness owners, their lobbyists, special interest groups such as the Farm Bureau, and the politicians who respond to them— actively oppose even the most basic improvements to labor practices. Because of knee-jerk reactions to farm labor improvements, even the provision of bathrooms and drinking water in the fields is still a fighting matter. Even though farmworkers are indispensable to U.S. farming, they often are deemed as parasites or victims within U.S. society rather than as contributors to its well-being. Many in the United States resent the presence of farmworkers in their communities, even as they depend directly upon farmworkers' labor for the very food they eat.

How can we allow these working and living conditions to continue even as the U.S. gross national product has expanded many times over and the stock prices of food companies have soared over the past quarter-century? Though hardly an excuse, too few consumers have learned what human misery and struggle their food represents, and sadly, consumer ignorance is bliss for food corporations. Therefore, while food is plentiful for consumers and profits for food corporations are high, farmworkers go without proper nutrition themselves. U.S. consumers on average spend less than 15 percent of their income for food and can applaud the freedom this gives them to spend more of their money otherwise.

Meanwhile, farmworkers have the lowest annual family incomes of any U.S. wage and salary workers, and 61 percent of them live in poverty. This is an increase from 1990, when 50 percent of farmworkers lived below the poverty line (Mehta et al. 2000). Despite their poverty and myths about farmworkers on welfare, few farmworkers actually use social services. Only 1 percent of farmworker households received Aid to Families with Dependent Children (AFDC), public housing, or general assistance in 1998, and only 10 percent of farmworkers received food stamps or Women, Infant, and Children (WIC) food vouchers. More than half of farmworkers are excluded altogether from participation in food stamp, Medicaid, and WIC programs due to federal legislation barring undocumented workers from receiving them (Mehta et al. 2000).

Problems of the Southeast

The southeastern region of the United States has long been a land of inequalities and contradictions. It was the region that in the nineteenth century depended most on slavery and that went to war to defend it. African American slaves made the southern plantation system successful, and slaveholders did not want to give them up to freedom.

Even after slavery was abolished, gaping disparities continued in the way African Americans and whites lived there. For more than a century after the Emancipation Proclamation, many former slaves and their descendants worked under egregious systems of debt-peonage and sharecropping supported by Jim Crow laws.

While plantation agriculture dominated the coastal plains and deltas of the Southeast, the Piedmont and other mountainous areas of the region were dotted with small farms. Many of these farms were subsistence homesteads owned by poor whites and later, especially with the coming of the U.S. Farm Security Administration in the 1930s, by African Americans. Even into the 1980s, the Southeast had more small farms than any other region of the United States (U.S. Department of Commerce 1996). As farming profits dwindled for these small farmers, many went to work in textile plants that relocated to the region in search of non-union and hardworking people.

Today, many small farms in the Southeast are rented to large-scale operations, and others have ceased to exist as farms. A combination of low commodities prices and a lack of access to credit and lucrative markets pushed most farmers of one hundred acres or less out of agriculture beginning immediately after World War II in 1945 and continuing to the present (Flowers 1990). Most small-scale farmers hire few farmworkers.

Meanwhile, plantation-style agriculture—large-scale farms owned by corporations or landed families—continues. Plantations in the region have shifted in nature to an industrial model of agriculture known as agribusiness, where factory-like conditions are commonplace. Often these agribusiness interests refer to themselves as growers, farm cooperatives, or farmers, thereby masking their resemblance to factory owners rather than to yeoman farmers. These growers often form associations that lobby for laws that favor them and often make it difficult for farmworkers to improve their livelihoods. It is important to differentiate between agribusiness interests and small-scale farmers and to rec-

ognize that small farmers are often victims of the same vertically integrated system that abuses farmworkers.

Large-scale agriculture hires the majority of farmworkers today. Indeed, according to agricultural activist Al Krebs, "a mere 139,560 of the
nation's 1.925 million farms have 77 percent of the total U.S. agricultural
labor expenses." As in earlier eras, the Southeast has many agribusiness
operations. Most of the large-scale poultry and hog operations, for example, have their strongest holds in the Southeast. Fruit and vegetable
production in the eastern United States is carried out mostly on huge
farms from Florida to southern Virginia. Overseers of slave days have
been replaced by labor contractors on these agribusiness operations, but
the relations between workers and crew bosses retain traces of those
heavy-handed arrangements of old.

The trend toward concentration of land ownership and loss of farms
is an international problem that plagues Latin American and Caribbean countries as well as the United States. Because of international
farm losses today, many destitute rural people and urban exiles one
generation removed from farms in Mexico, Guatemala, Haiti, or elsewhere come to the United States hoping to find more opportunities.
They often turn to agricultural labor in the United States because this
is the type of work they know and because low-paying jobs by U.S. standards have been relatively easy to come by, even when workers do not
possess documents that allow them to hold jobs officially in the United
States.

Thus, the region of the former slave states continues its tradition
of exploiting farmworkers. Of course, other regions are equally at fault
when it comes to farm labor rights, but the Southeast has a particular
legacy to live down. Even as African Americans gain access to limited
power in the region, Latino farmworkers feel the bite of an agribusiness
system reluctant to change its patterns of hiring and paying workers.
Too little has changed, and much remains to be done in this land where
freedom was relative and where too many still live with inequities from
the past.

Consumer Responsibility

In the United States in particular, we live in
a time when few people know where their food originates and how it
reaches their tables. Most people know less than ever about this most

basic link between the economy and the natural world even in an era of unprecedented access to information. Ours is a *selective* information age at best.

Farmworker abuses are not just a matter of ignorance, however. Mere education alone will not correct them. As agriculture is organized at present, low pay is part of the profit-bearing equation in the food system. Some attempts at reform through re-education meet with real and knowledgeable counter-education or resistance from powerful agricultural corporations. We know from experience that merely learning about and pointing out injustices imbedded in the food system is not enough to cause the system to change. Clearly some people want farmworkers to remain powerless in order to maximize profits. Resistance to change from the powerful in agriculture therefore requires working not just through education but also through policy changes and activism to attack the root causes of farmworker abuse. Improving farmworker conditions entails ideological and legal battles of advocacy and organizing.

"Don't bite the hand that feeds you," a common proverb, is an admonition so basic and self-preserving that even most animals understand it: survival requires that we refrain from harming those who provide our food. Yet while it is hard to disagree with this message, its salience can be lost in the complexity and enormity of the transnational food and agricultural system that provides our daily sustenance.

Since most U.S. citizens know almost no one whose hands directly touch their food in the field, the admonition that we refrain from biting the hands that feed us is lost in abstraction. Fewer U.S. citizens in each succeeding generation know someone who makes a living at farming or one who gets his or her hands dirty in the fields. Therefore many seem to think hands have little to do with their provisions. We just go to the grocery store to find our food. Even fresh fruits and vegetables are commonly wrapped in cellophane, giving the illusion that these are untouched by humans. As we buy and consume food, we fill our carts, pay the bill, and go home in good conscience, our exchange within the system being limited to aisles and checkout lines.

Even as consumers around the nation have become sensitized to manufacturing conditions and to unethical transnational business practices in poor nations, farmworkers have not benefited from this consumer awakening (see White 1998). It seems U.S. society is more sensitized to the ethics of international athletic shoe manufacturing than to domestic food production. However, given that more than four-fifths of farmworkers are now foreign-born and have few rewards for their labor,

FIGURE 0.2. *Loading trees for Texas. Creston, North Carolina. Photograph by Chris Johnson.*

it is no stretch of the imagination to claim that the United States has its own sweatshop system in its fields and food production.

To change these conditions, consumers and advocates must first educate themselves about these realities. This book is designed as a primer for such education about farmworker issues. After becoming aware of farmworker conditions, we must sow the seeds and reap the harvest of change as well.

What Future for Farmworkers?

As farms consolidate and managers control more production, we may see the numbers of workers in southeastern agriculture increase over the coming decades. This is particularly true as economic desperation increases for farmers everywhere and an international shortage of work for the poor—particularly in Latin America and the Caribbean—outpaces the willingness or ability of individual farm owners to invest in technology. Already this phenomenon is common in numerous agricultural industries. Because many agricultural producers seek to maximize their profits, it appears that menial jobs in the agricultural industries could rise in number even as those industries boast of their modern methods of production and as farms increase in size. Most family-owned farms are strapped financially, even while the food industry enjoys healthy profits.

Farm owners consider technology a good investment and an improvement to the economic bottom line only when they are forced to pay their employees more than it costs to buy and maintain the new equipment in question. To date, wages are so low for farmworkers that many companies avoid the extra costs of upgrading their equipment by hiring more workers who work for less than the cost of the investment. Thus, the persistence of an agricultural underclass—a seemingly inexhaustible international supply of workers who accept low wages—perpetuates U.S. agriculture's reliance on migrant and seasonal workers.

Of course, increased technology in agriculture probably will not improve the farm labor situation because new technologies often have meant increased mechanization and the related consolidation of farm ownership, worsening environmental pollution, and forcing farmworkers to work alongside dangerous machinery. Yet, perpetuating poverty by maintaining the present system is not the answer either.

Another option is, quite simply, to pay agricultural workers a just wage, ensure safer working conditions, and respect their occupation. This would require that agribusiness companies make less profit on the food dollar and/or that consumers pay slightly more for food in grocery stores. Already too much of the food dollar goes to chemicals, research and development, advertising, and packaging, while labor is a small percentage of what U.S. consumers pay in grocery bills. Yet, even if increasing wages and improving farmworker living conditions are reasonable requests, such changes will not come without a fight.

Organization of This Book

We focus on the following major areas of farmworker lives, labor, and advocacy: culture and identity, farm history in the Southeast, housing, health, education, organizing, legal issues, immigration, and guestworker programs. Accompanying each chapter are contributions from SAF interns and other advocates as well as from farmworkers themselves. Most photos in this book were taken by SAF interns.

In chapter 1, "Making Home: Culture, Ethnicity, and Religion among

Farmworkers in the Southeastern United States," Alejandra Okie Holt and Sister Evelyn Mattern describe the diversity of cultures and religions represented by U.S. farmworkers today. They demonstrate that farmworkers are far from a singular group and are diverse and active in shaping their own identities. An excerpt from Carmen Tomás's oral history interview titled "The Virgin of Guadalupe" precedes this chapter.

Chapter 2, "Layers of Loss: Migrants, Small Farmers, and Agribusiness" by Charles D. Thompson, Jr., links various layers of agricultural history in the South with that of Mexico. Part of Lucas Benitez's Sowing Seeds for Change symposium address precedes this chapter.

Chapter 3, "Standing Idly By: 'Organized' Farmworkers in South Florida during the Depression and World War II" by Cindy Hahamovitch, looks at agribusiness's reliance upon African American migrant workers in Florida in the first half of the twentieth century, providing an important link to the present situation with farm work. Preceding chapter 3 is the recollection "Life on Easy Street" by Rachel LaCour.

Chapter 4, "H-2A Guestworker Program: A Legacy of Importing Agricultural Labor" by Garry Geffert, unpacks the legal and ethical ramifications of guestworkers in the United States and shows why we should pay attention to this trend in agricultural work. Joe Bagby's transcript of Humberto Zapata Alvizo's song "*Rifaré mi suerte*/I'll Raffle My Luck" precedes this chapter.

Chapter 5, Greg Schell's "Farmworker Exceptionalism under the Law: How the Legal System Contributes to Farmworker Poverty and Powerlessness," details the specific U.S. legislation that has made farmworker abuse so prevalent. He makes the case that farmworkers should be given the same rights as other U.S. workers. This chapter follows an excerpt of Roman Rodriguez's testimony at the Commission on Agricultural Workers hearing.

Chapter 6, "Bitter Harvest: Housing Conditions of Migrant and Seasonal Farmworkers" by Christopher Holden, describes the particular conditions farmworkers on the East Coast endure on a daily basis and describes what advocates can do to secure better housing conditions. Preceding the chapter, "Wells Farms" by Rachel Avery and "The Conditions at the Camp Are Not Great" by Kris Adams show us further truths about housing and living conditions of migrant workers.

Chapter 7, "The Struggle for Health in Times of Plenty" by Colin Austin, describes the special challenges of health care, in terms of its availability and use by farmworkers. The anonymous poem "The History We Wrote This Summer" precedes this chapter.

Chapter 8, "Understanding the Challenges and Potential of Migrant Students" by Ramiro Arceo, Joy Kusserow, and Al Wright, addresses the barriers that migrant students face in schools as well as examples of programs addressing these problems. This chapter is accompanied by an excerpt from the short story "That Summer" written by Marcella Hurtado Gomez and the poem "Wonderful Youth/*Bella Juventud*" by Gloria Velásquez.

Chapter 9, "From Slavery to Cesar Chavez and Beyond: Farmworker Organizing in the United States" by Paul Ortiz, is a study of the history of labor organizing among farmworkers, particularly since World War II. An excerpt from Melinda Steele's interview with Sheila Payne, "I Don't Think People Give Up," accompanies this chapter.

The conclusion, "An Invocation to Act" by Melinda F. Wiggins, tells the story of farmworker advocates with whom she has worked and her own story of how she connects with farmworkers. She also recommends actions for advocates to take to support farmworkers. A short excerpt from Lucas Benitez's symposium address precedes this final chapter.

Appendix I, "Developing a Syllabus on Farmworker Advocacy," is a guide to course development. Appendix II is a list of organizations and agencies that work with farmworkers. Appendix III lists resources helpful for further reading and study. These appendixes, and indeed the entire work, are intended as tools of advocacy, though none of this information is to be considered exhaustive. Local agencies and organizations can add many resources to those listed and discussed here, especially information about their own geographical areas and fields of interest. Above all, we encourage readers to join us in seeking to change farmworker lives and labor conditions.

The Virgin of Guadalupe

Carmen Tomás, farmworker from Cherán, Michoacán, Mexico

Interview by Wendy Daniels Ibarra, 1999 SAF intern

We celebrate the appearance of the Virgin of Guadalupe on December 12 of each year. We have fireworks, Mass with wine and bread, and manzanitas. We have a lot of food in the house like tamales and sweets. I don't remember all of the foods, but I do remember the celebration. The celebration starts with the images of the Virgin in the procession in the streets and continues to the church.

I believe in the saints because whenever I have true faith, they give me miracles. The Virgin has helped me a lot.

I have gone to many churches including the Baptist church. One time the preacher came to my house and asked me why did I have the pictures I have of the Virgin. I told him that I have believed in the Virgin for many years and I will continue to believe in her. He told me that I should throw it in the trash, but I told him NO. My husband was very upset at what he said to me. Up until this day, I have never returned to that church because of what he said to me.

CHAPTER I

Making Home

Culture, Ethnicity, and Religion among Farmworkers in the Southeastern United States

Alejandra Okie Holt and
Sister Evelyn Mattern

Today, farmworkers are not the homogeneous group portrayed in Steinbeck's *Grapes of Wrath* in the 1930s. In this chapter we explore how farmworkers change and are changed by the cultures they encounter and the complex ethnic relationships of the United States. Until the 1960s most farmworkers along the East Coast were African Americans. Now Latinos make up the large majority of farmworker populations in most areas of the country. We focus on Latinos in general—and Mexicans specifically—because in total they make up almost 90 percent of the farmworker population. We also discuss other important groups of workers such as Haitians and seasonal African American farmworkers. We highlight aspects of farmworkers' lives that reflect their cultures and histories, as well as the processes of acculturation experienced by immigrant farmworker families.

Characteristics of Farmworkers

While 88 percent of farmworkers today are U.S.- or foreign-born Latinos, other ethnic and racial groups contribute to the farmworker mosaic. The National Agricultural Workers Survey (NAWS) is a study of farmworkers, field packers, and supervisors in crop agriculture that excludes H-2A guestworkers and unemployed agricultural workers. The most recent NAWS study includes a total of 4,199 interviews that were conducted from October 1996 to September 1998. It finds that 1 percent of total farmworkers are foreign-born Asian, 7 percent are non-Latino U.S.-born whites, 1 percent are U.S.-born African Americans, 1 percent are born in other foreign countries, and 2 percent are other U.S.-born. The survey finds that the primary language of 84 percent of farmworkers is Spanish, while 12 percent are native English-speakers, and 4 percent speak other native languages such as Tagalog,

Ilocano, Creole, and Mixtec. Most of the white farmworkers surveyed by the NAWS live in the Midwest and Great Plains and perform post-harvest and supervisory jobs. The NAWS survey reveals that 20 percent of farmworkers are women (Mehta et al. 2000).

NAWS groups seasonal and migrant farmworkers together, so the findings do not show the higher percentage of African Americans who labor as seasonal workers in the South. The survey presents only a macro-level picture of the composition of agricultural workers and does not reflect regional variations where certain racial or ethnic groups are present in large numbers. Unfortunately, extensive demographic studies on the ethnic and racial composition of the agricultural labor force by geographic region are not available.

African American Farmworkers

Up to the 1960s many southern African Americans left their home bases each spring and settled in northern agricultural communities for three to five months during the summer harvest season. African Americans migrated from Florida as groups of single men, while others traveled in family groups. Migrant workers would supplement the labor of local African American men and women, local high school students, and farm wives during harvest time. Some African American crews from Florida and Texas migrated to Georgia and the Carolinas and then to Delaware and New York through the 1980s (Griffith and Kissam 1995, 77). However, as early as the 1970s, many African Americans found work opportunities that allowed them to stop migrating and continue working as seasonal farmworkers in their own communities, while others moved to cities to find non-agricultural employment. Most African American farmworkers today work on southern farms on a seasonal basis. For instance, African American seasonal farmworkers continue to harvest sweet potatoes in eastern North Carolina in October after many Latino workers have migrated to other states for work.

Other African American workers continue to work in food production. For example, African American women have worked for generations processing Atlantic blue crabs along the Pamlico and Pungo Rivers in Beaufort County in eastern North Carolina. Many women who are now in their seventies and eighties started picking crabs when they were young children to help their families. They follow a tradition passed down by their mothers or grandmothers. In the past, crab picking was one of the few jobs available for women in this area of the state, other than harvesting vegetables or corn on nearby farms. For some time, white women weighed and packed crabs, while African American women did the picking. Now, few white women or men work at the crab houses. But young African American women are not following their mothers' and grandmothers' footsteps. This has resulted in an increase of temporary guestworkers from Mexico hired by some crab houses in North Carolina.

Most of the women who work in the crab houses of coastal North Carolina live near each other, but the beginning of the crab season and the opening of crab houses give them opportunities to exchange information about their families and friends. "There are updates on grandchildren, their appetites and illnesses, milestones, and setbacks" (Ruley 1994, 12). Many of the women have never traveled outside their coastal counties and have a deep connection to their communities and the natural resources around them, even living off fish from the nearby creeks. In addition to being vital to the region's economic survival, crab picking is a cultural tradition among African American women in eastern North Carolina. As the women age and their daughters and granddaughters find work elsewhere, this traditional labor force of the crab industry is diminishing.

West Indian, Haitian, and Asian Farmworkers

In 1943 agricultural producers began bringing British West Indians on a seasonal basis to harvest agricultural products in the eastern and midwestern United States. The British West Indies (BWI) Temporary Alien Labor Program was designed to supplement the larger Bracero contract labor program of 1942–1964 created by the U.S. government and Mexico. West Indians were employed in almost every region of the United States up to the late 1960s. After that, they worked primarily in the Northeast apple harvests and South Florida sugarcane harvests through the H-2 temporary guestworker program. During the 1980s, Jamaicans provided nearly 100 percent of the foreign labor in the apple harvest and 80 percent of the foreign labor utilized in the sugarcane harvest, with the remaining 20 percent coming from Barbados, Dominica, St. Lucia, and St. Vincent (Griffith 1986, 876). During this time, the seasonal recruitment of cane harvesters from the Caribbean region constituted the largest foreign labor program of its kind in the United States (Wood and McCoy 1985, 252). Even though the workers were provided with housing and employment, a Department of Labor investigation found that 65 percent of the workers paid on a piece-rate basis earned less than the equivalent of the federally mandated minimum hourly wage (DeWind, Seidl, and Shenk 1979, 393). The British West Indies program for sugar ended in 1992, due in part to labor abuses by employers and the mechanization of sugar production. British West Indian workers continue to be employed in the apple harvests in northeastern states, particularly the Hudson Valley of New York, and in tobacco. A small number of Jamaicans also currently work in citrus and watermelon harvests in Florida. However, Latino H-2 guestworkers, most of whom are Mexican, increasingly are being hired to replace West Indian workers in these same industries.

During the 1970s and 1980s, growers in the Southeast thought the influx of Haitians would alleviate their perceived agricultural labor supply shortage. However, Haitian crews from southern Florida rapidly began to find other employment, such as in poultry processing plants in the Delmarva peninsula or in construction, restaurants, and hotels in southwestern Florida. Some Haitian crews continue to migrate between Florida and Delaware, and settled-out Haitian workers continue to provide seasonal labor in those areas (Griffith and Kissam 1995, 78). A small number of Haitians still work in the citrus and watermelon harvests in Florida and the watermelon and tomato harvests in other states.

Southeast Asians worked as farmworkers in the post–World War II period in areas east of the Mississippi River. Although Asians no longer work in agriculture in large numbers, it is important to remember that Filipino farmworkers in California were instrumental in the creation of the Agricultural Workers Organizing Committee (AWOC) and the movement that led to the development of the United Farm Workers (UFW) union.

Laotians still form a significant proportion of the agricultural labor force in Florida and California (Mines, Boccalandro, and Gabbard 1992, 45–46). Small groups of Hmong, an ethnic minority from Laos, also have settled in Southeastern states. The Hmong fled Laos after facing persecution stemming from their participation in the "Secret War" as allies with the U.S. Central Intelligence Agency (CIA) during the Viet-

nam War. Some have found work in agricultural industries such as turkey and chicken processing plants in Minnesota and North Carolina,
while others have settled in Georgia and Wisconsin (Duchon 1997, 71).

The seafood processing industry in Bayou La Batre, Alabama, currently relies heavily on Indochinese workers. Before the influx in the
1970s of Vietnamese, Cambodian, and Laotian immigrants to this area
twenty-five miles southwest of Mobile, African Americans were employed in shrimp processing, while whites worked in crab processing.
In 1988 Asians constituted approximately 70 percent of crab processing
workers in this area, while 15 percent were white and 15 percent were
African Americans (Moberg and Thomas 1993, 87).

Since the 1980s, Cambodian refugees have worked as seasonal farmworkers in rural areas of New Jersey near Philadelphia. Prior to the Cambodian influx into this labor market, African Americans from inner-city
Philadelphia worked as day laborers in rural New Jersey. A recent study
determined that many African Americans left farm work before Cambodian refugees arrived, discrediting claims that the former were replaced
by Cambodians (Pfeffer 1994, 9).

Latinos

The NAWS found that 77 percent of the total
farmworker population in 1998 was born in Mexico, 2 percent was composed of other Latin American-born workers, and 9 percent was composed of U.S.-born Latinos (Mehta et al. 2000).

Latinos in the United States represent many cultures, nationalities,
and racial, ethnic, and religious backgrounds. Their main commonality
is the Spanish language. There are numerous ethnic labels used to describe persons of Latin American origin in the United States. Neither
scholars nor the population at large agree on a single term that is most
appropriate or correct. "Hispanic" is an English-language term that
means "pertaining to ancient Spain." The U.S. Census Bureau and other
government agencies adopted the term to identify all Spanish-speaking
and/or Spanish-origin populations in the United States. Many individuals consider this term an imposed identifier that denotes an artificial
political and national cohesiveness of the defined group. It also excludes
indigenous populations whose first language is not Spanish. Chicanas
and Chicanos refer respectively to women and men of Mexican descent
who were born or raised in the United States. Chicanos is also a broad

term that includes both males and females who claim Mexican heritage. The term was popularized in the late 1960s during the Chicano movement to denote a political and activist orientation that affirmed the need to struggle against the historical oppression of people of Mexican descent in the United States (de la Torre 1993, *xiii*). *La raza* is a term that was also adopted during the same period to convey the shared sense of unity, struggle, and cultural experience among Mexicans, Central Americans, and South Americans. *Latino* (or the feminine *Latina*) is a broadly encompassing term used to identify people of Latin American origin. It recognizes the cultural and linguistic commonality embraced by virtually all groups in Latin America, and it reflects the use of gender in the Spanish language. However, many individuals still choose to identify themselves by their nationality or ethnicity, as in being Mexican or Kanjobal.

Latinos constitute more than 10 percent of the U.S. population and soon will be the largest minority group (Finnegan 1996, 53). As defined by the Census Bureau, they include people from Mexico, Central America, South America, the Spanish-speaking Caribbean countries, Spain, and persons who identify themselves as Hispanic, Chicano, and so forth who are living in the United States.

Large numbers of Mexicans migrated to the United States during the Mexican Revolution of 1910–1920. By the mid-1920s, Mexican migrants who came to the United States through the Bracero program replaced farmworkers of Chinese, Japanese, Hindi, and other ethnic backgrounds in the West and Southwest who had been recruited at the beginning of the twentieth century. However, the largest wave of Mexican immigration began in the 1970s due to population growth, the devaluation of the Mexican peso, and the ensuing economic crisis, as well as land reform shortcomings in rural areas. In the 1980s, Mexican workers migrated to the United States in numbers greater than at any time since the 1920s (Lacy 1988, 110). At the same time, Guatemalans and other refugees from Central America began to work in the fields, in some instances replacing Mexicans. The Immigration Reform and Control Act (IRCA) of 1986 gave amnesty to millions of undocumented residents and inadvertently created a pull factor whereby individuals saw an opportunity to immigrate to the United States. Thus an act intended to solve perceived U.S. "immigration problems" created a larger population of undocumented workers entering the country.

In the U.S. South, most Latino farmworkers who have immigrated in the past twenty years face economic subjugation and prejudice along with a lower-caste status. Latinos have endured intense discrimination for an extended period of time. As part of the Treaty of Guadalupe Hidalgo of 1848, the Mexican government ceded California, Texas, Nevada, and Utah, and parts of Arizona, Colorado, Kansas, New Mexico, Oklahoma, and Wyoming to the United States for $15 million. This constituted more than half of the Mexican territory at the time (Shorris 1992, 39). When the treaty was signed, approximately seventy-five thousand Spanish speakers were living in the southwestern region of the United States. After the Mexican American War and the signing of the Treaty of Guadalupe Hidalgo, Mexicans who came across the border arrived as strangers in what had been their own land.

Until the civil rights movement, Latinos faced formal racial segregation and denial of the right to vote. A new consciousness and leadership is not yet apparent among most of the current farmworker population in the South due to constant migration, ethnic differences, and socioeconomic status. Earl Shorris speculates that if present trends continue, fifty years from now there will be a "Latino underclass of enormous size"—of perhaps twenty-five or thirty million people (quoted in Finnegan 1996, 62).

Latino Farmworkers

The availability of foreign labor, low wages, shifts in occupational opportunities, and migration to urban areas have led to a decrease in the percentage of African Americans working in agriculture, while the percentage of foreign-born farmworkers has increased. Since 1987 more Latinos than African Americans have worked on rural farms (Rochín 1995, 290). An ethnic shift has occurred as East Coast farmers increasingly employ foreign-born farmworkers to carry out harvest, pre-harvest, semiskilled, post-harvest, and supervisory jobs because of their availability and willingness to accept the prevailing low wages. The "Latinization" of U.S. farm labor occurs as the demand for heavy-hand labor on large, isolated farms increases and the influx of large numbers of Latin American immigrants continues (Mines, Boccalandro, and Gabbard 1992, 45). This Latinization continues to take place in the Midwest, Northeast, and Southeast. One example is the mushroom industry of Chester County, Pennsylvania. From the 1950s to the mid-1980s, the production tasks in this industry began shifting from Puerto Ricans and other U.S. citizens to Mexicans. An influx of Latinos

FIGURE 1.1. Ranchero *band playing at the Farmworker Festival in Newton Grove, North Carolina, 1996. Photograph by Chris Johnson.*

is also occurring in the peach-producing regions of Georgia and South Carolina. Mexicans replaced African American workers in the Georgia peach industry in 1983–1984 because foreign workers were available to work due to a freeze in Florida during that time. Mexican workers remained in the area and continue to be an important source of labor. This same process took place in South Carolina in the late 1980s. While Mexicans perform pre-harvest and harvest tasks, local African Americans and older white women perform post-harvest and semi-skilled work. Latinization is also taking place in the Piedmont region of North Carolina and Virginia, where Mexican workers replaced African American harvesters of flue-cured tobacco in the early 1980s. African Americans continue to transplant and hang leaves in barns in some tobacco-growing areas.

Presently, most Latino farmworkers in the United States are Mexican, but other nationalities also are represented. Starting in the 1980s, hundreds of thousands of indigenous Maya left Guatemala fleeing civil strife and terror. Many refugees went to Mexico, but the lack of assistance there drove some to the U.S. Maya communities that developed in Houston and Los Angeles and later in some areas of Florida such as Indiantown. Some Maya farmworkers living in Florida migrate annually to Alabama, Michigan, and New York to find employment. Others have found work in poultry plants and settled in communities such as Morganton in western North Carolina. The increase in the numbers of Maya farmworkers exemplifies a trend, as these and other indigenous groups from Latin America whose first language is not Spanish—such as the Mixtec and Zapotec of southern Mexico—are taking jobs as farmworkers in the United States.

Puerto Ricans were a prominent group of agricultural workers in the post–World War II period in areas east of the Mississippi River. Many Puerto Rican farmworkers labored in New York and New Jersey in the 1970s. In some areas in the early 1990s, Puerto Ricans still held agricultural jobs that were more desirable than those held by Mexican workers (Mines n.d.). In the 1990s Puerto Ricans were heavily recruited as farmworkers in the Southeast. Many of the Puerto Ricans who worked in North Carolina broke their contracts due to poor working conditions and because they could find more lucrative employment in other industries. This shows that even though Latinos continue to take jobs as farmworkers in large numbers, some Latino groups such as Puerto Ricans can readily move into other fields of employment.

Cultivating Their Own Cultures in New Communities

Today, immigrant farmworkers continue to maintain many institutions and norms of their native cultures even while living in isolated rural communities. By interacting with those in their new communities who share their customs and by communicating with family members or friends from home over the years, farmworkers continue to practice their own traditions. Immigrant farmworkers often assert and articulate their own cultures in a new land. In some instances this requires reinventing old cultural patterns. While the following examples mainly focus on Mexican farmworkers because of their significant presence as a cultural group, the limitations of this example are not meant to understate the rich diversity found among the farmworker population.

In Immokalee, Florida, some workers have been able to exercise political responsibilities that were part of cultural life in their home countries. Activities such as taking *cargos* (personal and political commitments or duties) in an organization, forming and running cooperatives, and organizing a hunger strike as a form of protest reflect a cultural and political expression ingrained in tradition (Asbed 1999). Spanish-language soccer leagues are common in many rural areas of the Southeast, with teams named after the players' home villages in Michoacán, Guanajuato, or Oaxaca. Some farmworkers who do not trust or cannot afford doctors visit *curanderos* or traditional healers who set up shop in U.S. towns. Healers provide traditional herbal remedies used in rural areas of Latin America. Throughout the United States, *tiendas*, or small family-owned stores, sell Mexican food products, *tejano* music, videos, and other expressions of popular culture. In rural areas, flea markets are popular weekend stops for groups of farmworkers. The concept of the flea market is similar to the Mexican *tianguis*, where vendors sell a wide variety of goods in temporary or semipermanent stands. The popularity of flea markets among farmworkers has boosted sales for ethnic entrepreneurs.

Another important cultural expression that farmworkers maintain is food. Many farmworkers prefer to pay a cook from their own country to prepare meals at the camp rather than eat other types of food. *Tamales*, *pozole* (pork and hominy soup), and *chiles* are found extensively in farmworkers' homes and labor camp kitchens.

Farmworkers bring traditional music and dancing with them across the border. For example, *corridos* are Mexican ballads performed by *conjuntos* (musical groups) and are popular among farmworkers and residents who live along the Mexican-U.S. border. Many of the songs celebrate Mexican heroes who do valiant deeds against Anglo oppressors. Migration is a common theme in popular Mexican songs such as *corridos* as well as in modern rock and roll. Songs tell stories of migration, its dangers, successes, failures, and reasons for leaving Mexico. These experiences are shared by millions of Mexicans. In *Shadowed Lives*, Leo Chavez points out how the song "El Otro México" composed by Enrique Franco of Los Tigres del Norte defends Mexicans who left to work in the United States as farmworkers and criticizes wealthy Mexicans who take their money out of Mexico (Chávez 1998, 30–31):

"El Otro México/*The Other Mexico*"

No me critiquen porque vivo al otro lado.
No soy un desarriagado. Vine por necesidad.
Ya muchos años que me vine de mojado, mis
costumbres no han cambiado ni mi nacionalidad.
Soy como tantos otros, muchos mexicanos, que

la vida nos ganamos trabajando bajo el sol,
reconocidos por buenos trabajadores, que hasta
los mismos patrones nos hablan en español.
¡Cuándo han sabido que un doctor, un ingeniero
que se han cruzado de braceros porque quieran
progresar! ¡O que un cacique deje tierras y
ganado por cruzar el Río Bravo! Eso nunca lo verán.
El otro México que aquí hemos construido es el
peso de lo que ha sido territorio nacional. Es el
esfuerzo de todos nuestros hermanos y latino-americanos que han sabido
    progresar.
Mientras los ricos se van para el extranjero para
esconder a su dinero y por Europa pasear.
Los campesinos que venimos de mojados casi
todo se lo enviamos a los que quedan allá.

Don't criticize me because I live on the other side.
I have not lost my roots. I came out of necessity.
Now it's been many years since I came as a *mojado,* my
customs have not changed nor have I changed my nationality.
I am like so many other Mexicans who
make a living working beneath the sun.
Renowned for being such good workers that
even employers speak to us in Spanish.
When have you heard that a doctor or an engineer
has crossed the border as a *bracero* because they want
to better their lives? Or a landowner leaves the land and
herds to cross the Rio Bravo [Rio Grande]? That you will never see.
The other Mexico that we have constructed here,
that is our burden, was once national territory. It's the
courage of all our brothers and Latin Americans that has improved our
    lives.
Meanwhile the rich ones go abroad
to hide their money and to travel through Europe.
Farmworkers like ourselves who came as *mojados* send
almost all of our money to those who stay behind.

Traditional Mexican music can be heard at *quinceañera* festivities that are commonly celebrated by farmworker families. During this traditional fifteenth birthday party for Mexican girls, families spend large

FIGURE 1.2. *The Segundo family at their daughter's quinceañera, 1999. Photograph by Luis Velasco.*

amounts of money—sometimes thousands of dollars—to celebrate this rite of passage when girls enter adulthood and become women (Finnegan 1996, 60). Entire towns are invited to the festivities, where guests eat traditional Mexican food and watch the girls waltz with their partners.

Festivals are important cultural expressions that bring community members together while they are away from their national or ethnic roots. The San Miguel fiesta in Indiantown, Florida, marks the end of summer migrant work in the North and the beginning of the harvest season in Florida. Several thousand Maya from different ethnic subgroups come together for this festival and have an opportunity to speak their own language. The festival started in 1982 as a small Sunday event. Today, it lasts three days and draws people from as far away as California, Oregon, and Guatemala. There is a Catholic Mass, a soccer tournament, a dance, and marimba music, and young women are selected as queens of the festival (Burns 1993, 53–57). In *Maya in Exile*, Allan Burns explains the cultural importance of events such as the San Miguel fiesta:

Family ceremonies such as baptisms and weddings provide a framework within which to organize small groups of people into bonds of ritual friendship. Larger events such as the yearly celebration of the patron saint

*of San Miguel Acatán provide a second field where new ways of organiz-
ing for survival in the U.S. can be developed. Voluntary associations and
clubs have also become common in the community as the Maya and other
Guatemalans have become more numerous (Burns 1993, 41).*

Women continue to practice traditional activities in Indiantown. A
group of women began a textile cooperative that produces traditional
items such as handbags. Maya midwives serve as important promoters
of prenatal health and nutrition in the community, even though legally
they cannot assist with the process of childbirth as they would in
Guatemala.

Mexican women who work in agriculture and those who work inside
the home continue to practice traditional cultural norms, such as the
cuarentena, where for forty days women follow dietary and sexual restrictions during the postpartum period. Women also use a *faja*, with
which they bind a newborn child's umbilicus to prevent umbilical-cord
bulging and entry of *mal aire*, or bad air.

Farmworkers have left a cultural legacy in the arts and literature for
generations to come. The renowned playwright Luis Valdez grew up in
central California in a farmworker family, harvesting crops until he was
eighteen years old. In the 1960s he founded El Teatro Campesino, an
internationally acclaimed farmworker theater group to support farmworkers on strike and to publicize the strike. Valdez recalled:

*I am a working professional who has managed to produce plays on every
level, first under the very rudimentary conditions with farmworkers on
the picket line, in churches, on flatbed trucks, outdoors as well as indoors.
These plays made it all the way to Los Angeles and Broadway and back,
and have been taken around the world to different countries in different
languages (Hanson 1997, 9).*

Acclaimed author Tomás Rivera was born in Texas to a Mexican
American migrant family. As a boy, Rivera and his family followed the
migrant stream from Texas through the Midwest and back. In his well-
received novel, . . . *y no se lo tragó la tierra* (. . . *And the Earth Did Not
Devour Him*), Rivera recounts a story of a young migrant farmworker
boy searching for his community's history and culture. Since its publication the novel has become one of the most important works of literature
dealing with the Mexican American experience in the United States.
Rivera's other works include *The Harvest* and *This Migrant Earth*.

Migrant and Seasonal Farmworker Religion

Religion provides expression to the cultures of seasonal and migrant farmworkers. The latter, now predominantly Latino, adhere to Roman Catholicism, evangelical Protestantism, and indigenous religious practices from Mexico, Central America, and the Caribbean. Some influence of African spirituality is also evident among migrant and seasonal farmworkers. Especially in the South, seasonal workers are likely to be rural African Americans. With some critical differences, their religious tenets and practices resemble those of the white Protestants who evangelized them in the eighteenth and nineteenth centuries.

Evangelical Protestantism devotes significant attention to baptism, revivals, preaching from scriptural texts, and music. In his memoir *The Substance of Things Hoped For*, Samuel DeWitt Proctor talks about differences between the white and black rural churches of his youth. "Whites emphasized God's holiness and judgment; blacks saw God as the liberator of the oppressed. Whites asked, 'What if you should die unsaved?' Blacks believed that God would help them to bear their daily burdens. Whites said that they wanted to be ready when Jesus came; blacks that God would make a way out of no way" (Proctor 1995, 24). Protestant farmworkers in the Southeast continue to encounter a God who will free them from the continuing slavery of fieldwork with minimal returns and give them the strength to endure it till He comes.

Gospel music in the black churches, almost as important as the sermon, chronicles a theological understanding of a mean world where God assures that the downtrodden will survive. "Go Down, Moses," "Blessed Assurance," "O Mary Don't You Weep," "Deep River," "Great Gettin' Up Mornin'," "We Walk by Faith and Not by Sight," "When I Was a Pilgrim," and "Dem Bones Gonna Rise Again" represent a small sampling of the rural black church's legacy of hope to the wider U.S. culture.

The prophetic preaching of the African American churches that emphasizes the liberation of oppressed people is the preaching that in Montgomery, Albany, Atlanta, and Birmingham put the churches in the forefront of the civil rights movement. But their country cousins in Jamesville, Virginia; Turkey, North Carolina; and Rhine, Georgia, have not led a comparable movement for the liberation of farmworkers. Even landowning black farmers have been rapidly losing their land in recent years because of discriminatory policies of local banks and federal agencies. Why have the churches not been able to stem the tide of black farmers' land loss or help rural farmworkers achieve economic justice?

For the past hundred years, rural African Americans have been moving to urban centers and until recently from the South to the North. This move has weakened rural black communities and, in specific ways, the rural black church. Many such churches have no resident full-time pastor and, indeed, share their "absentee pastor" with one or more other churches. Further, these pastors with several churches to serve often have to work at full-time jobs away from the church to support themselves. Consequently, a serious shortage of African American pastors plagues rural areas.

On the bright side, when the pastor is absent, lay leadership develops, and indeed strong deacons and deaconesses in many rural African American churches supervise the youth programs, visitation, fundraising, and building maintenance. Churches are usually the primary economically independent institutions in the rural African American community. They make their facilities available to community groups. They help sustain the network of family and friends who provide the safety net of personal loans, child care, and rides to jobs, doctors, and supermarkets that make possible poor people's survival in rural areas.

When it comes to community outreach and involvement in local economic and political change, however, rural black churches are handicapped by the pastors' inability to be present with the local community. A pastor's leadership is a limited resource. He—and it often is a he— comes to preach. The worship he leads will likely inspire the congregation to keep on keeping on, to believe in themselves and the eventual attainment of justice and equality. But his ability to move poor rural seasonal farmworkers beyond the needed tenacity to survive and on to effective action for their own liberation has thus far proved unequal to the task.

Migrant farmworkers in the eastern United States, now almost entirely Latino, are predominantly Roman Catholic, with increasing numbers of evangelical Protestants. Immigrants from Haiti, the Dominican Republic, Puerto Rico, and other Caribbean countries also bring the influence of African spiritualities in music and in voodoo, *santeria,* and other practices syncretized with Roman Catholicism.

Recent immigrants from Guatemala and neighboring countries also have brought *costumbre,* Maya religious traditions that have heavily influenced the practice of Roman Catholicism. Entire villages have moved to *El Norte,* as when the people of San Miguel Acatán in Huehuetenango in the Guatemalan highlands relocated to *el pueblo de los indios* (Indiantown), Florida, in the early 1980s. A welcoming church in that town drew Mayas from Oregon, California, and Central America. There, worship services feature marimbas and the Kanjobal Maya language, and priests play a more prominent role than is usual in Latino parishes. Similarly, a Seventh-Day Adventist community has drawn Mayas a little farther south to West Palm Beach.

Recent surveys indicate that although approximately 25 percent identify themselves as Protestant, many of them Evangelical or Pentecostal, most Latinos in the United States are Roman Catholic (Diaz-Stevens and Stevens-Arroyo 1998). The Roman Catholicism of Latin America and that of North America share a common hierarchical structure, the same sacraments, and the celebration of Mass, but the popular piety of Latino Catholicism makes for some dramatic differences.

Especially among poor Latino people, such as farmworkers, church attendance is important, but religious beliefs and practices are more likely to be passed on through the family. The Roman Catholic Church generally promotes infant baptism, but Latinos often delay the baptism of a child until the *comadre* (godmother) and *compadre* (godfather) and other members of the family's social networks can be present. If they are poor farmworkers traveling from several states or countries away, the sacrament may be delayed for a few years.

Just as religion for Latinos is more popular than official, with set forms adapted by the people to suit their circumstances, it tends to be more emotional than theological. At least one scholar, writing in *The Encyclopedia of Religion in the South*, says that Mexican Americans "recoil from the forbidding austerity of the American church" (Miller 1994). Especially after Vatican Council II, the gulf between the modernized Roman Catholic liturgy and the religiosity of Latino people has seemed to widen.

Latinos bring fervor to passion plays and *posadas*, processions, and fiestas. Individuals also have a special relationship with the saints they are named for, talking with and praying to them, especially during life crises. Pilgrimages (*romerias*) to shrines function as spiritual retreats. A mother whose child has survived a serious illness may lead her entire family on a thanksgiving pilgrimage to a shrine of a saint or *la virgen*. Members of the family may travel part of the way on their knees. In traditional piety, the saint or *la virgen* seems at times more important than Christ, whom passion plays and processions represent primarily as the suffering one whose death unlocks the door to personal immortality.

Our Lady of Guadalupe is the single most significant icon for the Mexican people. In 1531, at a time when the great Mexican nations had been defeated and demoralized by the Spanish, *la virgen* appeared as a *mestiza* woman to Juan Diego, a poor Indian. She introduced herself as the mother of the true God and asked that a temple be built where she stood, on the Aztec site at Tepeyac. With the Aztec glyph over her womb and her cloak full of flowers, she offered continuity with the past and a promise of love and protection. She sent Juan Diego to the church, her implicit message being that Indians could be baptized without leaving their own customs behind.

Since Vatican Council II in the early 1960s, the Roman Catholic Church has experienced some new theological emphases originating in Latin America. Liberation theology developed from small groups, *comunidades de base*, meeting to discuss Scripture and apply it to action on behalf of justice in the social and political environment in which they lived. Although criticized from within and outside of the church for some of its Marxist analysis of economic realities, the approach of yoking Scriptural reflection with practical action has survived in some Latino communities.

Lay *delegados*, trained to lead group reflections on scripture texts, and other pastoral agents who animate the community in religious and practical ways occasionally travel with communities of farmworkers or meet them in churches along the way. A few farmworkers from El Salvador, Guatemala, and southern Mexico have had exposure to the social analysis and leadership development this liberation approach fosters. They consider Archbishop Oscar Romero of El Salvador and other assassinated lay and religious church leaders as martyrs. They may well have Romero's picture enshrined along with that of Our Lady of Guadalupe. The solidarity fostered by liberation theology holds some promise that farmworkers may animate and organize the poor communities in which they live and work.

Because of widespread evangelization efforts in Central America in the past two decades, significant numbers of new immigrants arrive in the United States already committed to evangelical Protestantism, including Pentecostalism. Some Latin American churches now send "reverse mission" teams to North America. Although theologically at odds with Roman Catholicism, many of these churches nonetheless allow or incorporate traditional Latino piety often associated with Roman Catholicism into music, fiestas, pilgrimages, *cursillos* (retreats), and emphasis on family and community. They may forbid smoking, alcohol, and the use of cosmetics but use indigenous musical instruments such as drums, shells, flutes, guitars, and spontaneous, often sung, expressions of *"amen, aleluya, gloria a Dios!"*

Theologically, some evangelicals stress that the world is evil and its redemption difficult or impossible. What the individual can do is save himself or herself. Such a millennialist view does not normally lead oppressed people to organize themselves to overcome oppression. But the evangelical churches also tend to be egalitarian in structure, allowing women to preach, for example, and may provide a seedbed for leadership. Perhaps not coincidentally, Baldemar Velasquez, the charismatic leader of the Farm Labor Organizing Committee (FLOC), the tenacious and successful farmworker union now organizing in the Southeast, is an evangelical minister. Symbolic of the increasing presence of the evangelical churches in North Carolina, for example, names like Iglesia Hispana Bautista, Iglesia Evangélica Masonery Apóstoles y Profetas, Iglesia Sion Asamblea de Dios, and Iglesia Pentecostal Nueva Vida are common in rural as well as in urban areas.

Like rural African American churches, the Latino churches are places of cultural and soul survival for farmworkers. In a North American environment that values youth, efficiency, individualism, occupation, and "having" more than "being," Latino churches reinforce the traditional cultural values of the importance of the person, the family, the community, respect for elders, and "being" over "having." As they practice their religion, sometimes in a very public way, they not only remind their new neighbors of those traditional values, but they reinforce their own memory and practice of them.

For example, each December in the town of Clinton, North Carolina, a procession of hundreds of Latinos from Mexico and Central America follow behind a pickup truck converted into a shrine for *la virgen de Guadalupe* on her feast day. An article in the *Raleigh News and Observer* in 1996 noted that a lay worker from the local Roman Catholic Church said the procession was a way to unite the growing Latino community and to preserve cultural traditions important to their identity. Conceivably, the Latinos were also making a claim on the public space of a traditional southern town and, in so doing, altering its social fabric.

Changing Lives

Even though immigrant farmworkers have been able to hold on to many expressions of their culture, they have not been free of cultural impingement. Acculturation is defined as the cul-

FIGURE 1.3. *The baptism of Rodolfo, Jr., 2000. Photograph by Ana Viego.*

tural modification of an individual, group, or people by adapting to or borrowing traits from another culture. Assimilation refers to the process of being absorbed into the culture or mores of a population or group (Rumbaut 1997). Acculturation and assimilation are not neutral; usually oppressed groups assume the cultures of dominant groups. Immigrant farmworkers face changes in their lives associated with both acculturation and assimilation.

Immigrant farmworkers are able to preserve cultural patterns from their home countries through the creation of strong immigrant communities and institutions, vast ethnic networks, and continued transnational ties to their countries of origin. Many farmworkers are part of multilocal and binational families, with extended families and children residing in different countries. Transnational ties foster a cross-fertilization process, as immigrants bring new ideas to their home communities and are at the same time influenced by values and practices from home. This is particularly the case with farmworkers who travel frequently to their home countries. Among farmworkers, pre-migration cultural concepts and social practices prevail in the United States, but these do not continue unchanged. As farmworkers create new lives in the United States, they continue to draw on pre-migration family experiences, norms, and cultural frameworks. For example, the general patterns of interaction among members of a particular family will likely remain unchanged. However, faced with changes, many beliefs, values, and cultural symbols as well as behavior patterns undergo modification. Some former beliefs and social institutions may change only slightly. Foner argues that "to say immigrants change, however, does not mean that they become fully assimilated into American culture. Indeed, the classic concept of assimilation glosses over many complexities in the way immigrants and their institutions change in this country" (Foner 1997, 964). She argues that "in the U.S., where there is no undifferentiated monolithic 'American' culture, the recently developed concept of segmented assimilation describes the fact that immigrants assimilate to particular sectors of U.S. society." In the case of farmworkers, they are more likely to adopt some characteristics found in the way of life of predominately agricultural, working-class, rural communities. The cultures of immigrant farmworker families will increasingly differ both from the culture of their home countries and from mainstream U.S. culture. This can be thought of as a type of "creolization" process, as new and unique cultural and social patterns emerge.

Assimilation refers to the manner of incorporation of the periphery to the core society. However, assimilation is not necessarily a linear process of successive improvement of an immigrant's life in the United States. For example, low birth-weight rates are significantly more prevalent among more "acculturated" second-generation U.S.-born women of Mexican descent compared with first-generation Mexican-born women. This may stem from adoption of risky behaviors such as cigarette-smoking and drug and alcohol use (Rumbaut 1997, 925–928). The unavailability and lack of use of prenatal health care may also lead to the incidence of low birth-weight rates. Health practitioners have observed another pattern as immigrants' health has been negatively affected by an increase in the consumption of "junk" food.

Even though women continue to practice certain traditions, the patterns of breastfeeding may change among immigrant women employed in agriculture in the United States. Studies of Mexican agricultural migrants have found low rates of breastfeeding, a practice that is commonly found in rural communities in Mexico and one that can significantly affect children's health. De la Torre found that 32 percent of farmworker women preferred to feed their children formula due to reasons related to work (de la Torre 1993, 174). Forty-two percent of the women who combined breast- and formula-feeding stated that their work required them to include formula-feeding in their children's diet. The probability of breastfeeding declines when farmworker women work outside the home.

Even though the Maya of Indiantown have been able to hold onto elements of their culture, their identity has changed. According to Burns, "ethnicity is an identity that makes sense in contrast to the presence of other ethnic groups in a society." In the United States, where the Maya are one among many minorities, their cultural identity is now defined in relation to other groups. Outsiders have labeled the Guatemalan Maya as "migrant workers" and not as indigenous Maya. Some identify them with their jobs (farmworkers), their suspected legal status ("illegals"), and their nationality (Guatemalans). The capitalist economy forces their sense of identity as workers to the fore.

English proficiency is a measure of acculturation. Some studies have characterized Latino immigrants who speak English as well as or better than Spanish as being more acculturated in the host society than are their less English-proficient counterparts (Blank and Torrecilha 1998, 6). However, the full adoption of the English language may lead to a lessened use of the native language among young Latino immigrants or the adoption of a version of "Spanglish." McElroy noted that the continuum of accommodation or acculturation among settled-out Mexican farmworkers in northern California showed little correlation with economic success or whether the family lived in town or in a rural area. On the other hand, age group and length of time settled in the area proved to be more significant factors in the degree of acculturation. Farmworkers who have lived in this country for an extended period of time will be more likely to adopt U.S. ways of life (McElroy 1982). However, farmworkers who assimilate into mainstream U.S. society and forgo their own cultural practices and norms do not necessarily become more successful economically.

In the Southeast, where Latinos are a less visible group, discrimination against undocumented workers may contribute to their inability to incorporate into mainstream society. Many undocumented immigrants remain outsiders during the period of time they are in the United States and often return to their home countries after a brief stay. Many individuals who stay in the United States and who lean toward incorporation may find that their undocumented status and society's perception of them as "illegals" prevent them from full incorporation. Undocumented farmworkers who do not enjoy full incorporation may be more inclined to articulate cultural expressions in private, where they will be unnoticed by society at large.

Griswold del Castillo and de Leon stress that neither full Americanization nor total cultural retention have characterized Mexican immigrants in the United States. Lifestyles are "anglicized" by U.S. institutions, popular culture, and consumer goods, but the constant influx of new immigrants and residential segregation have reinforced Mexican culture. This ongoing immigration has both unified and fragmented the Mexican community in the United States. Ideological divisions and job competition among Latinos are offset by a shared culture, language, and experience of poverty and discrimination. Ties with new immigrants have resulted in the articulation of an increasingly inclusive identity through the acceptance of the term "Latino," which was fostered by the growth in the Central American and Caribbean-origin populations after 1965 (Griswold del Castillo and De Leon 1996).

Latin Americans are a people who have endured cultural juxtapositions for centuries. Mexican people still struggle with defining their identities following the Spanish conquest of what today is Spanish-speaking Latin America, and after the Mexican American War redefined territorial and cultural boundaries. Many *mestizos*, or Latin Americans of mixed ancestry, respect both their indigenous and colonial roots while at the same time discriminate against individuals who are darker than they, or *más indios*. Martinez states, "As *mestizos* lament the supposed loss of their Indian past, they see *Chicanos* and their supposed identity crisis as tragic. But those who see a 'loss of Mexicanness' in Chicanos don't know much about themselves. In many ways Chicanos are more 'Mexican' than the Mexico City middle class, whose gaze is ever fixed on New York and Paris . . . More than a loss of identity, what is happening is a continuation of the process of *mestizaje* in which Indians and Chicanos can put together a cultural package of their own choosing" (Martínez 1997, 37). For example, indigenous people from the Purépecha Plateau in Michoacán who speak Tarasco understand that the future and the past coexist in the present. They have settled in California and adopted Chicano and Anglo ways of life while keeping ties with family, their indigenous language, and their towns back home. They understand that to survive they have to change and to move (Martínez 1997, 37).

Networks and Family

Networks in general, and family networks in particular, play an important role in the adaptation, settlement, and living arrangements among Latino immigrants. An individual entering a farmworker community may already be part of a network of people from the same part of the country or even from the same town. Through this network, farmworkers may find out about social workers, lawyers, teachers, and other advocates when in need. Growers and crew leaders often rely on the recruitment of new workers by current employees who have established social networks. Family networks tend to stimulate and facilitate the migration process for many. Griffith and Kissam state that "social networks are the building blocks of the social infrastructure of migration; they are, by all accounts, the most important and comprehensive feature of farmworkers' lives" (Griffith and Kissam 1995, 49). Networks may be based on kinship, friendship, shared community of origin, ethnicity, national origin, common residence, or common job experiences. Farmworkers rely on this method of support for housing, transportation, financial assistance, labor market information, job contracts, and emotional support.

The demographic composition of farmworker groups has an impact on marriage and family patterns and results in cultural change. In farmworker communities with a disproportionate male-to-female sex ratio, males tend to marry outside their national groups, or a man may search for a wife from his home country. In fact, significant cross-marriage of U.S.-born Latinos to Mexicans occurs in the farmworker community. The 1997 NAWS found that 37 percent of farmworkers born in the United States were likely to be married to someone who was born in Mexico. About 7 percent of married Mexican-born farmworker males had spouses who were born in the United States (Mines, Gabbard, and Steirman 1997).

Significantly high rates of marital and family separation occur among farmworkers. Social and economic support from family, geographical proximity, and cultural traditions of the past lead to the importance of "familism" among Latinos (Blank and Torrecilha 1998, 3). The inclusion of extended family in households reflects social and cultural norms that encourage the incorporation of non-nuclear kin. Although culture alone is not a determinant of living arrangements, the high number of Latino farmworkers living away from spouses and extended family signifies a break from tradition due to employment, economics, and immigration patterns. Hiring practices significantly affect living patterns since many employers prefer to hire crews of men. The NAWS found that 45 percent of married farmworkers were living away from their spouses and children while doing farm work (Mehta et al. 2000). This proportion seems to have been increasing in recent years. Such a high rate of separation may be related to an immigration pattern among some Mexican male farmworkers employed in the United States in which they enter the country alone and later bring their spouses and children.

The 1997 NAWS also found that 56 percent of all farmworkers live with unrelated individuals. Half of male farmworkers live exclusively with people unrelated to themselves, while only one in ten women farmworkers live solely with unrelated persons. The survey also found that foreign-born workers are more likely than U.S.-born workers to share a residence with many (five or more) people. Twenty-nine percent of Mexican-born and 41 percent of other Latin American-born farmworkers living in a nuclear family setting have non-family residing with them. It is likely that non-family household members are coworkers or people from the same sending areas abroad (Mines, Gabbard, and Steirman 1997). It is evident that farmworkers have had to make significant changes in their living patterns while working in the United States. The lack of family structure that many all-male farmworker households experience can deter cultural and religious participation.

Changed Communities

Not only do immigrant farmworkers change while adapting to life in new communities, but residents of the communities where farmworkers settle also have changed from interactions with their new neighbors. Anthropologists use the term "transculturation" to describe the bridging of several cultures. It is a process that disregards the notion of partial and unidirectional assimilation into the dominant culture. Rather, the dominant culture changes and continues to change through its constant exposure to the cultural practices of the peripheral group. Transculturation refers to a form of cultural interaction in which some acquisition, some loss, and some cultural creations are combined and shared.

Even though many people overlook the contributions Latinos have made to culture and life in the United States, examples of their contributions abound. Colonial Spanish and Mexican-Indian settlers developed and diffused North America's first grapes, raisins, apricots, peaches, plums, oranges, lemons, wheat, barley, olives, and figs. They also adapted the New World products of cotton and henequen, as well as the indigenous staples of corn, beans, squash, tomatoes, chili peppers, avocados, vanilla, chocolate, and other fruits and vegetables that are cultivated in the United States today. After *mestizos* took control of the southwestern U.S. region from Spain in 1821, they along with the indigenous groups of the area developed western techniques of large-scale ranching and agriculture. They introduced water rights for areas adjacent to riverbanks as well as water irrigation systems used widely in the Southwest (Rochín 1995, 291–292).

The process of transculturation began many years ago and continues today. The United States increasingly sees the adoption of Mexican and Tex-Mex food and restaurants. U.S. consumers today buy more salsa than ketchup. Latin American music has become more popular in the United States. Salsa dance lessons are offered with increased regularity, and Latino musicians are top pop artists. Spanish language instruction in public schools is becoming more prevalent. The numbers of Latinos in rural areas impact governmental offices and social service departments in the South by demanding bilingual interpreters and social workers. Local law enforcement and fire departments in rural areas increasingly offer basic Spanish instruction and multicultural workshops for staff members. In North Carolina, the Department of Motor Vehicles recently translated its driver's license examination manual into Spanish as a response to pressure from advocacy groups and immigrant community members. For years, the United States has been economically dependent on Latinos. Now, mainstream U.S. society is linked more closely to Latinos on social, cultural, and personal levels.

Relations between Ethnic Groups

Stemming from the discrimination and oppression faced by many farmworkers regardless of their race and ethnicity, one could imagine that a sense of solidarity would prevail among farmworkers. However, tensions are common among various ethnic and national groups, arising from cultural differences and job competition. It may be that there are many examples of harmonious relations between different cultural groups of farmworkers, but if so, they have not been well documented. The Coalition of Immokalee (Florida) Workers is one exception.

Tensions between African American workers and immigrants in general can be traced back to the beginning of the twentieth century, when employers in the North pitted African Americans and immigrants from southern and Eastern Europe against one another in order to bid down wages and break unions (Diamond 1998, 455). The fear that large numbers of incoming immigrants would displace them was present among African American workers even in the 1920s. Blacks complained of the growing numbers of Mexicans coming north to work in the rapidly expanding agricultural industry in Texas and California. During that decade, African American journalist George Schuyler asked, "If the million Mexicans who have entered the country have not displaced Negro workers, whom have they displaced?" During the Depression, Mexican immigration was curtailed, and by 1935, more than four hundred thousand Mexicans had been deported. Some black leaders hoped that "with the repatriation of the Mexicans the labor market for colored workers will be considerably improved" (Diamond 1998, 458).

A current example of this tension is seen among crab pickers in North Carolina. As described earlier, African Americans dominated the crab-picking labor force for decades in North Carolina, but presently, younger African Americans no longer are taking those jobs. Crab plant owners are increasingly hiring Mexican temporary guestworkers to fill those jobs. In New Bern and Belhaven plants, women guestworkers from Mexico, most under forty years of age, and African American women in their seventies and eighties who have lived in the region for most of their lives work together. A Mexican crab worker stated that "*las morenas* [the black women] were given more freedom and could leave when they wanted to, while she and the other H-2B workers had to wait for the bus to come to take them home" (Robinson 1998, 33). The worker resented this. She mentioned that although all the workers came into the plant together, the Latinas and African Americans were then separated for work. When the interviewer asked the reason for this arrangement, she replied, "Because we didn't like *las morenas*." Perhaps both groups shared the sentiment. The newcomers do not have a connection to the area or know its history as the older African American women do. Cultural and linguistic differences prevent the two groups from learning about what they may have in common.

In agriculture, "many growers have been actively recruiting young Mexican workers into harvests, preferring them to West Indians, African Americans, and most other Latinos" (Griffith and Kissam 1995, 38). Growers prefer single-person households but also hire households consisting of nuclear families and single men or women who are related to the main family by kinship and friendship ties. As the use of the H-2A temporary guestworker program has become more prevalent, growers find it even easier to hire Mexican males.

In Indiantown, Florida, the Guatemalan Maya make up the majority of the migrant workers in the area. They work alongside Mexicans, Mexican Americans, African Americans, and Haitians (Burns 1993, 41). The Guatemalan Maya are the newest group and often the recipients of discrimination from other ethnic groups (especially whites). Mexican and Mexican American workers refer to the Guatemalans as *indios* (Indians), a derogatory term in Mexico and Guatemala. Employment opportunities also strain relations between groups, since the Mexican and Mexican American workers outwork the Guatemalans in the citrus orchards due to the Mayas' smaller stature. The Guatemalans have been denied work in the sugarcane industry, where workers from the Caribbean have been preferred in the past (Burns 1993, 134–35). Employers use tensions between groups to their advantage. "The big contractors foment tensions among the various ethnic groups—Puerto Ricans, Nicaraguans, Haitians, not just Mexicans—who work in the fields, making it impossible for a union organizer to pull the workers together" (Shorris 1992, 307).

In the community of Bayou La Batre in Alabama, Indochinese laborers who entered the crab-processing industry faced opposition by white residents who used to work in the same industry. White residents articulated opposition to the employment of Asians in this occupation in terms of the sanitary requirements of the work and the perception that "Asians are not clean" (Moberg and Thomas 1993, 93). However, state health inspections indicated that the cleanliness of the crab houses had not been altered as the composition of the labor force changed. Gradually, employers began hiring African Americans to work in the crab industry. As Indochinese workers entered the shrimp fishery business, anti-Asian sentiments heightened because this resulted in increased competition between U.S. and Asian fishermen for shrimp. Residents believed Asians had stolen jobs and displaced workers.

In addition to the difficult relations between community residents and Asian employees, differences related to nationality can be seen among Asians as well. Employers have capitalized on tensions between Vietnamese, Laotian, and Cambodian workers in Alabama. Some crab-processing houses divide their workforce among these different groups so that the workers are less likely to unite against the employer.

When the British West Indies Temporary Alien Labor Program was in place, growers preferred to hire Jamaicans instead of domestic workers or Puerto Ricans because they believed them to be better qualified and more experienced apple pickers (Griffith 1986, 880). U.S. farm labor organizations claimed that they were also easier for agricultural bosses to control and impossible to unionize. Domestic workers were judged on productivity standards set by the Jamaican workers, which resulted in the two groups being in direct competition with each other for the same jobs. Before World War II, local African American community members were the main source of seasonal labor in Florida agriculture (see Hahamovitch 1997). When they moved north to work in war-related industries, growers looked to replace them with foreign workers (Wood and McCoy 1985, 254). Many Jamaicans and Haitians were imported to replace African Americans.

Haitians who came to Florida during the late 1970s and early 1980s suffered from discrimination and were forced to rely on the resident Haitian community for housing, economic assistance, and other support during their initial years in the United States. In addition, immigrants from Haiti who arrived earlier often have discriminated against more recent Haitian immigrants. This has led to even more close-knit enclaves of Haitian farmworkers (Griffith and Kissam 1995, 46). Many growers characterized Haitians as "cliquish," more argumentative, and more likely to complain collectively about working conditions. Haitians have suffered as well from negative stereotypes and publicity related to the involvement of some Haitians in the drug trade (Burns 1993, 108). This has resulted in persistent discrimination toward newcomers by the core community of longtime Haitians residents.

The town of Immokalee, Florida, provides a microcosm where many ethnic and racial groups interact. African Americans have been long-time residents of the area, but changes in the community and the agricultural labor market have "undermined their once-dominant position in the East Coast farm labor market" (Griffith and Kissam 1995, 40). Haitians arrived in the early 1980s, and the Guatemalan population has increased significantly since the mid-1980s. On the other hand, Mexicans and Mexican Americans have been part of the agricultural labor force in Florida for at least twenty-five to thirty years, with significant numbers entering the citrus harvests in the early to mid-1970s and some coming to Immokalee as far back as the late 1950s.

In Immokalee, subsidized government housing complexes have been segregated by race and ethnicity. Most of the residents of Farmworker Village in Immokalee are Latinos, while new units were built specifically for African Americans (Griffith and Kissam 1995, 37). Many work crews are segregated by race or place of origin. The community's response to the growth in the ethnic communities and the ensuing growth in ethnic commercial establishments has been either to leave town ("white flight") or to reaffirm the community's identity through activities such as the annual African American festival in Belle Glade. "Struggles over community identity can lead to strained relations between host and immigrant ethnic groups, especially when, as in Immokalee, immigrant groups are perceived to contribute to crime, alcoholism, prostitution, drug abuse, and related concerns about the health and welfare of the resident population" (Griffith and Kissam 1995, 41).

However, a positive example of ethnic and race relations among farmworkers can be observed by examining the work of the Coalition of Immokalee Workers (CIW). In 1995, before many Haitian workers stopped harvesting vegetables, Haitian, Latino, and Maya members participated in the first general strike in the history of Immokalee. This "multiethnic, grassroots strike" provided the momentum to establish the coalition as an independent organization. The coalition built on the accomplishments brought about by the strike, including blocking the trend to further cut pay for tomato harvesters, organizing the hunger strike of 1997–1998, and securing the subsequent raises that workers received.

According to CIW organizer Greg Asbed, the thirty-day hunger strike, "like the general strike before it, again reflected a real victory in bridging divisions to bring about change." Among the hunger strikers, two were Maya Guatemalans, two were from Mexico, one was from the border in Texas, and one was from Cuba. The mobilization of the farmworker population was facilitated by the representation of the major Latino groups among the hunger strikers. Though the strike stands out as an example of successful organizing among diverse populations, coalition leaders have recognized that it did not solve all problems of racial division within the organization or the community in general (Asbed 1999).

Considering Culture

Even though most U.S. farmworkers today are Mexican, other groups have been part of the agricultural labor mosaic. In the mosaic of race, ethnicity, and national origin that contemporary U.S. farm labor encompasses, immigrant farmworkers continue to hold onto some cultural institutions. However, they face important changes in their lives associated with both acculturation and assimilation. In order to preserve their cultures, immigrant farmworkers in many cases have developed strong immigrant communities and institutions, vast ethnic networks, and continued transnational ties to their countries of origin. Networks in particular play an important role in the survival of Latino culture among immigrant farmworkers, especially since many are quite isolated in rural areas.

Farmworkers from all ethnicities and national origins continue to face discrimination and oppression. Those who work with and conduct research among farmworkers across ethnic and racial lines can foster a sense of solidarity among these groups. It is important to document and disseminate models that contribute to positive interactions between diverse groups of farmworkers. Also of importance are examples of ways in which farmworkers and the communities at large have learned from one another and dispelled cultural myths and stereotypes of farmworkers.

Advocates should consider the diversity of the farmworker population when devising strategies to ameliorate poor conditions faced by agricultural workers. A program that may be appropriate for Latino farmworkers might not be relevant to the needs of African American farmworkers. The background and cultural context of each farmworker may be a good starting point for analyzing his or her situation and working toward enfranchisement.

A review of the existing literature reflects a need for extensive studies that describe the ethnic and racial composition of the agricultural labor force by geographic regions. This is of particular importance in the Southeast, since the recent demographic changes among the farmworker population have not been recorded in full. Even though literature related to working conditions of farmworkers is rich, few studies describe the cultural traits of farmworker groups.

It is obvious that a depopulation of the country-side leads, finally, to social death. We can say that it will not reach that point. But still, we don't know that it won't. So far, there seems to be nothing which is likely to arrest it.
SIMONE WEIL, 1949

———

Sowing Seeds for Change symposium address, Gainesville, Florida

Lucas Benitez, farmworker and organizer

. . . A brief look at Florida headlines [in 1997–98] leaves little room for doubt that something is profoundly wrong in Florida agriculture as we head into the twenty-first century:

"Long hours, low pay: Workers file suit for back wages" (St. Petersburg Times, *May 1998). In a class action lawsuit against a major Florida citrus producer, orange pickers accused their employer of systematically bilking thousands of workers out of the minimum wage, paying some workers as little as $12 for a full day's work, sunup to sundown.*

"Florida harvests the too-young for field hands" (Associated Press, December 1997). *Child labor made a comeback, with children as young as 6 years old discovered "helping" their parents pick.*

"Slaves in America — Three plead guilty to enslaving migrants" (Naples Daily News, May 1997). *The most extensive slavery operation in the post–Civil War history of Florida was brought to justice in a joint investigative effort involving the farmworker community and the U.S. Justice Department, ending in twin fifteen-year sentences for two Southwest Florida crewleaders . . . for peonage and extortion.*

"This is just faster death — Six farmworkers stop eating to protest falling wages in fields" (Naples Daily News, *December 1997).*

. . . And yet all of this is happening during times of relative prosperity for agriculture in Florida. Headlines coming from the industry over the same period paint a very different picture for the growers:

"Farmers, ranchers earn most money in five years" (Fort Myers News Press, *September 1997*). *"Florida's farmers and ranchers raked in more than $6.1 billion in 1996, the highest level for cash receipts in five years, the state agriculture department announced Tuesday."*

"Tomato growers optimistic" (Fort Myers News Press, *September 1997*). *"The mood of growers, by and large, is better than it's been in a while."*

"Strong market to last awhile" (The Packer, *December 1997*).

. . . So what's going on here? Why must farmworkers continue to suffer the most miserable conditions in American labor while agribusiness continues to earn healthy, growing profits? Why are abuses from the past century still alive in Florida's fields today? And why hasn't this situation yielded to the best efforts of armies of attorneys, advocates, and reformers over the past thirty to forty years?

The answer lies in the relationship between farmworkers and their employers, a relationship that has not evolved in any significant way since the days of Tom Joad and *The Grapes of Wrath*. It is a relationship that is at its core unjust, and from that relationship stems, directly or indirectly, the entire array of substandard conditions—from falling wages to no drinking water in the fields, from pesticide poisoning to peonage—that we as farmworkers continue to suffer every day.

CHAPTER 2

Layers of Loss

Migrants, Small Farmers, and Agribusiness

Charles D. Thompson, Jr.

By reading the preceding passages in juxtaposition, the first by a European writer of a generation ago and the second by a present-day farmworker organizer in the United States, we find two seemingly discordant causes for concern. Simone Weil's major worry is the depopulation of the countryside brought about by the loss of farmers and the consequential decay of the social fabric. Lucas Benitez's address a half-century later, on the other hand, reveals a great divide between "growers" or "agribusiness interests" who have made billions in profits in agriculture and the farmworkers who live in poverty on or near these same farms. Benitez's most pressing concern is that farmworkers are forced to live with very little compensation for their labor in fields owned by those who are growing ever wealthier at these workers' expense. When we match Weil's concern with domestic out-migration from the countryside with Benitez's concern regarding injustices to farmworkers, the two concerns may seem hard to reconcile. However, in actuality, these are two components of a long-term degradation of U.S. agriculture and parts of the same damaged social fabric.

What Weil says about the decrease in population of farmers certainly has been true in this country, especially since 1949, when she wrote this passage. Over the past fifty years we have experienced tremendous, perhaps irreparable, damage to our society as tens of millions of farm people have been forced off their land in an exodus accelerated by factors including federal government policy, the rise of agribusiness, and natural adversity such as droughts and floods. However, contrary to Weil's worry, this has not meant the "depopulation" of the countryside as we might imagine it. In fact, the "farm" population in some rural areas is actually on the rise. But this is no cause for celebration, because as Lucas Benitez demonstrates, the countryside once peopled by small-farm owners has been rapidly repopulated by an underclass of non-owner agriculturalists who work long hours but own nothing.

Also operating in the same countryside, though sometimes in absentia, is an agricultural elite, a new class of powerful agricultural owners unmatched since the days of slavery.

Without question, as small farmers leave the land, society suffers. Family farming skills die out in a generation when none of the children can afford or want to take over the business. Rural schools have less local tax money to use when farms that once paid taxes go out of business. Rural churches and civic organizations also decline in membership and vitality. Weil was right about the tearing of the social fabric. What she could not foresee, however, is that as farms and their supporting rural institutions have declined in the United States, it is economic democracy, or equal access to resources, rather than population that suffers. A new socially and economically marginalized population has taken the place of small farmers who once had some say in the organization of their communities. Now the small farmers who remain are too few in number to constitute a political or economic force.

This loss of economic democracy means, as Florida headlines reveal, that while agriculture has increased in profitability in total dollars, fewer people than ever share this sector's wealth and power. No longer do small farmers control a significant portion of the ownership and decision making involved in crop and livestock production. No longer do small farmers have a significant voice in local politics. In their place are farmworkers who control nothing yet who provide the necessary labor by which the agricultural sector in the United States grows and profits. Because farmworkers have come to the fields even as small farmers have left them, recent increases in agricultural profitability in tomatoes and other commodities are due not to the entrepreneurship and hard work of those who might share this wealth, but rather to the contributions of an underclass who live in poverty while working in the shadows of the world's most productive agricultural system. Were numerous small farmers to share this same total farm income, an entirely different picture of rural economic health would result.

The present concentration in agricultural ownership is thus due to two interrelated trends: the depopulation of small farmers and the consequent use of temporary workers who have replaced their labor contributions on the now larger farms but who do not control any of the market as small farmers once did. As landless workers have replaced permanent owners, power and profit concentrates in fewer hands. Therefore, figures showing profits made in farming, as positive as they may sound to government officials and consumers, reveal little about who really pockets the money in the end.

Referring to concentrated agricultural interests merely as "growers" may actually mask the fact that the farms in question are often very large-scale companies with highly paid executives at the top of a pyramidal structure and many workers with few or no benefits at its bottom. These owners might best be described in industry terminology such as bosses and overseers rather than in agricultural terms such as growers and farmers. In fact, many fields and farms have become factories. And yet, as Benitez points out, in most other industries abuses like those experienced by farmworkers were outlawed long ago. One method that companies use to get around their legal and moral obligations to farmworkers is contractual agreements built on the claim that farmworkers work for growers and not for the companies. What companies avoid admitting is that many growers of numerous commodities from cucumbers to chickens have signed contracts with companies that make them de facto employees though they receive none of the benefits. This means growers and farmworkers can sometimes be caught in a similar squeeze. Sometimes, of course, individual growers are exploitative, but ending our analysis at the farm field masks the full truth of the agricultural economy.

Industrialized agribusiness takes in great profits, but not without human labor. Thus today, farm income accrues to huge agricultural interests in an agricultural economy nearly devoid of the little farms of Weil's day, while the harvest of many crops, especially vegetables and fruits, is still brought in by hand. Sometimes large numbers of farmworkers live and work on the very same land where small farmsteads once stood, even in the now run-down houses once owned and kept up by small farmers.

We should avoid making the agricultural economy seem neatly dualistic. We also must avoid making this analysis seem overly romantic and simple. While the Southeast has had large numbers of small farmers, it is also the region once dominated by slavery and subsequently by sharecroppers and tenants. In other words, the South has a long history of two-tiered farming, with an owner class and a class of slaves and later of renters. Small farmers predominated much of the region, but there were also planters, many of whose families have retained large holdings. It is a complex region with various layers of attempts at ownership and a long history of inequity and great losses. Despite the region's complexity, however, only a few hundred farm owners—and very few in commodities such as poultry and hogs—control agriculture in an area whose population was one-third farmers until the 1930s. Even if many of those who left farming once lived on too little income, their leaving means less, rather than more, freedom and wealth for many of the region's inhabitants today, particularly the farmworkers.

Although farmworkers often do the work farmers have done for thousands of years, there is a striking contrast between those who own and control farmland and housing, however modest, and those who own nothing. A world of difference exists between smallholders of Weil's day who made a meager living from their own work and workers who now labor on farms for poverty-level wages. Thus the issues affecting farmworkers are not the depopulation Weil described, but lack of power and stability among a large agricultural population.

Whippoorwill Farm

In 1984 my wife and I bought a small farm in North Carolina that I operated for nine years. During that time I heard many stories of farm losses even as I watched agribusiness, particularly the poultry industry, take hold of the county's economy. I also witnessed the replacement of farms with housing developments. I watched as the huge vacuum left by failing farms was filled not by families strongly associated with local agriculture but rather by new non-agricultural owners and/or farmworkers from far away. The story of losses on and around my own farm interwove eventually with stories of workers from Mexico who were displaced from full-time farming in their own country. Through one small place named Whippoorwill Farm, I learned about the broad structural forces that have afflicted agriculture in general. Thus this farm's story, as with much of the land throughout the Southeast, includes numerous layers of loss—losses that have only intensified with time's passage (Moore 1962, 75). Uncovering these layers personalized for me the cold statistics describing the unsettling of small farms and the restructuring of agriculture in the Americas.

While the farm tells a story of a certain depopulation, it also tells the story of arrivals of numerous newcomers, myself included, eager to find their own place in a new community and, in my case, the history of the Southeast. In our community I realized that two main populations replace small farmers when they leave their land: those who know little about agriculture but who seek the amenities offered by rural life or those who know a great deal about agriculture but who have no resources with which to buy land. On my farm I came to know many in both categories, and some in between.

We purchased our twenty-two acres from an absentee owner, a dentist I will call Dr. Radnor who held the farm in a portfolio of at least forty parcels. A decade before we bought the farm, it had fallen out of the hands of agriculturalists and into the hands of a land speculator. The farm was more than an hour's drive from Radnor's own home. He had no family connections to it, no agricultural ties, no reasons to buy that particular piece of land other than the fact that he could buy it cheap and make money by doing so. He put the small farm on the market because, in his words, it was "too far away to manage," though it was clearly a profitable decision as well. The farm had deteriorated while he owned it, yet he sold it at a profit after land values in the area appreciated—not because of farming but because of development. As Radnor had no particular attachments to the place, he told me without any sign of regret that he would have converted the land "into a trailer park" had no buyer come along when we did.

Radnor's farm interest was purely economic: the land represented capital and investment, not a place on which to live and work. His is a tale repeated innumerable times as farm families have given up due to the pressures of trying to make a living with increasing farm input costs and decreasing prices for what they sell. In North Carolina alone, more than 250,000 farmers have gone out of business since 1950 (USDA Economic Research Service). With our purchase, we rescued a single place from its conversion to non-agricultural usage, for a time at least. Yet this rescue meant nothing for the other places bordering ours, nothing that would change the structure of agriculture in general.

In the early 1970s, Dr. Radnor purchased the land from a widow, Mrs. Efland, whose husband had "found his dream place." After working away from farming for most his life and saving his money, in the 1960s Mr. Efland was finally able to purchase his "retirement farm" on which he planned to raise horses. The Eflands temporarily beset the trend toward housing subdivisions and development of the Piedmont by joining another increasingly popular southeastern trend toward small-scale horse farms. In doing so, they were able to keep the land in farming, but they did not plan to make money from it.

People like the Eflands have carried childhood memories of farming all their lives, but they earned the money to buy land in other more profitable pursuits, certainly not from farming. Many come to play at farming, an avocation that farmers who have had to struggle to make ends meet sometimes find amusing, sometimes depressing. Because of the plethora of part-time and hobby farms, the total number of farms remains artificially high. In actuality, concentration in agriculture is much greater than the simple counting of the total number of farms and farm acreage reveals. For example, two companies, Cargill and Archer Daniels Midland, control "60 percent of the export market for American grain" (Weiner 1999). Though the South has little grain industry, the same trends are occurring in vegetable and meat production.

Though the growth of hobby farms preserves farmland, the rise of "farmettes," as real estate agents call them, points to the loss of income-producing potential in agriculture. This means that small farming has become a retirement hobby rather than a way to make a living. Farms that go on the market in the North Carolina Piedmont and other rapidly developing regions in the Southeast rarely remain in the hands of farmers. Every farmer with whom I have spoken for the past twenty years through my field research in the Carolinas and Virginia has agreed that one cannot purchase land and pay for it by farming it, at least with conventional crops and livestock. For example, a modest-sized dairy farm by today's standards requires an investment of at least a half-million dollars. No one can milk enough cows to pay for land, equipment, livestock, and the interest on that kind of money. Thus, a dairy farm that is for sale is beyond the means of most farmers, particularly beginning and limited-resource farmers. Because of the kind of investment required, a decision to sell most often means the end of a family's farming lineage, and often the land is taken out of agriculture altogether.

Many farmers say in conversation that they believe the current decline in farm prices they receive will only last as long as there is competition in agriculture. When all the independent farmers are gone, the prices we pay for food will rise. By using large numbers of low-paid laborers and garnering market advantages, the mega-producers of agricultural crops already enjoy a competitive advantage over the smaller producers. If only corporations control agriculture, we can be sure that this will raise food prices as well.

Tragically, only a few years after completing his horse barn, Mr. Efland died after inadvertently uncovering a bees' nest inside the barn and sustaining multiple stings. After the sudden loss of her husband and therefore the end of his dream, Mrs. Efland moved to town, eager to sell the farm to anyone willing to match her relatively low selling price. Dr. Radnor was the first to arrive with the money, and he walked away with a good deal. Rarely do sellers and buyers discuss the uses of land or the intentions of the new owner. People usually speak in terms of price. Old hopes and plans of the previous owners rarely find new fulfillment once land trades hands. Dr. Radnor had no intention of continuing any of the Eflands' agricultural plans.

The Eflands had purchased the farm from the last remaining remnant of the Fawcett family, a widow left alone on the farm. The Fawcetts had made their living on tobacco, cotton, and a few other field crops. In the latter years they lived there, the Fawcett children had kept the farm from growing up in weeds. During the 1960s and 1970s all the children had taken what most rural North Carolinians call "public work." After the parents became too old to work the place, no family member remained who was both interested in farming and solvent enough to take over the place from the old folks. After Mr. Fawcett died, his widow had little choice but to build herself a small house on the corner of the property and put the rest of the farm on the market.

Though some of the family members have lived to regret their decision to leave the farm, at the time of the sale the Fawcett family's desire to earn cash outweighed any sentiment for the homeplace itself. For many farm households, the decades immediately following World War II were a time of escape from agriculture into the manufacturing sectors of the economy. Men returning from the war often avoided returning to farming; instead they filled the industrial plants spurred by the economic boom of the post-war years. As suburbs began to sprout up nationally, many industrial workers, especially in the land-rich Southeast, relied on the sale of family land as a means to buy new homes closer to their work. The small farm became less a place to depend on for sustenance and more of an economic nest egg.

The Fawcetts' story represents a common pattern in which land that once was "dirt cheap" transformed in the 1960s and 1970s into a rural family's most valuable source of wealth. Many an old farmer has been described as "cash poor but land rich," but let the old farmer die and the situation for the children may change drastically. This was true of the Fawcetts. After building their suburban-style dwellings that now line the road near the farmstead, as well as a house for their mother on the corner of the property, the Fawcett children sold their remaining land, converting terrain into dollars.

By the time the Fawcetts sold the old house under towering oaks, the farm's size had dwindled to just twenty-two acres from an original three hundred or more. In addition to the several parcels subdivided for children, the state built a second, straighter highway through the middle of the farm, and other parcels were sold off along both roads, including a large piece that was split from the main farmstead and sold in the 1980s as a horse farm to retirees from Ohio.

Following World War II, rapid mechanization of cropping systems along with the adoption of farm chemicals including new synthetic fertilizers hastened the transformation of the rural economy. Larger tractors and tillage equipment, along with innovative harvesting equipment, increased a single farmer's capacity to produce much more and thus rely less upon family and neighborly labor.

Especially since the war, as individual farmers have increased dramatically their capacity to produce a crop, neighbors who could not afford the technology became farm laborers or left agriculture altogether. In places where neighbors had once helped one another out of necessity, now a single farmer needed neighbors less and the neighbors' land more, as their machinery payments dictated additional production. Of course, some farms like Whippoorwill Farm dwindled in size because the land was no longer needed to produce agricultural commodities, but it remained in a family's possession for the sake of nostalgia, as a means of leaving something to the children, or simply as a place to live. By the 1960s and 1970s large farmers, spurred on by low-interest federal loans and tax breaks, began to consolidate others' operations into their own. Meanwhile, modern plant breeding paid for by tax dollars boosted production on many farms so much that the government instituted "soil banks" that encouraged many smaller farmers to take their land out of food production and to plant their land in pine trees. It had the effect of encouraging small farmers to cease production. In essence, the government sent the message to rural America that some farms and their owners were superfluous to U.S. agriculture's future. Because of boosted production made possible by federal farm policy, prices paid for goods at the farm gate fell dramatically. This made full-time work on small acreages harder than ever. Many full-time farmers became mere occupants of their own land as they shifted from intensive cropping to growing grass and pasturing a few cows, and to working at jobs off the farm. The economic boom outside of agriculture in the 1960s and again in the 1990s gave the farm progeny places to go when they left the farm, and so millions of them left.

Most of the Fawcett children took jobs in the manufacturing and service sectors. One son, for instance, manages a small chain of convenience marts. All that is left of their legacy of farming now lives in the memory of the remaining grandchildren or in an outbuilding or two. Even after I bought the place some fifteen years after Mrs. Fawcett's death, several of the then middle-aged grandchildren stopped by occasionally to see the farm and to tell me they missed the place and wished they had held on to their "grandma's house."

This story of the Fawcetts and their place is but one story of a small farm among millions given up to memory, another family that has joined nearly an entire generation of people who traded their agricultural skills for the regular work and wages gained off the farm. Of course, most of the Fawcetts, like many of their counterparts I have interviewed in the Carolinas, were not truly romantics about the pastoral life of farming. Rather, they said that because they knew the farm life and could remember working long hours in the tobacco fields, they did not want to raise their children under such grueling and uncertain conditions, particularly to receive such returns. Even while emphasizing the character-building qualities of hard work, they told me they no longer wanted any part of farm life.

As I researched the oral history of Whippoorwill Farm, I found Mr. Oldham, an African American man in his eighties who lived about a mile from the farm. He told me a story no one else in my community, most of whom were white, seemed to know: the story of the Peoples, an African American family who once owned the farm. While subsequent searches for records of the Peoples' ownership of the farm have yielded no conclusive evidence of their presence and Mr. Oldham has since died, I continue to think of the story as an essential part of the farm's history. Perhaps it was actually a composite of many stories, or a truth-revealing lesson for a new landowner. Perhaps it was from a memory slightly displaced, or the story of ghosts who haunt so much of the landscape of the region.

As Mr. Oldham told it, the Peoples had purchased the land following Emancipation in the late nineteenth century, a time when black landownership was possible, though never easy. The Peoples, dirt farmers like the early Fawcetts who followed them, raised row crops such as cotton and tobacco and worked the land with mules. Because farm loans for African Americans were nearly nonexistent and mules were too costly for them to purchase outright, the Peoples were forced to offer their whole farm as collateral for the purchase of a single team. After a bad crop year, depressed cotton prices, and discriminatory practices used against black landowners in general, the Peoples lost their entire farm to foreclosure on the loan.

Any success at all among African Americans was an affront to "privileges of whiteness" and grounds for elite whites to take back land they felt to be rightfully theirs. The story of the Peoples' success and failure in the difficult venture of landownership and farming is haunting, especially because land lost among blacks in agriculture is rarely regained. The number of African American farm owners in the United States has now dwindled to eighteen thousand from more than a million in 1920 (Smith and Poff 1997).

In 1920, 14 percent of American farmers were black, though a majority of these were tenant farmers. Since then, African American farmers have left farms in many areas of the Southeast at three times the rate of white small farmers, often with the encouragement of government loan officers (Smith and Poff 1997). In 1999 the U.S. Supreme Court ruled in *Pigford v. USDA* that the Farmer's Home Administration, the federal agency responsible for providing credit to small farmers, systematically discriminated against African Americans. Though this victory is a vindication of many farmers, few farmers I know believe that a majority of these people will return to farming as a result of winning this case. In fact, some agricultural experts, including some black farmers, have predicted the extinction of minority farm owners in this country within a decade. Currently there are only 175 black farmers under age twenty-five in the nation (Smith and Poff 1997).

While most African American landowners like the Peoples scrambled to survive with few resources and against white society's wishes, many blacks never owned the land they worked in the first place. This is due to the legacies of slavery that prevented African American ownership, for even after Emancipation, African Americans had little or nothing with which to start their own farms.

Despite notions of freedom championed by the Jeffersonian ideal of the yeoman farmer, farm ownership has remained a luxury unavailable to many of this country's inhabitants (C. E. Daniel 1981, 15). In the South more than in most regions, farm owners and those who could never own land have long rubbed shoulders in the fields. Even when small farms predominated the Southeast, class and racial differences among farm folk have been part of everyday life. Thus, even when Emancipation ended slavery officially, those who owned land continued as bosses, and in most cases those who had been slaves continued as day workers or sharecroppers for their former owners or those owners' descendants.

When slaves were freed, many became sharecroppers or tenant farmers who perhaps owned a mule, but rarely did they become landowners. They paid their bills with their own sweat and a share of the crop. Often no cash exchanged hands. Poor whites also worked as sharecroppers. They too were caught in a cycle of debt and repayment that kept them, along with some Native Americans left in small habitations in the Southeast, permanently dependent upon the landowning class. Because of indebtedness that people could seldom overcome through farming, and because there was little else to do in some rural areas, many families were forced to remain subservient to landowners year after year. The cycle continued for generations.

As recently as 1972 in the flue-cured tobacco belt of eastern North Carolina, 45 percent of farmers were tenants, though many of these paid rent in cash rather than as a share of the crop (Flowers 1990). Though these tenants earned cash for their crops, many continued to own little or no land. Since the 1970s, most of these tenant farmers have left agriculture, not because they have graduated to landowner status, however, but because they have been, as Linda Flowers puts it, "throwed away." She describes the appearance of communities without their presence as follows:

If a piece of land or person or a stretch along the highway looks "throwed away," it can be in no worse shape. Fields left unattended and overcome with cockleburs are "throwed away." Ramshackly houses with boarded up windows and rotten porches, or country stores that have bitten the dust are "throwed away" (Flowers 1990, xi).

These images are commonplace along the highways of the South, at least in those areas where commercial and residential development have not replaced the old farmsteads. While it would be naive to wish for that era to return, Flowers shows that sharecroppers in her community did possess important skills and farm knowledge, along with pride and a sense of community.

Many former tenants who could not immediately find work in industry have worked as seasonal, perhaps migrant, agricultural workers. Many of the black and white seasonal workers on farms today who harvest, drive tractors, and manage other responsibilities for landowners do so because their families were once sharecroppers. They grew up farming and have all the skills needed by farmers but remain poor because they cannot buy farms and the necessary equipment for profitability themselves. Throughout the South, African Americans and some poor whites continue to work alongside Latinos and Haitians who have taken over the most menial tasks on farms. It is common to see African American tractor and truck drivers working in fields with Latino harvesters.

When I tilled the same ground Mr. Oldham said the Peoples once owned, occasionally unearthing rusty mule shoes, I realized I had come upon signs of people much like those Flowers describes. Though the Peoples avoided becoming sharecroppers at first, they remained beholden to a system that kept them "in hock" and then threw them away like so much farm refuse. Each time I came upon those signs of prior habitation, of mules plodding over the ground on which I stood, and of the Peoples's irrevocable loss, I thought of a dream ending, of a hope dashed as a family lost its grip on the primary symbol of freedom available to former slaves—land. My land came at a greater price than I had realized.

Not even the Peoples's loss was the first layer of land forfeiture at Whippoorwill Farm, however. On several occasions when I was tilling I unearthed Native American projectile points, tools of a people who had used the very same land for hunting, perhaps even agriculture, long before Europeans and their African slaves began clearing land in the South. Many layers of leaving are still evident in this, and most other, southern ground.

Departures through U.S. history have always been followed by arrivals, often the arrivals of increasingly moneyed interests as poor, widowed, bankrupt, or race-baited black and Indian farmers have given up their tenuous holds. Yet, contrary to this trend, I was a beginning farmer with little cash and with less power than the previous owner—the land-speculating dentist. Financial obstacles befall anyone seeking to reverse trends of concentration and capitalization of agriculture, from a single individual wishing to buck the system and enter agriculture to a society struggling to reform its patterns of landownership. Despite the efforts some have made to resist land and power accumulation in this country, the problem continues apace.

In my own case I found that few services were available to help young beginning farm owners, even those like myself with plentiful farming skills. Most lenders and farmers alike told me in 1984 that the only way to start farming was to inherit the land and equipment. Numerous banks turned me down. Many lenders told me that they simply did not make farm loans anymore because they are too risky.

Though USDA's Farmer's Home Administration (FmHA) was mandated by Congress to make "Limited Resource Loans" to small and be-ginning farmers who could find no credit elsewhere, I was rejected on my first attempt to apply for a farm ownership loan. The main reasons given for this refusal were that my farm plan, which relied on direct sales of fruits and vegetables, was "atypical for the area" and that I pos-sessed "insufficient farm experience" to succeed. With multiple wit-nesses and with a large file of information, I showed that beginning farmers are by definition inexperienced. I also proved that I had experi-ence working for others. I showed that my plan would work precisely because it was atypical, particularly since so many other farms were fail-ing—more than ten thousand went out of business in North Carolina in the 1980s alone. I appealed the local FmHA board's decision. To every-one's surprise, I won the district director's approval. Some of my friends felt that I won simply because the agency wanted to avoid bad press. Their view seemed justified by the cynicism I heard from the loan offi-cer in my county who reported that a board member said, "You'll never get a cent of that money back," implying that the farm would not make money and that foreclosure was imminent.

Even with the agricultural establishment against me, I farmed fruits and vegetables using organic methods and reached a measure of success. Not only did I make my loan payments, but I accelerated my payment schedule. The ground, though quite depleted by decades of tobacco and cotton farming, responded to the organic matter and cropping patterns I employed. Simultaneously, new markets for specialty produce arose everywhere in and around Chapel Hill, where I trucked my produce, and my income rose each season. Many in the university community were eager for good food, particularly that grown without chemicals. Many also claimed to frequent our markets to support the beleaguered rural population. Thus my success was due to my being "in the right place at the right time." Had I been only a hundred miles to the south or east, far away from such a market, my situation would have been drastically different and I probably would have searched in vain for a lucrative local market for organic crops. Niche marketing will allow some farmers to thrive amidst an ever-concentrating conventional agricultural economy, but only in particular places. It is important to realize that one success-ful organic farm does not mean that changes can be brought about easily for an entire economic sector or that many people can return to the land to do the same thing. Structural changes in agriculture are much more difficult to attain than individual ones.

As Whippoorwill Farm's production rose, especially with labor-intensive crops like blueberries and blackberries, I needed help with harvesting. Relying upon the help of family and neighbors was not an option for me, either. In my search for help, I realized that generations of out-migration from farms to subdivisions and town life had sapped the local community of most of its potential workers. High school students from the subdivisions who wanted to earn money had neither skills nor stamina for long hours in the sun to succeed as farm helpers. Farmers, most of whose children had left the farms, were so few in number, so old, or so overworked that I could not ask them for field help.

My most devoted hired help was an African American woman in her seventies named Mrs. Degraffenreidt. She came to work in the afternoons with her two teen-age grandchildren. For an entire summer, Mrs. Degraffenreidt, her grandchildren, and I made do with extra help from a few other high school students. She became a talkative maven, chiding the rest of us to work harder as we toiled.

While our farm, along with my wife's all-important non-farm income, began meeting many of our family's financial needs, a large number of family farmers in the county were either selling out or looking desperately for crop and livestock alternatives so they could stay in business. In 1960 there were 212,000 farms in North Carolina. By 1980 there were 93,000, a loss of six thousand farms each year for twenty years prior to our arrival. Only 49,406 farms remained in the state in 1997, many of which were part-time or hobby farms. From 1992 to 1997, more than one farm a day went out of business in North Carolina (Williams 1999). Nationally, farm statistics are no better. For example, small farms with gross sales of $250,000 or less have declined 75 percent since the 1960s. The 1990s have seen a quiet continuation of what became known across the country in the 1980s as the "Farm Crisis." Joseph Belden says that every decade since at least the 1880s has seen a farm crisis, the most severe of them in the 1930s (Belden 1986, 1). Yet the 1980s crisis rang with a new finality, and many in the United States grasped that when the generation presently in farming goes, no more family farmers will take their place.

In the early 1980s the Rural Advancement Fund, a small nonprofit organization in North Carolina committed to preserving the family farm, began operating a crisis hotline for farmers. My wife and I worked for the organization at the time. The family-scale farmers who called the hotline voiced concerns much beyond the usual complaints that accompany farming. They were desperate, sometimes suicidal. Unless something changed, they said, they were the last of their families to farm.

They talked about actively preventing their children from entering farming. Farmers have been called eternal optimists for the way they face the weather's adversity. But deep pessimism has cast its shadow over family farming, even among family farmers who have remained in business since the 1980s.

Although farmers desperately sought financial plans that could save their farms from foreclosures and bankruptcy and though some people in banking and government tried to help, farm families in our county and elsewhere went bankrupt. Previously semi-independent beef, dairy, and tobacco producers, a group our county was once known for, turned to contract poultry production. Farmers throughout the Southeast signed their farms over to banks to build entirely new poultry houses the size of football fields in exchange for one-sided contracts to huge poultry integrators, large corporate entities responsible for chickens and turkeys, from eggs to market. In their search for growers, Perdue farms and other poultry integrators were flocking to rural counties in poorer, rural areas of Arkansas, North Carolina, and Mississippi to take advantage of the remaining small farmers' frantic search for ways to survive. Many farmers openly complained about the exploitation by the companies but felt they had no choice but to sign with the integrators.

The promise of regular paychecks from poultry operations, even though the huge poultry houses required outlays of more than a quarter of a million dollars and more than full-time work, enticed farmers into borrowing money and entering into a new business (Fesperman and Shatzkin 1999). Not surprisingly, when I was first rejected by FmHA for my atypical plan, the loan officer and the local extension agent mentioned that I should look into chicken production. Though I discarded the idea, many had no choice but to sign on. Chicken and turkey production have skyrocketed throughout the Southeast; feathers litter the roads from the large truckloads of birds hauled to processing plants in counties throughout the region. The smell of huge poultry barns wafts through the rural landscape and is inescapable to the passerby.

In the meantime, as many farmers have gone out of business or changed their way of making a living, a generally robust economy has masked their departure. During the 1980s a greater number of families left farming than during the Great Depression, but theirs was mostly a silent exodus.

FIGURE 2.1. *Children in a turkey barn in Sampson County, North Carolina, 1995. Photograph by Christopher Sims.*

A County's Repopulation

With the daily processing of tens of thousands of birds in our county came hundreds of processing workers. At first, unemployed farmers took the skilled chicken plant jobs, and rural people who had never owned farms provided the unskilled labor. Their rural, farm work-related backgrounds made them ideal workers in a chicken plant because they worked hard, could withstand grueling conditions, and worked for low wages. However, even with the surplus labor in the rural South, hundreds and then thousands more people were needed for the burgeoning industry in our county alone. As the poultry integrators were unwilling to raise wages to draw additional workers from domestic sectors, local labor pools quickly ran dry.

The poultry integrators began actively recruiting Latinos to work for them. They hired bilingual (Spanish/English) workers first, then asked these workers to help them hire other Latinos, such as migrant farmworkers from Florida. They hired Latinos although some of the long-term residents complained that the companies intentionally lowered wages and hired the outsiders as a way of avoiding wage raises to which the local residents knew they were entitled. This dynamic has bred resentment between African American, poor white, and Latino workers in many small towns, often hampering union organizing. Nevertheless, through word of mouth and family connections, Mexicans and Central Americans continued to arrive at the plants seeking work. Whole towns in Mexico responded to the call for poultry plant (*pollera*) workers.

Carloads of men and women, single and married, arrived to shoulder the load. By the mid-1980s, the lure of steady year-round income, though usually at minimum wage and in cold, wet, and dangerous conditions, brought Latinos and Latinas to our community by the thousands in a matter of a year or two. The Latino workers I knew complained privately of exploitative labor practices and of dangerous and unpleasant conditions within the plants, but they continued to work in them.

Many of these poultry workers also took part-time work after hours. During a particularly heavy work week on Whippoorwill Farm, I contacted a foreman at the local chicken processing plant to offer some part-time work. That afternoon a carload of men, all recently from Mexico, arrived at my door. They began working that afternoon, several of them still wearing the white coats and black rubber boots from the *pollera*.

The Handwork of Agriculture

The idea that machines have replaced farmers and farmworkers, at least for the non-grain crops, is a myth. While farmers have dwindled in number and machinery continues to increase in size and sophistication, human beings continue to do precise work that no machine can, in fruits and vegetables and in poultry and meat processing. Thus, it is not the handwork of agriculture that has disappeared, but rather the permanently self-employed people who once did this work who have gone. In their place are hundreds of thousands of temporary workers who have little say in the matter of food production. Though human, they are merely part of the necessary machinery of the "factories in the field" (McWilliams 1939). Their hard work and low wages are some of the reasons why poultry and other foods have become cheap and plentiful in the grocery stores today. While poultry corporations may give the impression that their birds are farm-raised and me-chanically processed, in actuality, hundreds of workers, many of them using their hands very rapidly in assembly lines, process every bird.

As Daniel Rothenberg observes, seasonal and underemployed farm-workers are not merely holdovers from an agricultural past but are "pro-foundly, if paradoxically, modern." He is worth quoting at length on this subject:

While the labor provided by farmworkers is traditional in nature—hoe-ing; weeding; pruning; and, above all, hand harvesting—the pressing need for large numbers of temporary workers is a function of the industrializa-tion of agricultural production . . . The industrialization and technological sophistication of modern agriculture has produced an increased need for temporary, itinerant laborers to provide the most traditional forms of hand labor. At the same time, the steady supply of low-wage laborers has pro-vided employers with little incentive for increased mechanization. As agri-cultural production becomes increasingly technological, with laser-leveled fields, genetically engineered seeds, and computer-controlled irrigation, and as farms begin to look more like other large corporations, the differ-ence between seasonal laborers and their employers becomes ever more striking (Rothenberg 1998, 12–13).

This means that farmworkers and processing workers are ever more indispensable as the control of agriculture falls into fewer and fewer hands, hands that are unlikely to get dirty or bloody with the tasks of laboring in the soil or cutting chicken parts. Often farmworkers do not know the owners personally, as managers, "coyotes," crew leaders, and others manage the everyday affairs of the fields, and owners work and live elsewhere. In turn, even as farmworkers are more necessary for agri-cultural production than ever, consumers seem unaware that farmers have been replaced.

The managers of large food corporations want us to believe in what Ingolf Vogeler called the "myth of the family farm" (Vogeler 1982). Ad-vertising executives want consumers to continue to hold in our minds, as we buy and consume food, images of rural yeomen who work hard to provide food for us with their own hands.

Meanwhile, farmworkers remain nearly invisible to consumers at all levels of agricultural production. What few consumers seem to know is that often there are no machines to do the delicate handwork still re-quired in picking fruits and vegetables and for butchering meats for sale.

They also do not know that in many cases it is still possible to hire low-paid laborers whose work is cheaper than investing in new technologies. Thus we see on food packages and television commercials farmers who appear to work alone in their fields. Never do we see migrant or seasonal farmworkers or poultry or seafood workers portrayed on a package as a means of selling a product.

Even if we no longer believe in the family farm myth, food companies perpetuate an alternate myth: that even though farms are increasingly consolidated and more mechanized, food production has become more efficient and touched by fewer human hands and therefore is somehow more hygienic and better for you. Stainless steel machines packaging food without human beings is a familiar televised scene. Food and farm advertisers purposely avoid showing the millions of landless and itinerant farmworkers who pick and process foods.

Perhaps the most important point to learn about these workers is that many who have flooded to agricultural jobs in the United States have recently come from farms themselves, some even hoping to return someday to their land in Mexico or Central America to farm again. This connection to a previous life on small farms gives many rural Latinos a work ethic the high school students who worked with me never knew and which the Fawcetts had tried desperately to escape. Their experience with rural work, gained from years of coaxing food from dirt and coupled with poverty, makes Latinos ready targets for a food industry hungry for hardworking laborers. Thus the pattern of farm labor and of rural dependency started with slavery and continued with sharecropping persists to this day and has become more transnational than ever. Now farm labor often comes from other failed farms or from not-quite-solvent farms in Mexico and Central America, perhaps Haiti and elsewhere in the Caribbean, rather than from the southeastern United States. Regardless of prevalent myths, our system of agriculture is still fueled by the losses of the underprivileged as much as by the successes of the wealthiest landowners.

I joined with the Latino workers who worked for me. We developed a relationship which reflects John Steinbeck's 1936 observations of interrelations between farmworkers and family farmers, the latter of which he defines as those tending between five acres and one hundred acres:

On the whole, the relations between the migrants and the small farmers are friendly and understanding. In many of California's agricultural strikes the small farmer has sided with the migrant against the powerful speculative farm groups. The workers realize that the problem of the small farmer is not unlike their own (Steinbeck 1988, 32–33).

The same workers who had settled semipermanently into our community sent all their extra "farm" income to their families at home in Mexico. Through our labor, our farms and lives became interconnected, though I always enjoyed the privileges of landownership and production in this country, while they did not.

Librado's Farm

My most enthusiastic employee and eventually my closest confidant of all my employees was a young man named Librado. While working, Librado often brought his wife and son to stay in or near the house. His wife would sit on our porch playing with their little son, or sometimes in the cooler afternoons they would all come to the field to watch as we worked. "I want to teach my son about farm work," Librado said. Of course, the child only played nearby, but this, according to Librado, would influence him to want to be a farmer. Librado had a commitment to farm work because it is work he loved. He also had an understanding of the management of crops that one cannot simply teach but that is gained through practice. Librado learned my farm operation quickly. He began to make suggestions for the farm, to help make decisions, and to do all the work when I was away selling at markets. Librado began to tell me of the longing he had to return home. At the end of his second year of work at the *pollera*, Librado informed me that he intended to return to Mexico immediately to farm. Librado intended to stay on his Mexican farm permanently if at all possible and to avoid entering the cycle of departures and returns that characterize the lives of many farmworkers. He had accumulated enough money to buy a pickup truck, chainsaw, weed trimmer, and a few other tools. His cash supply amounted to a few thousand dollars. He planned to take these tools and money to Guerrero, Mexico, to begin farming again and to put into practice a few techniques he had learned, or invented, in the United States.

Our parting was short. I said goodbye to Librado and his family as they drove away from our farm with the hope of returning to their own small farm. I have not seen them since.

Given the realities of survival of small peasant farmers in Mexico, however, Librado and his family may find themselves back in the migrant stream searching again for income that Mexican small farms can rarely provide. In fact, Mexican family farms are being systematically squeezed out of production by many of the same forces that have driven U.S. farmers out of business. Increasing farm size, made possible through the introduction of farm mechanization, chemicals, and fertilizers allowing a single farmer to plant more land, all of this encouraged by international farm policy, has displaced millions of peasant farmers who lack resources to purchase such tools. Many of these small farm families have had to become itinerant workers in Mexico. Some work for farms on both sides of the border.

The transnational push to consolidate and privatize land holdings is accompanied by the systematic political breakdown of land reforms instituted by the Mexican government following the Revolution of 1910–1917. This is especially evident in the evisceration of the right to communal land given by Article 27 of the Mexican Constitution and Agrarian Code (Collier and Quaratiello 1994, 84–85). Private interests have chipped away at progressive land-related laws. In addition, the North American Free Trade Agreement (NAFTA) has removed trade barriers, further destabilizing Mexican small farms by placing *campesinos* (small farmers) in direct competition with large private farming interests from the United States for both domestic and foreign markets. NAFTA came about through pressures from the United States to open the borders of Mexico to U.S. corporations. As a result of NAFTA, many U.S. corporate farm interests moved into Mexico to buy extensive acreage where land is inexpensive and to take advantage of that country's cheaper wage laws and less stringent pesticide laws. Many labor and environmental groups in the United States opposed NAFTA, as did peasant farmers in Mexico such as the Zapatistas, who rose up in protest in the state of Chiapas on the very day NAFTA took effect. They and others have contended that the Mexican government capitulated to international capitalist forces at the expense of Mexican farmers. The Mexican government, forced into dire straits by an economic crisis brought on by depressed oil prices, turned to international trade solutions to ease its pain. As a result, agricultural interests have been freed to exploit many of the same tactics as the U.S.-controlled *maquiladoras*. These U.S. manufacturing and now agricultural interests have employed many Mexican workers just over the border for only a fraction of the pay dictated by U.S. minimum wage laws (see Prieto 1997). In 1996, according to the National Union of Autonomous Regional Campesinos in Agriculture (UNORCA), these trends left 80 percent of Mexican small farmers—two and one-half million, a majority of the country's rural population—in danger of bankruptcy. According to UNORCA, the major obstacle to farm survival is "lack of credit" ("Mexican Farm Laborers Face 'Slave Labor'" 1998).

One factor that makes Mexicans leaving farms different from families like the Fawcetts is that there are no burgeoning service and industrial sectors in Mexico in which displaced farmers can find employment above poverty wages. When rural poor people in Mexico leave their land in search of something better or are forced off it by drought or overpopulation, often they feel their only recourse is to attempt to go to the United States, where at least a possibility exists of making some money.

As tenuous as their hold on land is, most small farmers in Mexico and Central America I have talked with still feel it is their most secure means of living and providing for their children. Many risk going to the United States to restore themselves and their families to agricultural production. For instance, of the fifty families with members who had been to the United States or who hoped to go I interviewed in the Guatemalan town of Jacaltenango in 1996, all of them spoke of coming back to Guatemala to buy more land and a house. These families taught me that an immigrant farmworker in the United States may send hundreds or even thousands of dollars home annually. In turn, the spouse, parents, or children of the workers buy land and homes. Even though *campesinos* in most of Latin America are used to living with much less than many U.S. citizens can imagine, few young families today are able to survive with so little. Thus, even as migrants send money home, few Latinos I have interviewed have been able to return permanently as Librado hoped to do.

In this small place called Whippoorwill Farm, numerous leavings have been linked not only to one another but to mass exoduses through the North American continent and beyond. I conclude that the most tragic part of this story is not simply that people leave. People always have left homes for travel elsewhere and to make better lives for themselves. Rather, the tragedy of these departures is that returns to farm ownership, particularly in the United States, are nearly nonexistent. These losses are not only about land but also about people losing knowledge and power. As large numbers of small farmers lose control of land, they are replaced with temporary workers who have no control over their destinies. Because of lack of continuity of farmers on the land and of a long-term vision, the environment also suffers as well because corporate interests often think in terms of short-term profits, not primogeniture.

Migration from farms typically means that skills and experience once applied to particular places have become free-floating and perhaps will never be applied again to a single piece of land. Agricultural skills with no ground on which to apply them and without children with the stability of place to learn them are lost completely in a generation. Ironically, today it is migrant farmworkers who possess the hand skills leftover from farm ownership elsewhere. Skills in harvesting, pruning, and hand cultivation are passed on—from those who own little or nothing to their children, who may never know what farm ownership means.

Farm Labor Forever

Only one year after Librado left, my family and I sold Whippoorwill Farm and I entered graduate school. Unlike many in this country and most in Mexico, Haiti, and most everywhere else, I had opportunities to do other work and pursue dreams as I left agriculture for full-time study. When we sold the farm after nearly ten years of hard work, it had become a rare commodity: a "working" and profitable organic farm of reasonable scale. Not surprisingly, five prospective buyers made offers on the farm the first weekend it was on the market. All of them were enamored with the possibilities of making a living at farming, though none of them had ever learned how. We sold to the most experienced of the five, hoping that the story of the farm we had revived would continue beyond us. Ironically, those who romanticize farming but who possess little or no skills to do it can afford to buy land, while those like Librado with many skills and farm experience cannot afford to buy any land in this country, let alone an improved farm like Whippoorwill Farm.

One of the reasons I decided to leave the farm was because I had grown weary of working by myself. I had no neighbors at home during the daylight hours. I worked alone most every day, at least until the poultry plant workers arrived in the afternoons. This silence in the countryside where most everyone gets into cars and goes somewhere else to work created a deafening calm. It was a silence after a storm that had blown millions of people from the landscape, sometimes in succession of generations, sometimes "layer after layer" of different families. I also heard the silence left by my own grandparents' departure from my own family's farm in the 1980s. It was from them I had learned to farm. No matter how hard I worked, I could never bring back my own relatives to work with me as I had worked with them as a boy.

In 1999 I learned that Whippoorwill Farm might go on the market again, since the latest farm venture had not survived. Who remained out there to buy it, especially as inflation and deterioration of the fruit planting had occurred? Who could afford the down payment on a farmstead in the suburbanizing Piedmont of North Carolina and possessed skills and stamina to do the work? Who with such qualifications also would be willing to stay home and work it? Who remained in our rural communities to teach anyone how to farm? Certainly no one from the farm families who left their traces on Whippoorwill Farm stayed behind to teach newcomers. Certainly no migrant worker who has come to work in the poultry plants can afford the time or space. Those who possess the skills most likely possess no capital for such a venture. Capital in agriculture, as in many other economic sectors, has moved further from the grasp of laborers' hands than ever. A single tractor can cost more than one hundred thousand dollars. Even a whole year's wages from the poultry plant could only buy a few acres, selling for more than five thousand dollars per acre in many rural parts of North Carolina.

Many layers of losses in southern agrarian history are found in the story of Whippoorwill Farm: the succession of land use from Native American to European, African American landownership and loss, growth of towns and cities and the urbanization of particular areas of the South, a rise in hobby farming; heightened interest in alternatives for both conventional and beginning farmers, the loss of farmland to non-agricultural uses, the rapid loss of farm-trained laborers to supply the farm market; the loss of indigenous knowledge of places and of farming techniques; and finally, the trend that this volume addresses most directly, the influx of Latinos and other immigrant workers into rural areas.

Whippoorwill Farm is located in the urbanizing Piedmont, and its future as farmland is questionable as the pressures of development bear down upon that area of the state. Zoning restrictions may save the land, but future owners may want to "grow" houses instead of crops. Meanwhile, in the less populous counties of the region, farms are growing ever larger. The average size of farms has risen, while the number of farms has dwindled. It is the small hobby farms, retirement farms, and tobacco farms with allotments that skew the state's average farm size to only 185 acres, as opposed to 588 nationally (U.S. Department of Commerce 1996). In reality, these little farms are rarely run by people whose primary occupation is farming, unless the person depends upon renting land to supplement the income on their own acreage or has found a niche market that by definition is limited. The average farmer who raises corn, soybeans, cotton, or most other farm commodities common to the region often must farm thousands of acres of their crops to make a living. Many farmers are caught in a whirlwind of debt for machinery that forces them to farm ever more acreage to pay for the equipment. Everywhere farmers chant the now-familiar refrain: the prices of farm inputs continue to go up while the prices we receive for our products go down or stay the same. Nearly unbelievably, for instance, the 1999 corn price fell below the 1930 price while prices paid for machinery, land, and other inputs continued to rise! While some agricultural economists might laud this achievement of American agricultural productivity, the reality of the situation is that family farmers pay dearly to hold onto their land, and still huge agricultural operations continue to replace smaller ones.

Farm Consolidation

The southeastern and mid-Atlantic states generally have become a stronghold of the corporate dominance of agriculture. As small farms have dwindled, large corporations, sometimes disguising themselves as family farms, have come to control commodities. Even "truck crops" traditionally produced in the Southeast by small farmers have become large-farm commodities, or commodities produced under contract to large companies. In Mount Olive, North Carolina, for example, the Mt. Olive Pickle Company divvies up contracts among growers—never for small-acreage contracts—and thus effectively eliminates the independent production of cucumbers. Of course, some farmers are amenable to the contract system because, as with poultry, it promises a particular price upon delivery. Mt. Olive provides seeds to the growers, processes and markets their products for them, and guarantees the growers a particular price per pound. However, as with any contract of an agricultural nature, pickle contracts are often much more advantageous to the company than the grower. There are many factors related to weather, insects, disease, and the international market—most all beyond the farmers' control but that can reduce the quality of the crop—that the buyer can use to justify paying lower prices for a crop.

In addition, growers must always sacrifice a measure of independence when they sign a contract with a powerful company that controls a huge portion of the market for a particular commodity.

As prices paid for nearly all farm products have dropped, consolidation in production continues unabated. This is paralleled by the concentration of food processing and marketing as well. Companies such as ConAgra, Cargill, and Archer Daniels Midland control the processing of numerous commodities, and these same corporations often control every single aspect of production and sales of some commodities, from the breeding or genetic engineering of seeds to the grocery shelf. This is known as vertical integration. Poultry production is a good example of this trend, as are hogs, grains, beef, dairy, and many fruits and vegetables. Even organic foods are increasingly produced by large, vertically integrated corporations.

When I spoke with farmers on the Farm Crisis Hotline during the 1980s and they discussed with me the possibility of losing their farms, many of them talked about loving farm life because it allowed them to make a living on their own land. They took pride in being their "own bosses." Now, few people with contracts talk about such benefits. In fact, many contract growers consider themselves less free and less secure than their factory-working counterparts. As one North Carolina tobacco farmer said upon contemplating the likelihood of tobacco going to contract-style farming, "It's like farming Perdue chickens, Perdue [the company's founder] makes all the money" (Allegood 1999). In a factory, laborers own nothing and therefore, in theory, may walk away from a job if a better offer comes along. Sometimes benefits such as health insurance and retirement packages are added incentives. In contract farming, however, farmers are owners without the power to control their investments. In effect, the companies use farmers' investments to make a profit, and the farmers are usually beholden to the companies. The companies dictate changes to the farm operations, and the farmers must obey or lose their contracts. Because of the huge investments in equipment and land, farmers cannot simply walk away from one company and sign a contract with another. Often there is no other company and even if there is, losing a contract with one company for reasons having to do with standing up to its representatives and demanding fair treatment is usually seen as belligerent behavior, effectively prohibiting a grower from finding any other contract. Too often a grower who rocks the boat loses any chance of gaining any contract (National Interfaith Committee for Worker Justice 1998). The loss of a farm contract usually means

FIGURE 2.2. *Farmworkers set out tobacco plants, 1999. Photograph by Chris Johnson.*

bankruptcy. These losses often put farmers who may appear to be independent on the same unsure footing with farmworkers. This means that in actuality the two groups do share concerns, and this can be used as an effective organizing tool.

Tobacco has been one commodity that has remained free of many contractual confines of poultry and vegetable commodities. This is true mostly because during the 1930s the federal government created the tobacco program as a means of salvaging the incomes of hundreds of thousands of small farmers throughout the South. The program effectively limited production to family-size units and kept the price of tobacco high through acreage allotments. This allowed thousands of farms to remain in production through the 1960s and beyond. Recently, health concerns have weakened tobacco's position with the progressive public otherwise prone to favor small farms over corporate ones. At the same time, mechanization of tobacco production combined with policy changes that allowed farmers to buy and sell their allotments weakened the program's effectiveness as a profitable small-farm crop. Yet there are still relatively small and profitable tobacco farms.

While a few farmers have found their niches and have succeeded in bucking trends toward "getting big or getting out," these are the exceptions. For the most part, family farmers are a beleaguered population, with dwindling numbers and consequently decreasing power in the political arena. In many cases, this is true of farmers who hire H-2A workers or migrant farmworkers. Farmers can sometimes be victimized by the structure of agriculture through macroeconomics even as they may exploit farmworkers microeconomically.

The corporate dominance of food production is a stark reality today. John Steinbeck saw this great exodus from the land in the 1930s and called attention to it (Steinbeck 1939). Numerous authors since then have marked agriculture's continued big-business dominance. Walter Goldschmidt gave us the landmark comparison of family farm and corporate agricultural economics entitled *As You Sow.* John Shover wrote *First Majority—Last Minority*, a documentation of the rural transformation he calls the "great disjuncture." Wendell Berry's book *The Unsettling of America* shows the effects of farm losses in rural America on both culture and agriculture. Jim Hightower's *Hard Tomatoes, Hard Times*, the famous exposé of the land grant universities' collusion in agricultural concentration, must also be mentioned. Where have the warnings from these works taken us? Perhaps only as far as Wendell Berry's recent title suggests: *Another Turn of the Crank*. This work reveals that trends toward farm loss continue unabated and that quite simply, "we are rapidly running out of farmers" and these farmers are clearly irreplaceable (Berry 1996, 4). Farmers of all ages are in short supply. Today, according to the Department of Commerce's agricultural census, their average age is fifty-five.

Although these works depict a dismal farm landscape, they do not identify U.S. farmers with the class of international rural peasant laborers who are losing land and autonomy across the globe. Perhaps because of the Jeffersonian ideal of democratic ownership and our tendency to see the economy as devoid of the trappings of feudalism, U.S. farmers usually are portrayed in a class by themselves among agriculturalists worldwide. How many times have we heard that a single U.S. farmer feeds more than one hundred people or that America's farm productivity exceeds that of every other country? How often have we heard of the U.S. farmers' independence? These emphases on autonomy and efficient production mask the similarities between the rural economies of the United States and other countries. In France, arguably as food self-sufficient as the United States, thousands of peasant farmers have left the land recently due to international market pressures associated with trade agreements. Yet this is not portrayed as part of the same problem that U.S. farmers are experiencing. In the United States the problem of people leaving the land is portrayed as a problem of efficiency. As John Berger points out, this is because U.S. farmers are construed as members of an economy where no one is classified as a "peasant," while in Europe a nomenclature of peasants is still common. He says U.S. farmers remain in a class by themselves because the "rate of economic development based on monetary exchange [in this country] was too rapid and too total" (Berger 1979, xxiii), meaning that the transition from a large number of small farmers to a relatively few landowners based on capitalization of agriculture has occurred here much faster than elsewhere.

The federal government's lack of response to these losses seems related to its inability to differentiate between total farm income and individual farms owned when assessing the health of the agricultural economy, as the headlines from Florida reveal. It is also due to a general lackadaisical attitude toward farm losses as long as food prices remain low. Because of the way these numbers are construed, we tend to think of farm loss as increased efficiency rather than as a component of the international exodus from farms. Thus, U.S. small farmers make their exodus quietly, while in France small farmers are organized and extremely vocal and they enjoy the support of the general populace.

Perhaps U.S. farm productivity supported by so few full-time farmers is positive by some standards. However, by considering farmers in this country as only independent entrepreneurs who are more a part of the owner class than the rural peasantry, we fail to see and respond to important political and economic parallels with other countries. In this way, lamentations over rural America make the problem of U.S. family farmers seem disconnected from those of Mexican farmers who have lost their land and livelihood, and thus many of us miss important associations that could lead to international trade reforms or to initiatives that would promote individual farm survival rather than overall profitability. Also, while U.S. citizens may mourn the loss of the nation's family farms, few take the extra step to link the loss to the situation of farmworkers who occupy the fields.

Griffith and Kissam show that an emphasis on family farmers and their crises is one-sided and that this emphasis gives the general public an inaccurate and nostalgic view of farms and farm population, usually focusing on "a reified lifestyle at whose heart and hearth lies the American family, usually of German or Scandinavian heritage." They claim that this type of attention has failed to raise the "public's consciousness about either the characteristics or conditions of U.S. farmworkers" (Griffith and Kissam 1995, 4). This one-sided focus emphasizes only the U.S. side of loss in agriculture, usually with a projected image of the male of European descent as its icon. This focus often overlooks the difficulties of many former inhabitants of land such as displaced owners or tenants, who are often people of color, who have contributed to farm life for centuries. Moreover, losses of farms are rarely portrayed as anything but U.S. families who are part of the rural middle class.

Complete stories of farm loss must concentrate on the long history of leavings and displacements that characterize much of this country's landscape. Farmworkers, though they are often seen as victims, are displaced along with many former farm owners in the United States. When we see large farms today, those that employ hundreds of low-paid farmworkers, rarely do we see the layers of loss that underlie these fields of shame. It is essential that we correlate family farmers in the United States with those in Mexico and elsewhere in order to grasp the reason we need farmworkers in U.S. fields today and why so many come from other countries.

One component of John Steinbeck's *Grapes of Wrath* that makes that particular story so timelessly powerful is that it portrays the Joads leaving their Dust Bowl farmland in Oklahoma in the 1930s instead of merely portraying their lives as they arrive as farmworkers in California, where the industrialization of agriculture had already taken hold. The two sides of the farm economy, the losers and the winners, appear together in the same scenes. Perhaps one reason we have felt so deeply moved by the story of the Joads is that they came from a farm of their own, albeit a sharecropper's homestead. With today's farmworkers, we often imagine them being nomads from nowhere. This is far from the case, however.

Though many farmworkers travel today, most have some memory of, or a connection to, greater stability elsewhere, even if from the memories of a previous generation. Even Cesar Chavez, well known as a farmworker and the founder of United Farm Workers, entered itinerant farm work because of his family's loss of its farm due to a foreclosure in Arizona (Griswold del Castillo and Garcia 1995, 3).

Advocacy across Borders

As farmworker advocates, we emphasize the exploitation of farmworkers, as opposed to farmers or agribusiness, as our primary focus. Unquestionably, farmworkers remain the most exploited population in agriculture. However, we must not conclude that the predicament of farmworkers is a new phenomenon or an isolated one. Rather the current era's treatment of farmworkers is but another layer of loss and exploitation added to those of the slaves, sharecroppers, small farmers, and other migrants who came before them.

Phillip L. Martin and David A. Martin have made it clear in their 1994 work *The Endless Quest: Helping America's Farm Workers* that simply helping farmworkers to escape farm work fails to address the structural problems inherent in agriculture. As farmworkers leave agricultural work, they are replaced by a seemingly endless supply of laborers who are fleeing agricultural and economic catastrophes elsewhere. Helping farmworkers out of agriculture only allows for others to replace them.

By seeing farmworkers as refugees from small farms in other parts of the same global system, and as part of the same exodus experienced in the southeastern United States, we can begin to place farmworkers in the context of numerous layers of loss. Just as easily we can see that the present agribusiness dominance of farm production has a long history. This view effectively eliminates national borders as a means of differentiating workers and farmers.

Using this analytical starting point, we also may come to the realization that solutions are no longer as simple as having one farmer improve the living conditions of the farmworkers on a single acreage, although this is certainly part of the solution, but we also will begin to think in terms of international forces and ways to combat them. This premise is different from a simple emphasis on a single farm loss or solely on farmworker exploitation on one site, but treats both the loss of farms and the current presence of farmworkers as different aspects of the same trend. This is a trend that means agribusiness is gradually taking away control and ownership of land and food production from individuals and families regardless of their country of origin and giving it to ever-fewer decision makers. Thus not only must we link layers of loss vertically within a single farm as with Whippoorwill Farm, but we also must search for linkages horizontally across international borders.

As we make these intellectual linkages, we can begin to see beyond statistics touting the overall farm income and read between the lines to see not only the misery the industry has caused its workers but also how the industry itself has shifted to an industrial model dependent upon farmworkers who have replaced small farmers in the U.S. economy. Most important, we will realize that the very structure of agriculture as it is organized today is made possible by an underclass of people who make it work. Without their losses and the concomitant consolidation of farms and the hiring of the displaced farmers, U.S. agriculture would grind to a halt. Fewer people understand how to farm and fail to have the work ethic required for such a venture. This means we as a nation have become dependent upon displaced farmers from elsewhere to do our hand labor in the fields. We eat because of their losses. U.S. agriculture depends upon the displaced. Indeed, it always has.

Life on Easy Street

Rachel LaCour
Niesen, 1999
SAF intern

With his deep, sandblasted voice, Robert Lee
Faison tells me about his life on Easy Street,
just between Dunn and Newton Grove, North
Carolina. Robert, a sixty-five-year-old African
American farmworker, bears the physical memories of a life of labor—a slouched, contorted
spine from years of bending low in green-yellow
leaves, cavernous grooves around the eyes, gifts
of squinting and sun, one lost pinkie finger,
and a toothless smile that reveals contagious
contentment and graceful strength.

Robert Lee Faison was born in 1933 in Dunn
and moved to a house off Easy Street when he
was five years old. He still lives on the same plot
of land, the land on which his mother's house
was built, on which he, his brothers and sisters
were born, on which he raised his own family,
and on which he has worked since he was twelve
years old.

Today, the family is gone and the old home
has gone through various stages of identity. Now
he lives in a labor camp, only ten feet from the
old home, with Mexican H-2A guestworkers.

As distinct as the weather-worn eyes and
protruding lower lip, Robert's life is one of
monumental routine—the monumental in the
mundane. His roots run deep, and he is the only
member of his family remaining on the land.
Surrounded by tobacco fields and the voices of

another language, Robert works hard in the only
life he has ever known: tobacco farming.

He is an ironic mix of rooted routine and willing adaptability. He has lived on the same land
for over sixty years but is learning Spanish from
the Mexican workers he lives and labors with.

"I know everything there is to know 'bout
'bacca." Robert's molasses-slow slang sticks in
my ears for ten minutes after he completes a
sentence. That's his life too—slow and steady,
a cycle of planting, priming, worming, cropping, harvesting, sorting, hauling, barning, and
curing tobacco. He is a breathing history book of
tobacco farming in North Carolina.

Now, too old to do the work he once did,
Robert drives a tractor during harvest month,
hauling flatbed loads of cut tobacco leaves
picked by migrant workers who live with him at
the camp.

He remembers the days when all the farmworkers were African American and the plows
were horse-drawn. He is a man of stories and
life-learned wisdom who has spent his life working in the fields of North Carolina.

In many ways, Robert is a forgotten hero. He
moves quietly, lives simply, and does his work
with incredible dignity. He is a constant in the
changing equation of American agriculture.

CHAPTER 3

Standing Idly By

"Organized" Farmworkers in South Florida during the Depression and World War II

Cindy Hahamovitch

If "organized labor" were defined as trade union activity, the story of organizing among African American migrant workers would be short indeed. They would appear to be the most powerless and marginalized of American workers. Denied the right of collective bargaining, disfranchised by both race and residency requirements, ignored by all but the most philanthropic labor unions, Atlantic Coast migrants would seem to epitomize the unorganized, if not the disorganized.[1] Certainly the experience of black farm laborers in South Florida during the Great Depression bears out such a characterization. Yet migrant farmworkers have power that industrial workers would envy: not only can they hurt a growers' profits by withholding their labor, but they can ruin a year's investment in a matter of days. The Second World War gave farmworkers the opportunity to wield this power. To farmers, the war brought the prospect of boom prices and the specter of spiraling wages. To farmworkers, it brought federal migrant labor camps, home bases to which they could retreat while they waited for crops to ripen and wages to rise. A tight labor market and guaranteed food and housing allowed black fieldworkers in South Florida to act militantly, bargain collectively, and organize successfully, without a union, a strike fund, a picket line, or a pamphlet.

Farmworkers living in Florida's migrant camps raised their wages, but in doing so they raised Leviathan. Accustomed to workers disciplined by the starvation wages of the Depression years, growers were outraged to find black workers uncooperative and organized. They demanded the importation of foreign workers who could be deported for refusing to work, and their demands were heeded. In 1945 alone, the War Food Administration put 178,000 importees and POWs to work in the nation's fields, while domestic migrants remained frozen in their home counties, denied the right to leave without the permission of county officials.

Thus the story told here can be broken down into three discrete

FIGURE 3.1. *Sixty-five-year-old tractor driver Robert Lee Faison has spent his life planting, harvesting, cropping, curing, and barning tobacco, 1999. Photograph by Rachel LaCour Niesen.*

phases. In the 1930s, a "factories in the fields" condition prevailed, as South Florida's truck farmers drove down farm wages by enlisting a reserve army of unemployed and displaced people. The construction of federal migrant labor camps beginning in 1940 inaugurated what might be called the "settlement house" stage. New Deal reformers designed these labor camps both to provide shelter and to convey to the nation's most down-and-out people the virtues of stability, thrift, and self-discipline. This stage ended in 1942, when growers demanded federal relief from what they called labor shortages, insisting in particular on their right to import foreign workers. The third stage we might call "the militarization of agriculture," as federal officials recruited, imported, housed, and moved a new reserve army of foreign workers. In doing so, they destroyed the embryonic organizing effort achieved during the "settlement house" stage.

Federal officials weighed in on growers' side after 1942 because southern farm employers claimed that labor scarcity was widespread and would prevent them from meeting war production goals. However, the question of whether a shortage of labor existed was inherently political. Florida's truck farmers were accustomed to an abundance of farmworkers; to growers, this abundance and the low wages it guaranteed seemed normal, natural, and necessary. Any change in the supply or price of labor could only be a change for the worse. Thus the growers defined as a dearth of labor any circumstance in which farmworkers were powerful enough to make demands upon employers.

Farmworkers, too, had a great deal riding on the price of picking a hamper of beans. As some black southerners joined the military or migrated north or west in search of higher pay and greater opportunities, those who remained behind depended upon rising wartime wages to help them do battle with Jim Crow and pull themselves out of the mire of the Depression. Higher wages for fieldwork meant that black families might be able to keep their children in school and out of the fields; black women might escape the drudgery of cooking and cleaning for white women; black men might enjoy the luxury of choosing one job over another.

Thus the struggle over labor supply during the war came to represent everything that farmworkers hoped for and growers feared. Farmworkers lost this contest, but the story of their defeat defies simple notions of migrants' powerlessness and passivity, challenging us to rethink the meaning of organized labor.

By the 1920s, vegetables, or "truck crops," as they were called, were Florida's most valuable products, despite the greater renown of the state's citrus fruit.[2] Land speculators made fortunes by buying newly drained tracts from the state for two dollars an acre and reselling them for ten times as much to distant buyers, many of whom did not know if they were getting arable land or alligator-ridden swamp. In 1926, a devastating hurricane flattened Miami and burst the land bubble, but a hardy few remained and prospered by putting their money in beans and sugarcane. Although the rest of the nation sank into the depths of the Depression in the 1930s, South Florida's truck-farming industry boomed, and the value of green beans, the state's principal crop, continued to climb.

What made South Florida's agriculture unique in the 1930s was that both its farmers and its labor force often were migrants. While central Florida's citrus orchards required years of patient tending before the fruit would bring a return, the brevity of the growing season for vegetables attracted suitcase farmers who would rent land from absentee owners or large operators and gamble on quick returns from a bean crop, much as the nation's rich were gambling at South Florida's race tracks. J. D. Abbin, a self-proclaimed "Florida cracker," smuggled bootlegged liquor and illegal Asian immigrants and then worked at a Ford plant near Detroit before trying his hand at truck farming in Lee City, Florida. In 1936, he heard there was "big money raisin truck," so he went "down there an rented me a piece-a land an putt in a crop uv tomatoers an beans." In a few short months, he had made "a killin. Cleaned up $2,000 cash money."[3]

By the time J. D. Abbin was gambling on truck crops in Lee City, the vegetable growers of South Florida were largely divided into two groups: very substantial operators who cut costs by doing their own packing and marketing; and tenants who planted a crop on borrowed land, sold it to a packer, took the money, and moved on.[4] The small landowners in between were gradually squeezed out by the costs of draining, irrigating, and fertilizing land that flooded when wet and caught fire when dry.[5] Both large-scale growers and small-scale tenant farmers, however, were dependent on migrant farmworkers for harvest and packing labor. Neither had much incentive to form personal relationships with such transient employees because the season was too short, the workforce too large, and the pressure to cut labor costs too great. Since growers hired by the day and paid by the crate or hamper, it mattered little to them how many farmworkers labored in their fields. "[If the tenant farmer] has a thousand hampers of beans to pick," a federal investigator noted in 1939, "he'd as soon that they be picked by two hundred workers as a hundred." The important thing was to get the matured beans picked "as quickly as possible and without regard for a full day's work for a specific number of laborers."[6]

Indeed, South Florida truck farming paid as well as it did in the 1930s because more and more poor people entered the state as the Depression wore on, driving the price of labor down. As Depression prices forced southeastern farmers to take millions of acres out of cotton production and as the boll weevil ate its way through neighboring Georgia, debt-ridden sharecroppers headed for South Florida's "Bean Deal," where there was work in winter and cash wages for day labor, however long the day and low the wage. Jacob McMillan, a white sharecropper from Georgia, came to Florida from Georgia "like a lot of them. I went broke, everything went to the bottom and I had to get away."[7] By the end of the decade, perhaps forty to sixty thousand entered the state annually in search of farm work, half crowding into Belle Glade and the nearby towns that hugged the southern shore of Lake Okeechobee, while the other half fanned out into smaller truck farming communities along the Atlantic and Gulf coasts of the state.

Like other white migrants, McMillan found work in a packing house. Black migrants had a virtual monopoly on stoop labor in the fields.[8] The influx drove wages down until they were "the sorriest" in the country, according to one veteran of harvests in thirty-three states.[9] So many people migrated to Florida seeking work and warmth in the 1930s that the state police set up a border patrol along the main highways, turning back "undesirables" who might flood relief rolls, while taking care not to offend tourists "in better automobiles."[10]

The press of unemployed and displaced sharecroppers into Florida meant that black fieldworkers competed for backbreaking stoop labor and the most primitive housing. In Belle Glade, where thousands of black workers gathered before dawn to board the trucks that would take them to the fields, the only guarantee of a day's work was to hurry onto one of the idling vehicles before they all filled up and pulled away. On some mornings, when the weight of the men and women packed upright in a truck was so great that the flatbed pressed down on the wheels and kept them from turning, the local police would oblige the driver by circling the vehicle and beating off workers who clung to the hood and boards, until the wheels could turn and the truck could pull out onto the fields.[11]

The same workers competed for places in Belle Glade's crowded flophouses and rented shacks. As one observer noted, they slept "packed together in sordid rooms, hallways, tar-paper shacks, filthy barracks with one central faucet and toilet, sheds, lean-tos, old garages, condemned and shaky buildings."[12] The development of the vegetable industry had so outstripped the pace of housing construction that one truck farmer remarked that when he arrived in Belle Glade in 1936, "colored people were paying 25 cents a night to sleep on a truck body, just an ordinary stake truck with bean bags on the platform and a tarpaulin over it, simply because there was no place for them to live."[13]

Farther south, farmworkers would live in housing provided by growers, but this meant they were less able to choose among employers; they worked for the farmer whose shack they occupied. When Mary Jenkins left Georgia for South Florida in 1935, she hoped for more excitement and independence than her parents' cotton farm could afford her. Arriving at Butts Farm in Broward County, however, she found nothing but a sea of beans, a thousand other poor black people like her, and a long row of pickers' shacks. It was the worst she "had ever seen," but with fifty cents to her name, there was no going back until the end of the season.[14] "We just got to live in the house where they people let you stay," Mrs. Johnnie Belle Taylor told a congressional committee in 1940. "Some have to sleep in cars and some few of them have a little tent along with them . . . We just have to take it as we find it . . . We just put up with most anyway, just to [be] working, trying to live."[15]

Local relief agencies were little help during the Depression, as residency requirements excluded most farmworkers from receiving aid. "These people have learned not to ask us for anything," one county employee said of black pickers in Belle Glade. Later in the decade, surplus commodities from the federal government became available, but state and county relief officials allotted them in such a way that they provided a subsidy to growers. When farm employers feared large outmigrations of workers due to freezes or floods, for example, they could bring workers to the local relief office and "certify" their need. Once harvests began, relief agencies up and down the Florida coast would cut African Americans off the rolls because, according to officials, they "wouldn't work as long as they could get relief." Thus federal relief, as doled out on the local level, benefited growers as much as it did pickers.[16]

New Deal relief measures began on a massive scale in 1933 but made no immediate difference in the lives of migrant farmworkers. In 1933, the Federal Emergency Relief Administration (FERA) set up a Federal Transient Program but explicitly excluded migrant farmworkers from its provisions, ostensibly so as not to subsidize industries "that existed and benefited in some degree because of the cheap labor supply furnished by migratory-casual workers." FERA was for "bona fide transients," not migrant farmworkers.[17]

Likewise, although the National Industrial Recovery Act (NIRA), enacted in June 1933, did not explicitly exclude agricultural labor when it granted workers collective bargaining rights, three weeks later Franklin Delano Roosevelt cut out farmworkers by presidential decree. Cannery and packinghouse workers, who were usually white, were deemed industrial workers with collective bargaining rights, but fieldworkers, who were far more likely to be people of color, were not.[18]

Despite their exclusion, or perhaps not knowing that they had been left out of the NIRA, farmworkers around the nation launched a wave of strikes the following summer, to which growers in many places responded with massive force. While central Florida's more sedentary citrus workers joined this organizational wave, bringing the membership of the newly formed United Citrus Workers to a peak of thirty thousand members by the end of 1933, black workers in the vegetable region remained unorganized. Passage of the Wagner Act in 1935 did nothing to improve their organizational prospects, as agricultural workers were excluded, this time explicitly, from its provisions.[19]

Over the next few years, Florida's black farmworkers struggled among themselves for the best picking, the fairest growers, the least brutal row bosses. Then, in the winter of 1936–1937, when growers slashed the piece rate for beans from twenty-five to fifteen cents a hamper, thousands of bean pickers refused to board the trucks at Belle Glade's loading area. "We been living up and down the east coast for years," one worker explained, and this "is the first time we have ever seen beans down to 15 cents. We go out and make maybe 30–40 cents a day, and again we might make $1.50 if we had real good picking . . . We wouldn't go to the fields at the low prices."

The outcome of this conflict starkly revealed the risks of an illegal strike in a glutted labor market where the employers were far better organized than their workers. While growers in New Jersey and California countered farmworkers' harvest strikes by waging small wars with armed thugs, tear gas, and guns, South Florida's truck farmers had only to open the floodgates to the Southeast's displaced sharecroppers and unemployed. After four days without labor, the growers got the bean pickers to return to the fields by promising to raise the hamper rate to twenty cents. Meanwhile, they alerted the state's border patrol to their "labor shortage." The border patrol settled the issue by flooding the area with labor, simply by "letting Negro hitch hikers through." Once there were enough destitute workers in the area to replace the strikers, the growers reneged on their promise. With exorbitant rents to pay, no strike fund, and no other means to survive in a region miles from urban soup kitchens and hundreds of miles from family members who might lend support, South Florida's bean pickers went back to work.[20]

Excluded from industrial labor law and beyond the reach of federal relief efforts, farmworkers could only appeal to Washington as supplicants who hoped to be treated as workers. Thus James Cheseburough, who had migrated to Florida from New Hampshire, wrote to President Roosevelt in 1942 to ask him to set a nine-hour day and a minimum wage of two dollars a day for farmworkers, to announce his decision by radio, and to "Please think a lot."[21] While Cheseburough ended his letter with a warning, reminding the president that he was still a voter in New Hampshire, his threat was an empty one, for most migrant farmworkers were disfranchised by residency requirements if not by race.

When New Dealers finally began to "think a lot" about the plight of migrant farmworkers, they did so not to cultivate working-class votes, but to prevent mass starvation on the nation's most productive farms. Moreover, their actions were triggered not by the migrants' power to wage harvest strikes, but by documentary photographers' exposés of migrants' poverty. The new policy, formulated by the Resettlement Administration in 1935 and implemented, beginning in 1936, by its successor, the Farm Security Administration (FSA), created a Migratory Camp Program to serve the American families who "were wandering from state to state in a desperate effort to earn a living as migrant farm laborers." In the eyes of the liberal reformers who created the camp program, migrant farmworkers were not workers at all, but wards of the state. They would be sheltered and rehabilitated, not organized or empowered.[22]

The FSA migrant program built both permanent camps in commercial farming centers and mobile camps that provided trailers and tents for migrating farmworkers. By 1936, twenty-six permanent camps that could shelter seven thousand families were in operation or under construction on the Pacific Coast. And in the spring of 1940, the first camps on the East Coast were finally opened in Belle Glade, with Eleanor Roosevelt in attendance. The Osceola Camp sheltered white packing-house workers and the larger Okeechobee Camp black field labor. By summer, there were three more camps in Florida; in 1941, union construction workers built two more as well as an FSA hospital.

The camp program's creators believed that migrant farmworkers were poor because they spent so much of their time and resources moving about and that they moved about because they were unwilling or unable to save enough to sustain themselves in the off-seasons. The purpose of the program, then, was not merely to provide shelter but also to teach farmworkers thrift and self-discipline so that they might escape the migrant life altogether. Therefore, in addition to showers, kitchens, laundries, and medical clinics, the camps offered nurseries and schools for the migrants' children, lessons in personal hygiene, canning facilities where residents could preserve vegetables for the summer months, and sewing classes where women learned to make mattresses and pillows. Those who used the canning facilities had to set aside one in six cans to be sold in the camps' cooperative stores, and proceeds from the stores helped to fund the camps' nurseries. Thus the camps' managers sought to teach residents to be self-sufficient and to manage their affairs.

To convey the skills of self-government in a migrant population that camp managers sometimes found to be a "real test," each site included an assembly building meant to be the "seat of democracy in the camp." Residents elected a camp council that set the rules of behavior for all members and had the power to evict residents who disrupted camp life. The councils fined residents who dirtied the latrines, chastised couples who fought in public, and evicted residents caught selling alcohol.[23]

Some black farmworkers remained suspicious of the camps, choosing independence over the scrutiny of the camp councils; they preferred the cultural freedom of Belle Glade's juke joints over the FSA's "wholesome" Easter egg hunts and table-tennis tournaments. But many others, particularly parents with children, found the camps a welcome alternative to the squalor of most migrant housing. While they praised the facilities, schools, recreational activities, and free lunches for children, they noted that the camps' greatest advantage was the sense of security they afforded by guaranteeing a place to sleep at little cost. Families had to pay just one dollar a week or, in lieu of rent, work a two-hour period maintaining the grounds of the camp. When summer came and it was hot enough in South Florida to bake even the heartiest plants, Mrs. Johnnie Belle Taylor would migrate north to pick truck crops in Georgia, but she would keep paying the low rent on her unit in the Okeechobee Camp so that she would be guaranteed a space upon her return. James Solomon, who lost his housing at U.S. Sugar Corporation on a day when he was too ill to work and spent the next three months in an overpriced Belle Glade boarding house, moved permanently into an FSA camp thereafter. When he injured his back cutting sugarcane after returning to work at U.S. Sugar, he simply found lighter work; injury or illness did not result in eviction from an FSA shelter.[24]

For more than a year after the first camps opened in Florida, growers seemed to dismiss them as a harmless experiment in uplift that served only a small fraction of the migrant population. Some clearly accepted the camps as a sort of growers' subsidy, like the occasional relief provided by county and state agencies in the 1930s during freezes or floods. One noted that the camps seemed to produce "a much more reliable type of laborer." Luther Jones, realtor, farmer, and owner of the Belle Glade Herald, commented, "The idea is good and everybody is in favor of it," although he ridiculed camp managers for addressing black residents as equals. Growers in Frostproof, Sanford, Hollywood, and South Broward, Florida, all requested FSA mobile camps in 1941.[25]

In the context of a glutted labor market, local growers seemed largely supportive of the camp program, but by the winter of 1941–1942, when the draft and the expanding war economy increased the demand on the nation's labor supply, the camps took on a very different and far more significant meaning. Because truck farmers hired migrants only for the harvest season, they had no way to know how much labor would be available until the harvest was upon them. Thus they panicked early and loudly. And the more growers worried about real or imagined labor shortages, the more camp residents took advantage of their fears to bargain wages upward.

The camps provided farmworkers with all they needed to organize and wait out growers while crops ripened in the fields: a steady source of cheap food and housing from which they would not be evicted so long as they obeyed camp rules. Even the camps' assembly halls could be put to new uses. And although the FSA staffers were not permitted to advocate or encourage unionization in the camps, nothing said they had to discourage it or evict residents who were on strike.[26] Thus farmworkers did not have to picket, protest, or even affiliate with a labor union to force up wages. They only had to decide among themselves what they considered a reasonable rate of pay, and then wait while the highly perishable truck crops ripened under Florida's glaring sun. This they did, and growers responded immediately and vehemently.

In February 1942, L. L. Stuckey, chair of the Florida Farm Bureau's Vegetable Committee, complained to the U.S. secretary of agriculture on behalf of South Florida's largest growers that "50 percent of the crops are wasting in the fields on approximately 30,000 acres of winter vegetables and 25,000 acres of sugar cane with 1,000 farm laborers idle in the communities and a majority of those working effectively employing delaying tactics."[27] The manager of the Everglades Farm Labor Supply Center noted that when growers dropped the piece rate for beans, the bulk of the camp's 872 workers refused to leave for the fields. Another grower sent a telegram to Washington, insisting furiously that while she had "not struck nor sat down," her labor force had done so several times. A Pahokee farmer declared in *The Miami Herald*, "We just don't have the labor. The people we do have, both white and Negro, simply will not work for us. Tons of beans are rotting in the fields." Mrs. Ruth Edgeworth of Belle Glade noted, "We've tried everything but holding a gun to their heads, and still they won't work."[28]

Accustomed to workers disciplined by the starvation wages of the Depression years, growers were outraged to find black workers collectively uncooperative. Farmworkers had not vanished into the armed forces, nor had they all been swept up into the industrial war machine; but they were not behaving in the manner to which growers had become accustomed. Growers blamed the camps as much as the farmworkers' themselves, for, in their minds, the camps coddled the workers, relieving them of the need to work. James Beardsley of Clewiston reported rumors that farmworkers could stay in the camps and pay their rent by "pushing a lawnmower along on the grass." Officials of the U.S. Sugar Corporation protested to camp managers that their employees had "stopped all work and were loafing while housed in the camps." The sugar executives could hardly have been placated when camp managers replied that it was "not within [their] power to require individuals to work at any specified point." In a sense, the growers were right: while the camps did not relieve farmworkers of their need to work (the camps provided only the most basic subsistence, after all), they did allow farmworkers to refuse work at a price set unilaterally by growers. The camps allowed their residents time to stall, and in truck farming a few days could mean the difference between a crop that made its way to market or to the armed forces and one that rotted or dried on the vine.[29]

Florida's truck farmers' protests found a receptive audience among conservatives in the wartime Congress. As soon as the United States entered the war, Republicans and conservative Democrats—dubbed the "economy bloc"—had begun demanding drastic cutbacks in spending not related to defense and an end to New Deal "experimentation." Long the object of conservative attacks on the New Deal, the FSA found its head on the budgetary chopping block early in 1942. Its efforts to resettle farm families living on spent soil, create farm cooperatives, and offer low-interest loans to small farmers all were doomed. What saved the agency, at least temporarily, was the importance of its migrant camp program to the labor needs of the nation's truck farmers. The FSA's advocates fought for the agency on the grounds that the camp program contributed to the war effort and that only an expansion of the program's mobile camps would facilitate the efficient movement of "Migrant Soldiers on the Food Production Front."[30]

As a result, the FSA was saved but transformed. Congress authorized the expansion of the Migratory Camp Program and extended the life of the FSA for another six months so that it could continue to run the program, even as all other FSA programs died a swift death by defunding.[31] The camp program had been designed to provide farmworkers with the means and motivation to stop migrating, but in the winter of 1941–1942 FSA officials began to facilitate migrancy in the name of the war effort.[32] In January, the FSA and the U.S. Employment Service (USES) signed a joint policy statement to coordinate farm labor supply activities. The USES would identify labor needs and areas of surplus and recruit farmworkers willing to move from one region to another. The FSA would get them there and provide food and shelter along the way. Both agencies advertised the plan widely in the hope that growers would not restrict planting the following spring in anticipation of labor shortages. By the summer of 1942, 46 permanent and 43 mobile camps were in operation, 6 more mobile units were under construction, and 140 more sites to be used by 90 additional mobile units had been proposed.

This plan seems to have placated growers in small truck-farming regions along the Atlantic Coast. When asked by the FSA to provide "good testimonial stories which show the need of our migrant camps," many were happy to oblige. The mayor of Elizabeth City, North Carolina, noted, for example, that he had heard "nothing but universal praise" for the camps and that all the farmers with whom he talked "were most gratefully pleased in that they eliminated the necessity of frequent trips into Elizabeth City in an endeavor to recruit labor."[33] Isolated from each other and too small to hire their own recruiters, these growers depended upon the arrival of migrant workers in time for very short harvest seasons. With defense industries drawing away workers and tire and gas shortages impeding the mobility of those who remained, operators of small truck farms along the coast were glad to have the federal government take charge of domestic farmworkers and organize their travels into efficient troop movements. They could only nod their approval when FSA workers arrived to assemble a mobile camp in advance of an impending harvest.

South Florida's growers, however, were not placated in the least, although USES officials continued to insist that they could meet all growers' labor needs. The presence of year-round, permanent FSA camps had already undermined the power growers had wielded over Belle Glade's bean pickers during the strike of 1936–1937. The last thing these growers wanted was for the FSA to take a direct hand in the supply and removal of their accustomed workforce. When, in October 1942, FSA officials in Florida arranged for the out-migration of several hundred farmworkers to the Campbell Soup cannery in Camden, New Jersey, growers were outraged, calling it the "most high-handed act of labor piracy ever perpetrated in this state."[34]

Some growers determined to maintain control of their labor supply by resorting to time-honored labor recruitment methods. U.S. Sugar Corporation managers kidnapped, imprisoned, and shot at workers, for example; and the sheriff of Glades County took prisoners from the county jail and put them to work without pay on his farm.[35] However, although some growers were not above the use of force, most chose to wage their war against migrant farm labor and the FSA's camp program in Washington under the auspices of the American Farm Bureau Federation. At their behest, the Farm Bureau fought not to dismantle the camp program but to turn it over to local control and to use camp facilities to house foreign workers who could be deported for striking.

By the winter of 1942–1943, South Florida growers and the Farm Bureau had devised an alternative both to shooting at farmworkers to keep them in the fields and to accepting farmworkers provided by the FSA under contracts that required growers to pay a minimum wage. The growers by then had heard that the FSA was supplying California and Arizona growers with Mexican nationals, and they demanded the same treatment.[36] South Florida's growers demanded foreign workers who could be deported for refusing to work. They began to insist that the government allow them to hire West Indians, who had worked in limited numbers in South Florida since the 1880s. After January 29, 1943, when truck farmers met in Homestead, Florida, near Miami, to discuss ways to stabilize wages, Secretary of Agriculture Claude Wickard received more than fifty telegrams from South Florida potato, bean, and tomato growers, demanding imported farm labor. One woman insisted that she wanted "6 Bahama Laborers and need them now. Bahamians are far better help than riffraff now walking our roads and shooting craps in our fields."[37] L. L. Chandler of Dade County's Farm Bureau called the FSA program impractical, bound by red tape, and "dripping" with social reform. "Yet . . . just 48 miles across the Gulf Stream," he continued, "are some 18,000 men, willing laborers who want to come to Florida . . . and despite the fact that Mexican labor is permitted to enter this country . . . we haven't yet had one Bahaman laborer offered to us." He insisted that Florida's farmers had planted every possible plant and seed needed for the war effort, "despite the fact that labor has struck on him," endlessly putting the farmer "across the barrel" and the government, "who could control it," did nothing.[38]

The growers' persistent agitation was effective. In April 1943, the Farm Bureau won passage of a bill designed to remove the Migrant Labor Program from the hands of New Deal liberals and eliminate the program's minimum wage, maximum hours, and housing standards. Public Law 45 permitted the retention and expansion of the farm labor recruitment program, so long as its managers did not use it to improve farmworkers' working and living conditions. The new law turned over the renamed Farm Labor Supply Program to the War Food Administration (the wartime version of the grower-dominated Department of Agriculture) and committed it to the importation, transportation, and housing of foreign workers. No one, not even federal officials, could transport domestic farmworkers out of a county without a release signed by a local county agricultural extension agent.[39]

In 1943, the Farm Labor Supply Program delivered 8,828 Jamaicans to East Coast growers. In the first six months of 1944, it imported over 15,000 more. In the last year of the war, the Labor Supply Program moved only 11,000 domestic farmworkers nationwide, while it supplied growers with 56,000 foreign workers and 122,000 prisoners of war.[40]

The camp managers' reports reveal clearly that the foreign workers brought to South Florida did not simply compensate for labor shortages created when American workers were drafted or departed for industrial jobs. Rather, foreign workers displaced domestic laborers, forcing them out of the camps that had been such a boon to their organizational efforts. In the fall of 1943, managers at the Okeechobee Camp for black labor reported that Bahamians were imported despite an adequate domestic labor supply the previous year. "[T]he farmer had more than necessary labor" in 1942, one staff member noted; with the addition of the Bahamians, "many farm laborers were without day work." In 1944 another Okeechobee Camp official reported that the camp was "filled to capacity" for the bean harvest; "daily we turn down hundreds of applicants who are so anxious to call this their home."[41]

Some camp managers lamented the exclusion of domestic workers, and even some growers protested "regulations which prevented American citizens being housed in Federal farm labor supply centers." But such sentiments were rare. As the manager of the Pahokee Camp pointed out, reserving the camps for foreign workers allowed for more efficient use of space, since domestic workers' children took up room without providing labor. The imported foreign workers were all adults. In 1942, he noted, the Pahokee Camp, while full, had housed only 213 residents old enough to work. In 1943, if the camp were to be used for Bahamians only, it could house at least 800 "easily."[42]

Barred from many of the federal labor camps that had been their winter homes for three years, African American workers also found that, on many farms, they were hired only as a last resort. Growers in the Fort Pierce area preferred Bahamians, citing their attendance, tractability, adaptability, productivity, and conduct. The local camp manager reported that most employers "considered Bahamians, all things considered, as superior to native American workers," adding that "most of the Bahamians were quite contented and happy. It is said that they are that way by nature anyway."[43]

Even where African Americans kept their billets in federal camps, they lost their monopoly on fieldwork and therefore their ability to control wages by agreeing among themselves to stay out of the fields. In Belle Glade, Caribbean and African American workers lived in separate camps about a mile apart. Growers depressed wages by driving from one camp to the other, telling one group that the other had promised to work for less. There was no labor shortage, recalled Rev. David Burgess, the Southern Tenant Farmers Union's "minister to the migrants"; the Farm Labor Supply Program, as he saw it, was merely a bald effort to break strikes and lower wages.[44]

Imported farmworkers also struck, but when they did, growers merely had to summon War Food Administration officials to have them "repatriated" and replaced. Thus, in 1944, the Pahokee Camp manager reported that "approximately 75 workers held a strike against the 50 cents an hour paid them which was the prevailing wage at that time." After a hearing, the three leaders "were turned over to the Border Patrol for deportation." No other trouble occurred after that, he noted.[45] Camp managers were baffled when the supposedly pliant West Indians refused to work at the proffered wages; some concluded that they were simply picking up bad habits from African Americans. Reports for the week ending June 10, 1944, revealed that on average, 23 percent of the West Indian workers refused to work for various reasons.[46] All were repatriated.

As a weapon against farmworkers' militancy, the Labor Supply Program was an unmitigated success. In 1945 the Fort Pierce Camp manager reassessed the value of African American labor, reporting that the "domestic colored did a swell job in harvesting the vegetable crop." "They never once asked for higher prices than prevailed in that area," he noted.[47] In some ways, the war experience was a reprise of the 1936–1937 bean pickers' strike but on a much grander scale. This time, however, when growers complained of a labor-supply problem, the state highway patrol could not simply open the border and let job-seekers flood the state. Instead, federal officials opened the nation's borders to Latin American and Caribbean job-seekers and then enforced labor discipline through the deportation process.

Denied the right of collective bargaining, farmworker movements were easily defeated. Thus the workers were unable to oppose an immigration policy tailored to growers' needs. At the end of the war, Congress ordered the Farm Labor Supply Program's temporary camps dismantled and its permanent camps sold to growers' associations for a dollar each. At the same time, Congress extended the life of the importation program in the East and the much larger bracero program in the West. Although public outcry during the 1953–1954 recession resulted in the deportation of more than a million Mexican workers from the West Coast, Congress continued to sanction the use of foreign workers in agriculture, reinventing the World War II Labor Importation Program as the H-2 Program (the name refers to section H-2 of the 1952 Immigration and Nationality Act).

In the 1950s, African Americans continued to dominate the ranks of farm laborers in Florida, but foreign workers willing to toil for lower wages gradually displaced them. One by one, H-2 workers from Jamaica, refugees from Haiti, and, since the 1970s, often undocumented Mexicans and other Latin Americans pushed African Americans out of the farm labor market.

With undocumented workers laboring alongside legal immigrants and H-2 workers subject to deportation if they protested their rate of pay or living conditions, opportunities for organization were few. Proof that private power and public policy combined to squelch black farmworkers' militancy came in a 1978 labor dispute near Tampa. In a stark reversal of earlier struggles, 136 Mexican tomato pickers walked off the job to protest wages and conditions, and growers quickly recruited several hundred African Americans to break the strike.[48]

African American farmworkers' wartime struggle did not fail for lack of organization. It was the growers' ability to enlist the aid of federal authorities that crushed their promising but short-lived initiative. Yet the consequences of African American farmworkers' wartime defeat were profound—and not just for them, but for all farmworkers on the East Coast of the United States. Because farmworkers were unsuccessful in their organizing efforts, their living and working conditions remained desperate. Belle Glade won infamy in the 1980s as the nation's poorest city and as the capital of the AIDS epidemic in the United States. Moreover, a recent study found that African American migrants along the East Coast were three hundred times more likely to have active tuberculosis than the average American.

Sporadic reform campaigns led to state laws regulating crew leaders and housing and, finally, to the inclusion of farmworkers in federal minimum wage, unemployment insurance, and workplace safety legislation. These provisions were rarely enforced, however, and even if appropriations committees had been generous with funding for enforcement (and they were not), there still would not have been enough inspectors to check for housing, labor, and pesticide violations on every farm in the state. If farmworkers had enjoyed the right of collective bargaining and if they had been successful in organizing, they might have been able to take advantage of such protective legislation. But so long as they feared displacement and deportation, they could not afford to protest inadequate conditions or report employers' violations of health and safety laws to state authorities. To make matters worse, farmworkers still lack political leverage. Now dominated by an immigrant workforce, Florida's farmworkers remain a disfranchised population.[49]

The story of Florida's farmworkers is not a sort of throwback to nineteenth-century labor relations, with labor unorganized and federal officials determined not to intervene in an unequal struggle between capital and labor. Farmworkers did organize, and federal officials did intervene in farm labor relations on a massive scale—first by feeding, housing, and attempting to uplift them, and then by setting wage ceilings, shuttling farmworkers from field to field, prohibiting American farm laborers from moving to better-paying jobs, and replacing militant migrants with farmworkers recruited under no-strike contracts. Leaving growers with permanent access to foreign workers in the postwar period, Congress made it unlikely that Florida farmworkers will organize effectively in the future.

Notes

1. Labor historians have largely ignored migrant farmworkers on the East Coast of the United States, doubtless because they produced no tradition of trade unionism, no Cesar Chavez, no national boycotts. Florida's citrus workers flirted with the American Federation of Labor several times during this century, and some black field workers joined the Southern Tenant Farmers Union in the 1940s, but the former movement spurned all but the most sedentary white workers, while the latter was a fleeting phenomenon. A few exceptions to the neglect of this topic: Louis Persh, "An Analysis of the Agricultural Migratory Movements on the Atlantic Seaboard and the Socio-Economic Implications for the Community and the Migrants, 1930–1950" (Ph.D. diss., American University, 1953); Jerrell H. Shofner, "The Legacy of Racial Slavery: Free Enterprise and Forced Labor in Florida in the 1940s," *Journal of Southern History* 47, no. 3 (1981): 411–426; Donald E. Grubbs, "The Story of Florida's Migrant Farm Workers," *Florida*

Historical Quarterly 40, no. 2 (October 1961): 103–122; and Sandra M. Mohl, "Migrant Farmworkers in America: A Florida Case Study" (master's thesis, Florida Atlantic University, 1981).

2. U.S. Census Bureau, 14th Census, 1920, vol. 6, pt. 2, p. 375; U.S. Census Bureau, 16th Census, 1940, Agriculture, vol. 1, pt. 3, South Atlantic, p. 682; and Joan Pascal and Harold G. Tipton, "Vegetable Production in South Florida," U.S. House of Representatives, Select Committee Investigating National Defense Migration, Hearings . . . , 77th Congress, 1st Session, 1941 (hereafter cited as NDMH), pt. 33, p. 12893.

3. J. D. Abbin, quoted in Federal Writers' Project Life Histories, reel 1, Southern Historical Collection, University of North Carolina at Chapel Hill.

4. South Florida tenancy rates fell during the 1930s, but they were still extremely high. In Broward County, the tenancy rate was 70.9 percent in 1930, 68.9 percent in 1935, and 59.5 percent in 1940. In Palm Beach County, the tenancy rate was 54.6 percent in 1930, 50.3 percent in 1935, and 34.9 percent in 1940. At the same time, harvests on farms of more than 500 acres increased in Broward County from 15.7 percent to 41.1 percent and in Dade County from 18.9 percent to 38.3 percent between 1929 and 1939. Census Bureau, 16th Census, 1940, Agriculture, vol. 1, pt. 3, South Atlantic, County Table 2, Farm Tenure.

5. One of Belle Glade's more successful truck farmers estimated in 1942 that it would take 640 acres and $35,000 in equipment to start a profitable farm in the Everglades. The larger enterprises cut costs by packing and shipping their own crops. Those who had to pay packers gradually went bust and became tenants. Pascal and Tipton, "Vegetable Production in South Florida," 12911.

6. In March 1940, approximately 2 percent of Florida farms hired almost 50 percent of all the seasonal labor employed, according to Harry Schwartz, Seasonal Farm Labor in the United States (New York: Columbia University Press, 1945), 9. See also Terrell Cline to John Beecher, May 14, 1939, National Archives and Records Administration (NARA), Record Group (RG) 96, Box 20, File RP-M-85-183-01; and Pascal and Tipton, "Vegetable Production in South Florida," 12911.

7. Cotton prices dropped 50 percent in the three years after World War I, and then the boll weevil arrived to finish the job. Georgia lost two-thirds of its cotton crop to the boll weevil in 1922 and 1923. By 1925, Georgia cotton planters had taken nearly 3.5 million acres out of production, decreasing by that amount the acres requiring sharecroppers to farm them and day laborers to work the harvests on them. Resettlement Administration staffers surveyed 690 workers in winter of 1936–1937 and reported that 79.3 percent were from southern states, 39.7 percent were from Georgia, and 10.4 percent were from Alabama. NDMH, pt. 33, Belle Glade, April 25, 1942, pp. 12651–12653; Aubrey Clyde Robinson and Glenore Fisk Horne, "Florida Migratory Workers," June 1937, NARA, RG 96, Box 9, AD-124, Region 5, Migratory Labor, 1940.

8. Testimony of A. Frederick Smith of the Florida Industrial Commission in U.S. Congress, House of Representatives, Select Committee to Investigate the Interstate Migration of Destitute Citizens, Hearings . . . , 76th Congress, 3d Session. (Washington, D.C.: USGPO, 1941), pt. 2, pp. 483 and 583 (hereafter cited as Tolan Hearings). See also Memorandum, John Beecher, research supervisor, Resettlement Division, Region 5, USDA, to Max A. Egloff, chief of research and

investigations, Labor Relations Division, May 15, 1939, NARA, RG 96, Box 20, File RP-M-85-183-01, Monthly Reports.

9. NDMH, pt. 33, 12739–12742.

10. Robinson and Horne, "Florida Migratory Workers," 45–46; and Charlton W. Tebeau, *A History of Florida* (Coral Gables, Fla.: University of Miami Press, 1971), 403.

11. Lawrence Will, *Swamp to Sugar Bowl: Pioneer Days in Belle Glade* (St. Petersburg, Fla.: Great Outdoors, 1968), 189–193. See also Robinson and Horne, "Florida Migratory Workers."

12. The observer was Marjory Stoneman Douglas, *The Everglades: River of Grass* (New York: Rinehart and Co., 1947), 356–357. See also Grubbs, "Story of Florida's Migrant Farm Workers," 106–107; and testimony of Howard Haney, NDMH, pt. 33, 12604.

13. Testimony of Howard Haney, NDMH, pt. 33, 12604. See also Douglas, *River of Grass*, 356–357; and Grubbs, "Story of Florida's Migrant Farm Workers," 106–107.

14. Mary Jenkins, interview by Arthur S. Evans, Jr., and David Lee, in Pearl City Oral History Project, Boca Raton Historical Society Library, Boca Raton, Fla., 1984–1985.

15. NDMH, pt. 33, 12625–12628.

16. Robinson and Horne, "Florida Migratory Workers," 45–46; Tolan Hearings, pt. 2, 483–488; Testimony of Dorothea Brower, District Welfare Supervisor, West Palm Beach, Fla., April 29, 1942, NDMH, pt. 33, 12792–12795.

17. John N. Webb, *The Migratory and Casual Worker*, WPA Research Monograph 7 (Washington, D.C.: USGPO, 1937), ix–x; John N. Webb, *The Transient Unemployed*, WPA Research Monograph 3 (Washington, D.C.: USGPO, 1935), 48; Philip Elwood Ryan, *Migration and Social Welfare* (New York: Russell Sage Foundation, 1940), 8–10; Ellen C. Potter, "After Five Years—The Unsolved Problem of the Transient Unemployed, 1932–37," included in the testimony of Bertha McCall, general director, National Travelers Aid Association, Tolan Hearings, pt. 1, New York City Hearings, 54; Doris Carothers, *Chronology of the Federal Emergency Relief Administration, May 12, 1933, to Dec. 31, 1935*, WPA Research Monograph 6 (Washington, D.C: USGPO, 1937), 25 and 81.

18. FDR's decree excluded agricultural workers generally, but later scuffles between the National Recovery Administration and the Department of Agriculture resulting in a distinction between those who worked outside the "area of production" (i.e., processing workers) and those who worked within the area of production (fieldworkers). Austin P. Morris, "Agricultural Labor and National Labor Legislation," *California Law Review* 54 (1966): 1939–1989.

19. See Cletus Daniel, *Bitter Harvest: A History of California Farmworkers, 1870–1941* (Ithaca, N.Y.: Cornell University Press, 1981); Stuart Jamieson, *Labor Unionism in American Agriculture*, Bulletin No. 836, U.S. Department of Labor, Bureau of Labor Statistics (Washington, D.C.: USGPO, 1945; reprint, Arno Press, 1976); and Cindy Hahamovitch, "In the Valley of the Giant: The Politics of Migrant Farm Labor, 1865–1945" (Ph.D. dissertation, University of North Carolina at Chapel Hill, 1992), 240–261.

20. Robinson and Horne, "Florida Migratory Workers," 40.

21. January 20, 1942, RG 16, Office for Agricultural War Relations, General Correspondence, 1942, NARA, Box 145, File Employment 3 Wages (January 1–July 31).

22. "History of Farm Labor Activities of the Farm Security Administration," U.S. Department of Agriculture, War Food Administration, NARA, RG 287, FSA Publication 132; Memo to Paul H. Appleby, assistant to the secretary, from John Fischer, director of information, FSA, December 9, 1939, RG 16, Secretary of Agriculture, E17 General Correspondence, Camps, Migratory Labor, 1939.

23. C. B. Baldwin to Senator Claude Pepper, July 29, 1941, NARA, RG 96, Box 9, AD-124, Region 5; "Community and Family Services Bulletin," February 28, 1941, RG 96, FSA, Migrant Labor Camps Correspondence 1935–1943, Box 16, File RP-M-169, Publications; John F. O'Malley, Elba, N.Y., Narrative Report for Period Ending October 4, 1942, RG 96, Migrant Labor Camps Correspondence, 1935–1943, Box 19, File RP-M-183, Migratory Reg.

24. NDMH, pt. 33, 12574–12577, 12625–12638.

25. Ibid., 12603, 12672–12674; and NARA, RG 96, Correspondence Concerning Migratory Labor Camps, 1935–1943, Box 2, Region 5, File RP-85 M-060, Projects 1941.

26. The acting director had noted as early as 1938 that the FSA "does not attempt either to encourage or to impede the formation of labor organizations. It is true, however, that residents of the FSA camps enjoy certain protection of their civil liberties which often is not available to migrant workers living on private property or in the numerous 'ditch bank camps.'" Memo for Paul H. Appleby, Acting Administrator, June 10, 1938, NARA, RG 16, Secretary of Agriculture, E17 General Correspondence, Camps, Migratory Labor.

27. NARA, RG 224, Box 51, File C2-R36, Narrative Reports Farm Labor Supply Centers, Florida, May-December 1944; and L. L. Stuckey, Chairman, Vegetable Committee, Florida Farm Bureau Federation, Pahokee, Fla., to Claude R. Wickard, February 10, 1942, NARA, RG 96, Correspondence Concerning Migratory Labor Camps, 1935–1943, Box 7.

28. NARA, RG 224, FSA Correspondence, 1943–1944, Box 75, File 4-FLT-R57; David Burgess, quoted in "The Joads—Still Out of Luck," *New Republic* 110 (1944): 46.

29. Testimony of James E. Beardsley, Clewiston, Fla., April 26, 1942, NDMH, pt. 33, pp. 12565–12566; Paul Vander Schouw, Supervisor, Florida Migratory Labor Camps, January 1942, NARA, RG 96, Migratory Labor Camps Correspondence, 1935–1943, Box 20, File RP-M-85–183.

30. NARA, RG 16, Office for Agricultural War Relations, General Correspondence, 1942, Box 188.

31. Sidney Baldwin, *Poverty and Politics: The Rise and Decline of the Farm Security Administration* (Chapel Hill: University of North Carolina Press, 1968).

32. Ibid., 329–331; N. Gregory Silvermaster, Director, Labor Division, FSA, to C. B. Baldwin re. Proposed Expansion of FSA Camp Program to Meet Agricultural Defense Production Needs (undated), NARA, RG 96, Correspondence Concerning Migratory Labor Camps, 1935–1943, Box 2, Region 5, File RP-85 M-060, Projects 1941.

33. Jerome B. Flora to Howard H. Gordon, Regional Director, FSA, Raleigh,

N.C., August 31, 1942, NARA, RG 96, Migratory Labor Camps Correspondence, 1935–1943, Box 16, File Migratory, 84–160.

34. Harry L. Askew, Chairman, Joint Industry Committee, to Hon. Marvin Jones, War Food Administration, August 9, 1943, NARA, RG 224, General Correspondence, 1943–1944, Box 61, File 6-R15-Florida, July–December 1943.

35. *Tampa Tribune*, November 5, 1942.

36. In early 1942, Secretary Wickard had traveled secretly to Mexico to negotiate the terms of a labor importation agreement with the Mexican government. According to the agreement, transportation would be provided when growers signed a contract that they would pay prevailing wage rates (but not less than 30 cents an hour), that they would guarantee employment for 75 percent of the contract period, and that certain minimum standards of housing and sanitation would be available. Workers accepting such a contract would be guaranteed their transportation costs and would be furnished food, medical care, and living facilities during the trip; and if the employer failed to pay the agreed wage rate, the government would provide subsistence. NARA, RG 96, Correspondence Concerning Migratory Labor Camps, 1935–1943, Box 7, File Migratory–120, A through G. See Kitty Calavita, *Inside the State: The Bracero Program, Immigration, and the INS* (New York: Routledge, 1992).

37. NARA, RG 224, FSA Correspondence, 1943–1944, Box 75, File 4-FLT-R57.

38. U.S. Congress, Senate, Committee on Agriculture and Forestry, Hearings before a Subcommittee on the Food Supply of the United States, 78th Congress, 1st Session, pt. 1, 237 and 241.

39. U.S. Congress, House, Committee on Appropriations, Hearings . . . Farm Labor Program . . . 1943–1944, cited in Wayne D. Rasmussen, *A History of the Emergency Farm Labor Supply Program, 1943–1947*, Bureau of Agricultural Economics Monograph 13 (Washington, D.C.: USGPO, 1951), 42, 58, and 62–63. See also Baldwin, *Poverty and Politics*, 394. The major opposition to the bill came from the NAACP and the Southern Tenant Farmers Union; neither organization was in a particularly good position to influence Congress. See, e.g., *Atlanta Daily World*, May 4, 1943; and H. L. Mitchell to Frank P. Fenton, June 13, 1944, Southern Tenant Farmers Union Papers, Southern Historical Collection, Univ. of North Carolina at Chapel Hill.

40. Rasmussen, Emergency Farm Labor Supply Program; RG 224, General Correspondence, 1943–1944, Box 61, File 6-R15, Jamaicans, 1944.

41. Reports by Sadye E. Pryor, Home Management Supervisor, Okeechobee Center, September 1943; and Henry O. Earwood, Okeechobee Camp Manager, October 1944, RG 224, General Correspondence, 1943–1944, Box 51, File C2-R36-Florida.

42. Paul Vander Schouw, Monthly Narrative Report, August 1943, RG 224, Box 51, File C2-R36, Florida.

43. S. C. Merritt, Manager, Fort Pierce, Farm Labor Supply Center (FLSC) Report for October, November 5, 1945, RG 224, General Correspondence, 1945, Box 78, File Camps 11–1, Florida FLSC, 1945; and John V. Wright, Manager, Fort Pierce FLSC, January 1944, Box 51, File C2-R36-Florida.

44. Rev. David Burgess, interview by Cindy Hahamovitch, May 1990, Newark, N.J., audiotape recording in author's possession.

45. George E. Winston, Pahokee FLSC, Report, April 1944, RG 224, General Correspondence, 1943–1944, Box 51, File C2-R36-Florida.

46. RG 224, Box 59, File 6-A19, Agreements, January 1944; and Box 78, File Camps 11–1.

47. Sherwood Brantley, Fort Pierce FLSC Manager, January 31, 1945, RG 224, General Correspondence, 1945, Box 78, File Camps 11–1, Florida FLSC, 1945.

48. Fifty-one Latino protesters picketing the entrance of Fulwood Farms were arrested by forty sheriff's deputies, some armed with riot sticks. Ronnie Fulwood evicted twenty families who participated in the strike. J. P. Schuck, director of the Florida Mediation and Conciliation Service, urged Fulwood to meet with the strike leader, arguing, "We don't want this thing to rage into a wildfire that will spread across the state." *New York Times,* April 20, 1978, 13.

49. On farmworkers and tuberculosis, see *New York Times,* April 3, 1991; on AIDS in Belle Glade, see *Los Angeles Times,* January 28, 1993, A5; and on exposure to pesticides, see *New York Times,* August 19, 1990, 12. See also "Migrant Workers Straining the South's Health Safety Net," *Raleigh (N.C.) News and Observer,* October 29, 1989.

Rifaré mi suerte/ I'll Raffle My Luck

Humberto Zapata Alvizo, farmworker and musician

Interview by Joe Bagby, 1999 SAF intern

Ahora que estoy tan lejos
de la tierra en la que nací,
oh, mis queridos padres
cuanto habrán sufrido por mí.

Mi pobre vieja madre
que me dió tantos consejos,
con lágrimas en sus ojos,
me dió su bendición.

No llore más, madre.
Esté bien; no sufra.
déjeme rifar me suerte
buscando mi fortuna.

También dejé a mi amor,
a quien le prometí regresar.
Sé muy bien que me esperará.
Estoy seguro que Dios me lo concederá.

Me gustaría ser esos pájaros
y volar adonde tú estés
cruzando valles y montañas
y llegar a donde están los seres que yo amo.

Milagrosa Virgen María
conoces bien mi sufrimiento.
De rodillas, iré a verte
si me permites regresar a mi casa.

Now I'm so far
From the land where I was born,

Oh, my beloved parents
How much you have suffered for me.

My poor old mother
Who gave me so much advice,
With tears in her eyes,
She gave me her blessing.

Don't cry any more, Mother.
Be well; don't suffer.
Let me raffle my luck
By seeking my fortune.

I also left my love,
Whom I promised I'd return.
I know damn well she'll wait for me.
Surely God has to concede me this.

I would like to be those birds
And fly to where you are
Crossing valleys and mountains
To get to my loved ones.

Miraculous Virgin Mary
You know my suffering well.
On my knees, I'll go to see you
If you let me return home.

CHAPTER 4

H-2A Guestworker Program

A Legacy of Importing Agricultural Labor

Garry G. Geffert

That part of the agricultural industry that depends on hand-harvest labor has never completely adjusted to the adoption of the Thirteenth Amendment to the Constitution, the amendment that abolished slavery. Unlike other industries, many people who control hand harvest agriculture have not attempted to use modern labor management techniques to recruit and retain workers and have not felt it necessary to pay a living wage to their laborers.

Among the industry's strategies for retaining its version of a reliable and stable workforce in place of slaves were the contract labor laws enacted in the former Confederate states in the last half of the nineteenth century. Under those laws, a worker who failed to complete his contract was arrested and sentenced to work off his fine for his former employer and thus was held in involuntary servitude. The last of these laws in Florida was not declared unconstitutional until the 1940s (Daniel 1972).

A first effort to control the newly freed slaves occurred shortly after the end of the Civil War when a group of Virginia farmers met on Turkey Island in an effort to systematize their labor management policies. They agreed to offer a uniform wage rate to the freedmen and declared "that toward all freedmen in our employ we will act justly and we will consider the following wages very liberal, and that we pledge ourselves not to exceed them" (*Congressional Globe* 1886). The agreement set uniform deductions that would be taken from workers' pay, specified charges that would be deducted for fuel, set pay periods and rations, and declared that one month's pay would always be "held in arrears." The agreement also provided that "No hand will be employed who has been discharged for misconduct or violation of contract."

When General Oliver Otis Howard, the assistant commissioner of the Freedman's Bureau for the area, was informed of this agreement, he declared:

*The freedmen referred to in the resolutions are at liberty to enter into just
such agreements or contracts as they please, and with whomsoever they
please, and they will not be restrained from receiving as high wages as
they can get (Congressional Globe 1886).*

Then, General Howard employed the occupying Union troops to assure
that the Turkey Island agreement would not be enforced (*Congressional
Globe* 1886).

Though times have changed, unfortunately the U.S. government,
through the Immigration and Naturalization Service (INS) and the U.S.
Department of Labor (DOL), with the full blessing of Congress, administers a farm labor program that bears striking similarities to the Turkey
Island agreement. This present-day labor arrangement is known as the
H-2A agricultural guestworker program. This program, which gets its
name from the section of the Immigration and Naturalization Act that
created it, 8 U.S.C. § 1101(a)(15)(H)(2A), allows the importation of foreign
workers and sets wages and work terms that, while stated as minimums,
in practice are maximums.

However, the H-2A program does not satisfy some growers who continue to seek new programs that supply laborers over whom they have
greater control and who have fewer protections. They seek programs
even more repressive than the Turkey Island agreement.

A Brief History of Agricultural
Guestworker Programs

Until 1917, immigration from Mexico to the
United States was largely unrestricted. Then, as now, workers went
where jobs were available. Railroads and farms near the border employed
Mexican immigrants. Even at the beginning of the twentieth century,
wages in Mexico were lower than the wages paid in the United States.
This, combined with the depressing effect of a large labor supply spurred
on by the influx of Mexican immigrants, had a negative effect on wages
in the United States and thus helped keep growers' labor costs down.

By the end of the nineteenth century, farmers in the Southwest had
begun relying on workers from Mexico as a source of low-cost labor.
But under the influence of anti-alien sentiment, Congress enacted what
then were the strongest restrictions on immigration in the Immigration
Act of 1917. The act cut off much of the Mexican labor force. It imposed a

literacy requirement and increased the head tax for immigration to eight dollars, making it virtually impossible for most of those who had been engaged in contract labor to enter the United States. As men went off to fight in World War I, farmers complained of labor shortages. These factors led to the creation of the first formal guestworker program, also in 1917. Most of the eighty thousand guestworkers admitted under this program came from Mexico, although a few were also admitted from Canada and the Bahamas. They worked mainly in sugar beets or cotton.

Under the 1917 program, farmers were required to pay "the current wage" of those similarly employed and to comply with state laws regarding housing. Guestworkers were admitted to the United States for up to six months, with a possible extension for an additional six months. Family members could accompany the guestworkers. Farmers applied for permission to employ the guestworkers and were permitted to hire them only upon showing a labor shortage. While guestworkers were prohibited from working in any unauthorized jobs, they could work for other authorized employers. Farmers were required to withhold a portion of guestworkers' wages and deposit them in a bank to assure the workers would comply with the terms of admission. Farmers were also required to pay the cost of workers' transportation back to the border.

There was little enforcement of any of the provisions of the law after the guestworkers were admitted, and many workers remained in the United States after their jobs ended. Some remained because the farmers refused to pay their return transportation.

The World War I program lasted until 1921. However, immigrant workers remained in the United States to work in the fields, as immigration laws were not enforced. The Depression forced many U.S. residents who had lost jobs in other segments of the economy to seek work in agriculture. This ended the perceived need for immigrant workers, and Mexican nationals were forced out of the workforce and repatriated.

The buildup of the defense industry and armed forces as the United States entered World War II led to renewed complaints of labor shortages from farmers. The Farm Security Administration (FSA) argued that there were enough workers to fill the need if only the farmers would pay a decent wage. The FSA set up labor camps and acted as labor recruiters for farmers. The availability of these FSA houses at low cost led workers in some areas to refuse to work for the paltry wages offered by farmers. Many farmers, especially in the South, refused to negotiate with African American or Mexican American workers and complained that they needed a reliable workforce. The complaints resonated politically with

federal representatives, and thus the United States and Mexico negotiated an agreement under which guestworkers, called Bracero workers,
were admitted directly from Mexico to the United States in September
1942 to work specifically in sugar beets in California. In 1943 workers were admitted from the Bahamas and Jamaica under separate intergovernmental agreements. The Bahamian workers were housed in the
FSA camps, displacing the domestic farmworkers (Hahamovitch 1999).

In 1947, after the end of World War II, the wartime agreements were
allowed to lapse, and the Caribbean and Mexican programs diverged.
While the Mexican program continued to be governed by international
agreements until its end in 1964, the intergovernmental agreements
with the Caribbean nations were replaced by private agreements between U.S. employers and representatives of the Caribbean governments. The British West Indies Central Labour Organization (BWICLO)
served as a liaison in these agreements (and continues to do so today, although now under the acronym WICLO, because the "British" has been
dropped).

The Bracero program operated until 1964, when, in response to media
exposure of the abuse of workers in the program, Congress refused to
extend the law authorizing it. That did not, however, end the use of
imported labor in agriculture. Instead, over time many farmers, particularly in California and the Southwest, continued to employ Mexican nationals, although many were undocumented workers who were
neither U.S. citizens nor legal permanent residents.

The H-2 Program

In 1952 Congress repealed the Immigration Act
of 1917 and replaced it with a new Immigration and Nationality Act.
This act authorized the issuance of nonimmigrant visas to various categories of aliens, including an H-2 visa for persons entering the United
States to perform temporary labor or services. The statute did not define
the conditions under which these visas could be issued but merely directed the attorney general to consult with appropriate agencies before
issuing the visas. By regulation, the attorney general designated the U.S.
Department of Labor as the appropriate enforcement agency. Consultation was provided in the form of a certification from the secretary of
labor that (1) U.S. workers were not available and (2) the wages and working conditions offered would not adversely affect U.S. workers.

FIGURE 4.1. *Man waiting at the border of Matamoros, Mexico, and Brownsville, Texas, 1997. Photograph by Chris Johnson.*

Although the H-2 administrative scheme was similar to the requirements for admission of Bracero workers, Bracero workers were more readily available, and as a result, the H-2 program saw little use during the 1950s and early 1960s apart from the Caribbean workers who labored in the East Coast apple and sugarcane harvests.

It was not until 1964, when the Bracero program ended, that the H-2 program became more widely used. At that time DOL promulgated regulations governing the procedures for issuing H-2 labor certification. These regulations adopted verbatim the terms of the Bracero program's standard work contract (terms originally designed to protect Mexican workers from abuse) as the minimum terms necessary to ensure that the admission of H-2 workers would not adversely affect the wages and working conditions of U.S. workers. These regulations also continued the special minimum wage requirement (called the adverse effect wage rate) begun under the Bracero program.

The original H-2 regulations remained largely unchanged from 1964 until 1978, when, under the Carter Administration, the regulations were strengthened. The most important change was the addition of a requirement that rates paid for specific measurements such as bushels or crates increase each year in proportion to the adverse effect rate. The Carter

Administration also went to great lengths to recruit U.S. workers for H-2 jobs and limit the use of the program (Semler 1983).

With the change in administrations in 1980, attitudes toward the H-2 program changed dramatically. Under President Reagan's DOL, many of the protections of the regulations either were not enforced or were weakened. This was especially true of the wage protections, which were litigated extensively throughout the first half of the 1980s (Semler 1983).

Overview of the H-2A Program

Congress ended a decade-long deliberation over changes in immigration law when it adopted the Immigration Reform and Control Act of 1986 (IRCA). Parts of IRCA directly affected agriculture. First, IRCA gave legal permanent residency status to undocumented aliens who could prove they had performed agricultural work during a two-year period under the Special Agricultural Worker, or "SAW," program. Second, Congress created a successor to the H-2 program (codified as 8 U.S.C. § 1101(a)(15)(H)(ii). This new "H-2A" program is very similar to the original H-2 program, with some changes designed to streamline the application process for growers and the elevation of certain minimum work terms from regulatory to statutory language. The H-2A provisions became effective in June 1987.

The H-2A program is supposed to work like this: the grower files a job offer with the local employment service system; the job offer contains the details of the job and promises the wages and other terms and conditions of employment required by DOL's regulations. The regulatory minimum wages and employment terms are meant to be floors, set to prevent the use of foreign workers from causing an "adverse effect" on the employment of U.S. resident farmworkers. The job offers are supposed to contain not only the employment terms to be offered to U.S. workers but also those to be offered to foreign workers.

The statute requires that U.S. workers—which include U.S. citizens and legal permanent residents—be given preference for jobs, and it requires that growers make efforts to recruit workers in the United States. At the same time, the U.S. interstate employment service system is supposed to refer U.S. workers to the job openings with growers. If these recruitment efforts have not filled all the jobs by thirty days before the date on which the work begins, then DOL certifies the grower for the difference. As a result of the certification, the grower is allowed to import

H-2A workers to meet the shortfall. U.S. workers retain their preference for the jobs, and any U.S. worker who is able to do the job and who also applies for the job in the first half of the work contract period must be hired by the grower.

In reality, the system works quite differently. And though H-2A workers are less than 2 percent of the total agricultural worker population, the program has resulted in U.S. workers being excluded from jobs and has maintained a legacy of U.S. farm owners importing agricultural labor from other countries.

H-2A Program—The Statutory Standard

The H-2A program, like other visa programs, is administered by the U.S. attorney general acting through the INS, a branch of the Department of Justice. In creating the H-2A program, Congress recognized that an uncontrolled influx of foreign labor could have disastrous effects on U.S. workers, causing job displacement and depression of wages and working conditions. Accordingly, IRCA prohibits the attorney general from granting H-2A visas unless the petitioning employer has first applied to the secretary of labor for a certification that:

(A) there are not sufficient workers who are able, willing, and qualified, and who will be available at the time and place needed, to perform the labor or services involved in the petition, and

(B) the employment of the alien in such labor or services will not adversely affect the wages and working conditions of workers in the U.S. similarly employed (IRCA § 218(a)(1), 8 U.S.C. § 1188(a)(1).

This standard is very similar to the prior H-2 standard but is more restrictive to U.S. workers, as it requires not only that they be able and available, but that they "be available at the time and place needed." This phrase makes clear that a farmer can get H-2A workers even if there is a labor surplus in another area of the country—or even the state.

DOL's H-2A regulations require an agricultural employer who anticipates a labor shortage for a particular job to file a "temporary labor certification application" with the DOL at least forty-five days prior to the date that workers are needed. This application consists of an offer of employment setting forth the terms and conditions of work applicable to the job. DOL's regulations set the minimum terms and conditions of work that must be offered and paid to U.S. and foreign workers in order to ensure that the importation of foreign workers will not adversely affect similarly employed U.S. workers. Only if the employer's H-2A application meets the minimum requirement that the job will not adversely affect U.S. workers can DOL make the required certification.

Once the required terms of work have been offered by an employer, the secretary of labor tests the labor market to determine whether U.S. workers are available to fill the employer's needs. To do this, DOL circulates the employer's job offer through the U.S. Employment Service Interstate Clearance System and requires the employer to engage in private "positive" recruitment efforts. If after a brief recruitment period these efforts fail to locate enough U.S. workers to fill all of the employer's labor needs, the secretary of labor can make the second part of the required certification that U.S. workers are not available.

After the labor certification has been issued, an employer petitions the INS for temporary nonimmigrant visas for the foreign workers he or she wishes to import. INS regulations govern this visa process and require the employer to demonstrate that the job qualifies for H-2A visas (by presenting the DOL labor certification) and that the foreign workers selected by the employer meet the job qualifications specified by the employer.

Once issued, the visa gives the foreign worker permission to enter the United States to work only for the petitioning employer and only in the job for which labor certification was granted. Work for other employers or in other jobs may be grounds for revocation of the visa.

The U.S. Supreme Court said in its 1982 decision on *Alfred L. Snapp and Sons, Inc. v. Puerto Rico* regarding the nearly identical visa petitioning process under the old H-2 program:

The obvious point of this somewhat complicated statutory and regulatory framework is to provide two assurances to U.S. workers, including the citizens of Puerto Rico. First, these workers are given job preference over foreign workers for jobs that become available within this country. Second, to the extent that foreign workers are brought in, the working conditions of domestic employees are not to be adversely affected, nor are U.S. workers to be discriminated against in favor of foreign workers.

This statutory and regulatory framework is also intended to protect foreign workers from exploitation. In fact, the minimum terms of work that must be provided by H-2A employers have their origins in the work terms negotiated to protect Mexican Bracero workers during the 1950s.

The two statutory conditions that must be certified before foreign workers may be imported—the unavailability of U.S. workers and no adverse effect—are absolute minimums. They cannot be waived no matter how desperate an employer's need for workers might be or what business justification is offered for not complying with the statutory requirements. For example, in *Elton Orchards v. Brennan* (1974), H-2 apple growers in New Hampshire challenged DOL's policy of referring recruited U.S. workers to one H-2 orchard at a time until that orchard's labor needs were filled rather than distributing U.S. workers evenly among all of the New Hampshire H-2 orchards. The growers complained that DOL's policy denied equal protection to the orchards whose labor needs were filled with U.S. workers because all orchards needed at least some experienced foreign workers as a matter of business necessity. The court rejected that argument:

*We recognize that [the farmer's] business depends on proper harvesting of its crop during the brief span of weeks when the apples are ready, and that there may be good reason for appellee's wish to be able to rely on the experienced crews of British West Indians who have performed well in the past, but here that preference collides with the mandate of a congressional policy. To recognize a legal right to use alien workers upon a showing of business justification would be to negate the policy which permeates the immigration statutes, that domestic workers rather than aliens be hired wherever possible (*Elton Orchards, 508 F2d at 500).

Courts have even more strictly enforced the proposition that if a farmer complies with the two certification requirements as defined by the DOL regulations, then the farmer is entitled to import foreign workers regardless of how many U.S. workers might be available at higher wages or benefits. The result of this view is that the regulations act not only as minimum protections for U.S. workers but also as maximum protections. U.S. workers who demand better working conditions than those set by DOL are by definition not "available" for work and have no right to job preference over foreign workers who are willing to work at those DOL terms. For example, in *Hernandez-Flecha v. Quiros* (1978), Puerto Rican workers who were ready, able, and willing to accept jobs with H-2 employers were denied employment and their jobs were filled by foreign workers because Puerto Rican law required that they be offered slightly more favorable work terms than those set by the DOL regulations as the minimum necessary to avoid an adverse effect on U.S. workers. The Puerto Rican workers argued that the DOL conditions were merely minimum conditions that did not preclude them from demanding more. The court squarely rejected that position arguing that if U.S. workers could demand more than the minimum necessary to meet the requirements of the statute,

it requires little reflection to see that the statute would be used to require employers to meet whatever demands might be made by domestic workers. The effect, indeed, the necessary effect would be that the alien market would never be reached—the employer would have to pay whatever the domestic workers sought, it being obvious that if there were no limits on the price that could be asked, workers could always be found (Hernandez-Flecha, *567 F.2d at 1156*).

The court concluded that for the H-2 scheme to work, U.S. workers could not seek more beneficial terms than those set by the DOL regulations without forfeiting their right to job preference over foreign workers, regardless of their reason for seeking more beneficial terms.

The H-2A statutory terms are supposed to represent a balance between workers' and growers' interests. As the court in *Rogers v. Larson* (1977) noted, U.S. resident workers would be protected most effectively if no aliens were admitted to work, as the labor supply would then be considerably less so that wages and working conditions should improve. On the other hand, growers would best be assured a labor force if aliens were admitted without any restrictions. The H-2A program, said the court, strikes a balance between these polar positions.

The regulatory scheme created by DOL and INS further defines the balance point below which employers may not go without losing their right to import foreign workers and above which U.S. workers may not go without losing their right to job preference. However, under the statute, DOL's duty when adopting regulations is not to weigh the competing interests of employers and workers and attempt to strike its own balance between those interests. IRCA already has struck that balance, and DOL's duty is to carry out the statutory mandate that foreign workers not adversely affect the wages and working conditions of U.S. workers. This is an irreducible minimum that must be met, whatever balance point between worker and grower interests DOL may think is preferable. If an employer cannot offer terms that will protect U.S. workers from the adverse effects of foreign labor, then the employer's interests are irrelevant—even if it means that the employer must go out of business.

U.S. Employment Service

Although not itself a foreign worker program, the U.S. Employment Service (USES) Interstate Clearance System has been used in conjunction with foreign worker programs since the 1940s as the primary mechanism for measuring the availability of U.S. workers. The USES was created by the Wagner-Peyser Act of 1933 to help relieve unemployment during the Depression. The USES, a branch of the DOL Employment and Training Administration (ETA), directs and funds a network of public employment service offices in each of the fifty states. These local employment service offices operate as a no-fee labor exchange to help unemployed workers in one part of the country find available jobs in other parts of the country. State employment service offices also administer a variety of other federal programs such as unemployment compensation.

The recruitment functions of the USES are carried out in the following manner: employers in need of workers file job offers called "clearance orders" with their local employment service office. These clearance orders are first used to recruit workers locally. Unemployed workers are encouraged to sign up with their local employment service office and are notified when jobs for which they are qualified become available. If there is an insufficient number of local workers to fill a particular job, the job order is circulated or "cleared" to employment service offices in other parts of the state (intrastate clearance), and if workers are still needed, it is cleared to employment service offices in other states (interstate clearance).

As a condition for using the free recruitment services of the USES, employers are required to offer certain minimum terms and conditions of work specified in the USES regulations. Among other criteria, an employer is required to state all of the material terms and conditions of work in her or his job offer and to assure that the wages and working conditions offered are not less than the prevailing wages and working conditions among similarly employed agricultural workers in the area of intended employment nor less than the applicable federal or state minimum wage, whichever is higher.

Like the wage protections of the current H-2A program, the USES prevailing wage requirements are designed to "prevent the use of the interstate system as a vehicle for undermining prevailing wage rates in the area of intended employment" (U.S. Attorney General 1959, 409). The H-2A regulations protect local workers from unfair foreign competition, and the USES regulations protect local workers from government-assisted out-of-state competition.

The job offer circulated through the clearance system operates as an enforceable contract when accepted by a worker. However, neither the state employment service nor the USES is a party to the work contract.

The USES has operated in essentially the same manner since it was established in 1933, although it is used less and less by non-H-2A employers. It is the central administrative instrument by which DOL determines whether U.S. workers are available for H-2A jobs and hence is increasingly treated by DOL as a subdivision of its foreign worker program. The flaw in this system is that most farmworkers would never use the USES to help them find work. Therefore, the DOL cannot determine, through this method at least, how many workers are available in a particular area.

H-2A Contract and Regulation Terms

With limited exceptions, the IRCA statute does not specify particular terms of work that must be offered to U.S. workers. Rather, IRCA sets a general standard that the terms of work offered must be sufficient to ensure that the importation of foreign workers will not adversely affect the terms and conditions of work of similarly employed U.S. workers. Thus, in theory, IRCA requires employers to offer whatever terms are necessary to ensure that no adverse effect will occur. In practice, DOL's H-2A regulations define the terms which DOL asserts are necessary to avoid an adverse effect and, unless they are arbitrary, capricious, or operate in a manner contrary to the purposes of IRCA (i.e., allow an adverse effect), those terms are the only ones which must be offered. Proving that DOL work terms or policies are arbitrary or contrary to law is difficult.

Most of the substantive employment terms come from the H-2A regulations:

1.   *Work Contract.* The employer must provide both H-2A and U.S. workers with copies of the work contract no later than the day the work commences. This contract must contain all of the work terms required by the regulations. If no contract is provided to the worker, the required terms of the job order and the application for temporary alien agricultural certification are the work contract. Even if there is no approved certification or the employer has specifically refused to offer the H-2A terms, those terms are implied in the visas and the employer is contractually bound by them absent specific waiver of those terms.

2.   *Housing.* Employers are required to provide housing free of charge to all workers "who are not reasonably able to return to their residence within the same day." This is one of the few protections specifically required by IRCA. The housing may be, at the employer's option, rental or public accommodation-type housing. In the past, DOL generally considered thirty miles as a reasonable commuting distance, although this is not a fixed rule. The housing must meet federal, state, or local housing codes. The employer must pay any charges for rent directly to the owner of the rental property. The employer must document compliance with local or state housing standards.

3.   *Workers' Compensation.* The employer must provide workers' compensation coverage for its employees. However, in several states, agricultural workers are not covered by workers' compensation. Employers in those states must provide insurance covering injury and disease arising out of and in the course of the worker's

employment, at no cost to the worker. The insurance must provide benefits at least equal to those provided under the state workers' compensation law, if any, for comparable employment.

4.   *Tools/Employer-Provided Items.* The employer must provide free of charge all tools, equipment, and supplies required to perform the duties assigned to the worker except where the employer can demonstrate that it is common practice in the area, crop activity, and occupation for workers to provide tools and equipment. This exception may only be invoked if it is approved in advance by DOL. An employer may charge a worker for his refusal or negligent failure to return tools or for willful destruction of property.

5.   *Meals.* The employer must provide workers with three meals per day or furnish free and convenient cooking and kitchen facilities to the workers that will enable workers to prepare their own meals. In 1994 the maximum an employer could charge workers for meals was $6.81 per day unless a higher amount is approved by DOL. These charges are revised annually by the percentage change in the Consumer Price Index.

6.   *Transportation.* Employers are required to reimburse U.S. and foreign workers for the cost of transportation and subsistence "from the place from which the worker has come to work for the employer to the place of employment." The amount can be no less than the most economical means of obtaining the transportation, and the subsistence payments must be at least equal to the daily food charge.

      Reimbursement of these costs is due after the worker has completed 50 percent of the contract period—workers who quit or are terminated for cause before the 50 percent point are not entitled to reimbursement. The daily food charges are minimums for reimbursement purposes. Growers must pay the worker's actual expenses if the expenses are higher than the minimum meal charge.

These transportation and subsistence costs must be *advanced* to U.S. workers if it is the prevailing practice among non-H-2A employers in the occupation and area of employment to advance transportation costs to workers or if advances are made to foreign workers. Growers must also advance costs to U.S. workers if they collaborate with a third party, including a foreign government, to advance costs to foreign workers under circumstances only where the growers bear the risk of loss if the foreign worker fails to complete the first half of the contract. The employer may recoup transportation advances through payroll deductions, but these deductions must be returned to workers upon completion of 50 percent of the contract.

If a worker completes the total contract period, the employer must provide or pay for the worker's transportation and daily subsistence from the place of employment "to the place from which the worker, disregarding intervening employment, came to work for the employer."

The employer also must provide daily transportation from the living quarters to the work site free of charge to nonlocal workers who qualify for free housing. Local workers must pay their own way to the work site.

7. *Three-Quarter Contract Guarantee.* The employer must guarantee work or wages for three-quarters of the workdays during the contract period. However, if a worker is not hired until after the contract has begun, the three-quarter guarantee period begins with the first workday after the worker's arrival at the job and ends with the last day of the contract or any extension

thereof. Where there is no written work contract, the guarantee is measured by the approved
visa period. The guarantee basically works as
follows: if the contract is for eight weeks, the
employer must give the worker the opportunity
to work for at least six weeks. If the employer
only provides five weeks of work, he must pay
the worker an additional week's wages.

If a worker is paid on a piece rate basis, his
or her average hourly earnings on the piece rate
are used to calculate the value of the contract
guarantee. A grower may claim credit toward the
guarantee if a worker refuses to work when work
is available.

Workers who voluntarily abandon their jobs
or who are terminated for cause are not entitled
to the three-quarter guarantee if the employer
notifies the employment service of the termina-
tion or abandonment.

8.   *Records.* Employers are required to keep records
of the number of hours of work offered each
day, the hours worked by the employee, the
beginning and ending time, the rate of pay, earnings per pay period, the worker's address, and
the reasons for any deductions from pay. If the
hours worked are less than the hours offered, the
reason for the discrepancy must be recorded.

All records, including field tally records and
supporting summary payroll records, must be
made available to DOL and to the worker and
representatives designated by the worker. The
employer must keep these records for at least
three years.

9.   *Hours and Earnings Statement.* The employer
must provide to workers, on or before each payday, a statement showing the total earnings of
the pay period, the hourly rate or piece rate, the
hours of work offered and worked, itemization of

all deductions from pay, and the daily number of units picked on a piece rate.

10.   *Rates of Pay.* Employers have the right to choose what method of payment they will offer to workers, but whatever method is used, the rate paid must not be less than the adverse effect wage rate (AEWR), the prevailing rate, or the state or federal minimum wage, whichever is highest.

The AEWR is a special hourly wage rate set annually on a state-by-state basis to ensure that foreign workers do not adversely affect the wages of U.S. workers. It is set at the regional U.S. Department of Agriculture's average farm and livestock wage.

The prevailing wage rate is a crop- and area-specific wage that must be paid by all employers who use the employment service whether or not they apply for H-2A workers. It is generally the median rate paid according to the most common method of payment used in a crop. Thus, if a majority of the growers in an area pay by the piece for a particular crop activity, the prevailing wage in that crop will be the median of the different piece rates paid. If growers generally pay by the hour, the prevailing wage will be the median hourly rate.

11.   *Frequency of Pay.* Employers must pay in accordance with the prevailing practice in the area of intended employment or twice monthly, whichever is more frequent.

12.   *Contract Impossibility.* If before the expiration of the work contract the worker's services are no longer needed for reasons beyond the control of the employer (fire, hurricane, act of God), the employer may terminate the work contract. In such cases the three-fourths guarantee applies to whatever portion of the contract elapsed before the "act of God." The employer must at-

tempt to transfer the worker to other comparable employment acceptable to the worker, offer to return the worker to the place from which the worker came (disregarding any intervening employment), and reimburse the worker for the costs of transportation and subsistence to the place of employment. The employer is required to notify the DOL and employment service office in writing of the "act of God." In addition, the work contract must specify "the exclusive manner in which the guarantee may be abated due to weather conditions or other acts of God beyond the employer's control."

13. *Payroll Deductions.* The employer may make all deductions required by law and any other reasonable deductions as long as those deductions do not violate state or federal law. Thus an employer may deduct the costs of transportation advanced to the worker at the beginning of the season, although these deductions must be reimbursed after 50 percent of the contract has expired, but the employer may not make this or any other deduction if it would reduce the worker's wage below the minimum wage.

14. *Equal Treatment.* The H-2A regulations require equal treatment for U.S. and H-2A workers. Thus any benefit provided to H-2A workers, whether required or not, must be provided to U.S. workers.

Federal and State Employment-Related Laws

The H-2A and USES regulations both require an employer to assure that it will comply "with applicable federal, state, and local employment-related laws and regulations, including employment-related health and safety laws" (20 C.F.R. § 655.103[b], § 653.501 [d][2][xii]). Thus, these laws are incorporated into the H-2A

FIGURE 4.2. *Fifteen-year-old H-2A worker Mario from Michoacan, Mexico, is always seen with his headphone, bandana, and cap, 1999. Photograph by Rachel LaCour Niesen.*

contract and are enforceable through that contract. If state or local laws offer greater worker protections than the federal law, they rather than the federal law control. Only in the event of irreconcilable conflict between federal and state law would federal law prevail.

In some circumstances growers will specify additional benefits not required by law in their clearance orders, visa petitions, or the contracts with foreign workers. Any such work terms are automatically part of the job contract and must be offered to all workers, U.S. and H-2A alike.

In addition, employers are allowed to impose job qualifications for applicants under certain circumstances. In general, the employer can impose experience requirements or seek job references if it is the normal practice in the area for an agricultural employer to hire only experienced workers or to require references. Employers also can impose productivity minimums for keeping jobs if certain conditions are met, but only if those standards are no higher than the standards required by the employer in 1977 or the first year the employer entered the H-2 system. Productivity standards may be increased if the employer can demonstrate to the DOL that technological, horticultural, or other labor-saving means justify an increase in the minimum productivity level. In any event, productivity standards may not be higher than those normally required by employers in the area.

H-2A—The Reality

Agribusiness apologists point to the H-2A regulatory scheme as proof that farmworkers in the United States are well protected from any wage depression or loss of jobs due to the importation of workers from other countries with depressed economies. However, in practice, U.S. workers find themselves excluded from jobs with H-2A employers, while wages and working conditions for farmworkers lag behind the rest of the U.S. economy for work that is far harder than most.

Once the DOL makes its decision to allow a farmer to use H-2A workers, the farmer has no incentive to engage in recruitment. The grower knows he or she will have H-2A workers to fill the job. DOL formerly had to make that decision twenty days before the date on which workers were needed yet, as a result of recent legislation, now must decide thirty days before the date of need. That means that growers avoid any need to recruit at the time U.S. workers are most likely to be looking for their next jobs.

H-2A workers come with built-in advantages for growers. They are relatively easy to recruit. WICLO for years managed the recruiting of Jamaican workers for the sugarcane and East Coast apple harvests. Similar mechanisms are now employed in Mexico, although the Mexican government does not directly participate in the H-2A program as did the governments of the West Indies. For employers, obtaining a full crew of workers is often as easy as a telephone call. The workers arrive when the grower wants them, and no sooner, eliminating the need to provide shelter for workers before the harvest begins. Equally important, H-2A workers leave in an organized fashion as soon as the work ends.

The H-2A workers are, in the growers' view, more reliable. The wages the H-2A workers receive for their work on U.S. farms is far greater than what they could earn in their home countries, while for U.S. workers agricultural earnings are among the lowest. For crops like apples, piece rate earnings fall toward the end of the harvest, when there is only cleanup work to do. Often near the end of the harvest, U.S. workers are free to leave for better-paying work elsewhere, and they often do leave unless the employer provides some incentive to stay. H-2A workers, on the other hand, have to stay and work, or they risk losing their contracts and the cancellation of their work visas.

Growers who use H-2A workers are free of what little competition there is for agricultural labor. They offer only the minimum wages and work terms required by the DOL regulations. If they cannot get workers at those terms, they have access to a pool of foreign workers who are desperate for jobs. An employer who uses only U.S. workers, on the other hand, must respond to the laws of labor supply and demand. One of the problems with the H-2A regulations is that, as discussed above, DOL's minimum work terms are also maximums. Any worker wanting a higher hourly wage does not count as an available worker under the H-2A regulations, no matter how skilled she or he may be.

Further, the visa bonds H-2A workers to a single employer. By law, an H-2A worker cannot work for anyone else. U.S. workers, as guaranteed generations ago by General O. O. Howard in Virginia, are free to go to work for the farmer across the field if that farmer offers a higher wage or better housing or some other benefit.

The H-2A worker's dependence on his or her employer also undermines enforcement of the regulations, as the General Accounting Office (GAO) found in 1997. According to the GAO report, "H-2A guestworkers may be less aware of U.S. laws and protections than domestic workers, and they are unlikely to complain about worker protection violations . . . fearing they will lose their jobs or will not be hired in the future" (U.S. General Accounting Office 1997). Their fears are not imaginary. To illustrate, the Florida sugarcane growers operated a "no return list" to weed out complainers and other undesirable workers. Compounding the problem, DOL lacks staff and resources to adequately police the program. GAO found evidence that H-2A workers were not receiving the three-quarters guarantee, yet DOL had not received complaints nor found any violations.

Even when DOL stumbles upon a violation, it is loath to impose any penalty. For example, in 1985 the *Frederick County Fruit Growers Association v. McLaughlin* case showed that virtually every East Coast H-2 apple grower paid less than the wage rate required by the DOL and that each had promised to pay. Yet DOL failed to impose penalties on any of those growers following this case.

When H-2A workers contact an attorney, other obstacles arise. There is no explicit cause of action to enforce the work terms of the H-2A regulations, and H-2A workers are not covered by the major farmworker protective statute, the Migrant and Seasonal Agricultural Worker Protection Act. This means that an H-2A worker cannot enforce what rights he or she may have in federal court and cannot recover the statutory penalties that other U.S. workers can recover. H-2A workers also cannot avail themselves of federal court procedures, which are generally more accommodating than state court rules to litigants who live far from the courthouse. That leaves H-2A workers to state law contract actions, which usually must be tried in the county where the farmer lives. In a contest decided by a jury of local citizens between a fellow citizen and a worker from another country who may speak a different language, many advocates believe the worker is at a significant disadvantage. The difficulties and expense of bringing the worker back to the United States for trial or even pretrial proceedings add yet another hurdle. U.S. workers do not have these same obstacles, although they frequently have other significant barriers to obtaining justice.

Given these factors, it is not surprising that agricultural employers will spend significant sums to hire attorneys and agents to draft job descriptions that make their jobs seem as unappealing as possible or that contain new and onerous experience or productivity requirements, discouraging U.S. workers from applying for or staying with the jobs. Growers also use other tactics to keep U.S. workers out of the jobs. For example, some make U.S. workers take pre-employment tests or administer those tests in ways that allow guestworkers to pass at much higher rates than U.S. farmworkers. U.S. workers often are fired for failing to meet work standards not even applied to guestworkers (Geffert 1993).

While not the stated intent of the legislation, the result is that two groups of poor workers—guestworkers and U.S. farmworkers—find themselves pitted against each other in a system in which only the employer wins. Still, the agricultural industry is not satisfied. In 1997 and again in 1999, 2000, and 2001, bills drafted by agricultural interests have been introduced in Congress that would create yet another agricultural guestworker program, but this time without even the minimal protections of the H-2A system.

Growers' organizations have made demands for a new guestworker program in an attempt to avoid the minimal wage and working conditions that agricultural employers call "burdensome," even though the GAO has found that there is a surplus of agricultural labor in the United States already (U.S. General Accounting Office 1997). Growers complain that U.S. workers will not take the jobs. But the jobs require hard physical labor for short periods of time, provide no fringe benefits, and pay low wages that have risen slower than the rate of inflation (Commission on Agricultural Workers 1992). The 1986 IRCA created a special commission to study conditions in agriculture. Representatives of the agricultural industry heavily dominated the commission (Geffert 1993), yet the commission said that no new guestworker program should be established. Instead, the commission recommended that the agricultural industry adopt modern labor management practices and improve wages and working conditions. When IRCA was passed, the farm lobby claimed that farmworkers would leave agriculture after they got their legal permanent residency visas. The farmers said they would be forced to improve wages and working conditions in order to retain workers. However, a GAO study found that no such change had taken place (U.S. General Accounting Office 1989).

More recently, the agribusiness lobby has claimed that a new guestworker program would help control unlawful immigration. However, the evidence says just the opposite: guestworker programs encourage unlawful immigration (Congressional Research Service 1980). Alternatively, a fair work program might encourage compliance with immigration laws.

For the agribusiness lobby, however, it seems all that matters is access to a pool of labor without having to pay living wages, improve working conditions, or meet government standards required of other industries seeking a competent workforce. So far, the bills introduced to create a new agricultural guestworker program have failed. In part this is because of a general anti-immigrant sentiment in Congress, because of representatives who are concerned about fair policies for farmworkers, and in part because the Clinton Administration opposed the bills. Farmworker advocates must help ensure that future administrations likewise will resist political pressures from powerful agricultural interests as the latter seek to eliminate the few protections farmworkers possess. Only through these protections will farmworkers have a fighting chance at better conditions.

Testimony at Hearing before the Commission on Agricultural Workers

Roman Rodriguez, Florida farmworker

After just ten years I've seen changes, but I haven't seen any changes in favor of the farmworkers. I've seen everything going the other way. About seven years ago, we used to get rides to work. We used to get supplies for work. And now we are not getting anything. Plus, after we got all this taken from us, we've seen so many changes that are all against us . . . I don't know if it's the same with lower Florida, but I'm an organizer for the farmworkers of central Florida, and I've seen so many cases where the farmers fire the people just because they are asking if they can give them a few more cents per hour, per bunch, or just if they think they deserve a little bit more because of the job that they are doing. The first thing we heard is that they are fired just because of doing that. We have no rights to ask for anything that we think we deserve. I don't think that's fair.

They won't even listen to us. They have some of these crew leaders in front of us [so] we won't be able to go in front of a farmer and tell him what we need or what we want. He was going to send somebody to tell us that we were fired before he can listen to us.

I'm [making this testimony] because I really don't like the things that are going on around my family. I have most of my family working in the same conditions, and I'm really hoping that my being here will help to make a little change. I'm hoping that I'm talking to the right people to at least start the change. And I thank you for listening to me.

CHAPTER 5

Farmworker Exceptionalism under the Law

How the Legal System Contributes to Farmworker Poverty and Powerlessness

Greg Schell

Workers Unprotected under the Law

Every few years, surveys are published ranking jobs in the United States. Invariably, these surveys identify migrant farm work as the single worst profession. Farm work is unattractive for a number of reasons. The work usually is seasonal, leaving many farmworkers without employment for weeks on end between harvests. The work itself is arduous in nature and oftentimes performed in unpleasant weather conditions. However, farm labor is principally distinguished from other low-skill jobs by the extremely low wages paid and the primitive working and living conditions offered.

U.S. society was dramatically altered in the first half of the twentieth century through progressive legislation that revolutionized the industrial workplace. However, major agricultural organizations such as the American Farm Bureau Federation and its state affiliates, as well as groups representing growers of particular commodities, have vigilantly guarded against the extension of these basic labor laws to farmworkers. While they are forced to absorb rising costs for fertilizer, seed, pesticides, and farm equipment and to sell their perishable commodities at a market price subject to wide fluctuations, growers often have been able to control wages and other labor costs. While farmworkers themselves ordinarily have been disorganized and disconnected from the political process, agribusiness interests acting on behalf of large fruit and vegetable producers have always exerted substantial influence in legislative and administrative arenas and have been able to shape most governmental policies that impact farmworkers' wages and working conditions. In recent years, groups such as the National Council of Agricultural Employers, the Western Growers Association, and the Florida Fruit and Vegetable Association have emerged as effective advocates for the interests of large-scale growers and as antagonists to farmworkers with regard to labor matters. As a result, farmworkers in many respects find themselves trapped in the sort of living and working conditions that characterized much of industrial labor in the late nineteenth century.

It has proven extraordinarily difficult to overcome these longstanding laws excluding farmworkers from the same legal rights enjoyed by other workers in the United States. As an alternative strategy, farmworker supporters have concentrated their reform efforts on passage of laws specifically designed to ameliorate the distressing conditions under which farmworkers live and toil. While these well-intentioned efforts certainly have helped alleviate some aspects of farmworker life, they have done relatively little to address the primary problem farmworkers face in the legal arena—the concept of agricultural exceptionalism that pervades federal and state law.

Origins of Agricultural Exceptionalism

In the nineteenth-century United States, the living and working conditions faced by farmworkers were not markedly different from those of industrial workers. Both groups found themselves in an ever-expanding labor market filled by a constant stream of immigrants willing to accept backbreaking jobs at low wages. The work was characterized by low wages, child labor, long hours, and enormously hazardous working conditions.

Beginning with the reforms of the Progressive Era in the late nineteenth century and culminating in the federal labor legislation of the New Deal period, an extraordinary transformation occurred with regard to industrial labor. First at the state level and later at the federal level, child labor was severely restricted or outlawed altogether in most industries. Hours of work were sharply limited, with the development of the concept of overtime pay as a means to discourage employers from requiring workers to toil for more than forty hours per week. Workers' compensation laws were adopted to ensure that workers injured on the job received medical benefits and compensation for their lost wages while convalescing. Occupational safety and health legislation, coupled with a workers' compensation insurance system that rewarded employers with lower premiums if their employees had fewer accidents, created powerful incentives to curb the most dangerous working conditions. Federal and state minimum wage acts were adopted to correct "conditions detrimental to the maintenance of the minimum standard of living necessary for health, efficiency, and general well-being of workers" (Section 2, Fair Labor Standards Act of 1938, codified at 29 U.S.C. §202[a]). Finally, and perhaps most important, with the passage of the National Labor Relations Act in the mid-1930s, industrial workers were granted the right to collectively bargain for their wages with protection against reprisals from their employers.

As a result of these developments, the living standards of industrial workers changed dramatically. Armed with the protections of the new National Labor Relations Act, industrial unions won numerous contracts in a wide range of occupations. Union wage rates and fringe benefits enabled industrial employees to enter the prosperity of middle-class living. Even at non-union jobs, wages and working conditions improved as employers competed with union plants for employees.

Farmworkers did not benefit from this period of dramatic transformation of the industrial workplace. Instead, as labor laws were passed to improve the conditions for workers, the doctrine of "agricultural exceptionalism" developed. Virtually every labor protective standard passed on both a federal and state level prior to 1960 excluded agricultural workers. As the lot of industrial workers consistently improved, the earnings of agricultural workers lagged further and further behind. By the end of World War II, a marked gap existed between the protections enjoyed by industrial workers and the nineteenth-century conditions endured by farmworkers.

At the same time, agriculture was rapidly changing, with a corresponding rise in the need for temporary labor. Improvements in refrigeration and transportation, combined with technological advances such as the development of citrus concentrate, resulted in a growing demand for fruit and vegetable workers. While the picking of some crops, such as cotton, was taken over by machines, these new devices proved too rough on most fruits and vegetables to serve as a viable alternative to hand-harvesting. Consumers were unwilling to purchase fresh produce bruised from mechanical handling. Thus, most fresh fruits and vegetables continued to be harvested by hand, as did tobacco, a major cash crop in the Southeast.

A handful of states adopted laws regulating the most obvious abuses of farmworkers, such as transportation in unsafe and overcrowded vehicles and housing workers in units lacking electricity or running water. However, these modest reforms were largely restricted to states with strong, progressive labor laws, such as New York, New Jersey, and Michigan. In most states, the power of agricultural interests overwhelmed any efforts at reform, leaving most farmworkers beyond the purview of any governmental regulation.

This was most noticeably the case in the southeastern states, which were among the largest users of hand-harvest agricultural labor. Despite the large number of migrant workers employed in them, Georgia, South Carolina, Alabama, Tennessee, Mississippi, and West Virginia have not adopted laws setting minimum standards for farmworker housing. No southern state has adopted a minimum wage law applicable to farmworkers. Georgia and Florida remain the only two states that lack laws mandating that employees be paid promptly for their labor. Mississippi still exempts farmworker children from its compulsory education laws.

In most agricultural states, farm interests historically have been disproportionately powerful in state legislatures. Prior to 1962, states were generally free to allocate their legislative seats on factors other than population. In most states, this resulted in the concentration of extraordinary political power in the hands of rural legislators at the expense of representatives from more populous urban and suburban areas. Although they generally were home to a shrinking minority of the population, the rural areas controlled many state legislatures. This proved an effective damper on legislation at the state level designed to benefit farmworkers. Agricultural lobbyists convinced sympathetic legislators that their farmers would be at a competitive disadvantage compared to other states if substantial new production costs were added in the form of higher wages and increased protections for farmworkers. It was only in 1962, in the case of *Baker v. Carr*, that the U.S. Supreme Court struck down legislative apportionment schemes that were not based upon population. The Supreme Court determined in that case that the fundamental concept of "one man, one vote" required that legislative districts be drawn so as to ensure that each district had a roughly equal number of citizens.

At the federal level, a similar dynamic resulted in the exclusion of farmworkers from most federal laws protecting employees. The peculiar structure of Congress accentuated the influence of its members from rural districts, particularly those from the South. Until the latter part of the twentieth century, the South remained predominantly rural, and its legislative representatives heavily influenced national politics on behalf of agricultural interests. Because most of the farmworkers in the rural South prior to 1960 were African American, any legislation on behalf of farmworkers tended to be viewed as undermining the hierarchical and racially charged social order preserved throughout the South with various Jim Crow laws.

In order to pass the New Deal reforms in the 1930s and 1940s, President Franklin D. Roosevelt needed the support of the southern members of Congress. Although nominally Democratic, most southerners in Congress at the time only reluctantly supported an activist federal government, fearing federal intervention in civil rights matters. To secure these needed votes for critical New Deal programs, proponents had to agree to exempt agriculture. One scholar has forcefully argued that most of the agricultural exemptions were prompted by racial concerns (Linder 1992).

Over the following decades, efforts at eliminating agricultural exceptionalism usually floundered. While the farm population continued to decline as a percentage of the U.S. population, agricultural interests remained influential both in the state houses and in Congress. Farm groups have been quite effective in conveying an image of wholesomeness, relying on Americans' nostalgic belief in the basic goodness of the family farm. Indeed, despite the fact that most farmworkers now are employed by large corporate growers, much of the population still views American farmers as the subjects in Grant Wood's classic portrait, "American Gothic"—hard-working, decent folks struggling to make ends meet on their small plots of land. Advertising images projected by food producers have contributed to this phenomenon, portraying farmers as small family-based operations.

Farm interests also have succeeded to a large extent in depicting American farmworkers as a group different and apart from other employees. Lobbyists describe farmworkers as natural-born wanderers who revel in the informality of agricultural work, enjoy working outdoors, have no long-range goals, and live for the day. In fact, as farm lobbyists depict them, farmworkers chafe under the sort of regimentation common in more tightly regulated settings. Thus, the argument goes, farmworkers neither need nor desire rules, standards, and regulations relating to their work. According to this erroneous depiction of farmworkers, agricultural producers are neither greedy nor exploitative and instead are simply catering to the wishes of their farmworker employees.

Farmworkers and their advocates are ill-equipped to overcome the political efforts of agribusiness. Agricultural workers are one of the most politically impotent groups in U.S. society. Farmworkers are scattered about the country, never constituting a large enough voting bloc to affect elections. Political participation by farmworkers became more difficult in the 1990s, especially as the percentage of undocumented aliens in the farm labor workforce grew. By the late 1990s the National Agricultural Worker Survey estimated that more than half the farm labor workforce was comprised of undocumented workers. Outside of the electoral cycle, farmworkers also are constrained in their efforts to influence the policies that impact their lives. Many farmworkers do not view their occupation as a lifelong career and as a result are unwilling to invest the time and energy necessary to support organizations seeking to improve conditions for agricultural workers.

The increasing transience of the farm labor force over recent decades has exacerbated the legal and political problems affecting farmworkers. Prior to the enactment of the federal civil rights acts, many minorities residing in rural areas were forced to remain in farm labor jobs because few other opportunities were available to them. School desegregation and fair employment laws of the 1960s provided many new options, especially for African Americans in rural areas. Increasingly, the farm labor workforce is comprised of immigrants, both documented and undocumented. Collective efforts at reform often become bogged down because of ethnic tensions between immigrant groups and unfamiliarity of immigrants with the U.S. economic and political systems.

Given these obstacles, it is not surprising that few viable organizations comprised of farmworkers have emerged. These farmworker membership organizations have often struggled to build coalitions with potential allies such as organized labor. While they often have supported legislative initiatives to improve farmworker conditions, labor and religious groups have not sustained their support for farmworker issues among the many other issues they address, in part because of the relative invisibility of farmworkers in society.

Persistence of Agricultural Exceptionalism

Arrayed against the highly effective lobbying efforts of agricultural interests, the relatively small and disorganized farm labor advocacy groups normally are seriously outmatched. During those rare and all too brief periods when national attention focuses on them, farmworkers are able to attract some attention from legislators to the myriad problems. Otherwise, farm labor advocacy groups find them-

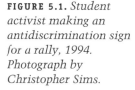

FIGURE 5.1. *Student activist making an antidiscrimination sign for a rally, 1994. Photograph by Christopher Sims.*

selves in a largely defensive situation, struggling to block agribusiness-backed legislation that is detrimental to farmworkers. The bulk of this legislation has been enacted at the federal level, with more modest advances occurring under the laws of a number of states, particularly those in the Northeast and along the Pacific Coast.

A. FEDERAL LAW

The majority of the employment rights enjoyed by most U.S. workers are provided under federal law. Many of these laws trace their origins to the New Deal period in the 1930s, when congressional majorities were marshaled to enact a number of proposals that had evolved decades earlier during the Progressive Era.

Farmworkers were excluded from every major piece of labor legislation enacted during the New Deal, notably those laws that established minimum wages, maximum hours, and workplace safety standards, and those that limited child labor. Slowly, a few of these exemptions have been diminished or even eliminated. However, farmworkers remain outside the scope of many basic labor law protections that most U.S. workers take for granted.

In many instances, these modest legal protections have only been extended to farmworkers employed on larger farms, with migrants employed on relatively smaller operations still exempted from the law. Many tobacco farms, for example, which generally employ fewer than a dozen full-time workers, remain exempt from all federal labor laws. Likewise, many smaller fruit and vegetable farms in the Southeast, such as those producing watermelons and pickling cucumbers, are not subject to these laws. Roughly one-third of the nation's farmworkers are employed on small farms that are not subject to federal law, with far higher percentages in some states.

Wages   Perhaps nowhere is the enormous disparity between the relative political power of agribusiness and farmworkers better illustrated than in the struggle over wages. The Fair Labor Standards Act, one of the centerpieces of the New Deal, established minimum wages for most workers in the United States. The Fair Labor Standards Act (FLSA) also was designed to discourage excessive hours of work through its requirement that employers pay their employees enhanced overtime wages for any time worked in excess of forty hours during a week.

At its inception in 1938, the act exempted farmworkers altogether. In 1966, after prolonged agitation by farmworker advocates, farmworkers finally were included in the law's minimum wage provisions, although at a lower rate than other workers. By the late 1970s, forty years after most workers were guaranteed the minimum wage, farmworkers at larger farms were guaranteed the federal minimum wage. However, farmworker advocates have been unsuccessful in extending the other major provisions of the Fair Labor Standards Act to farmworkers.

First, farmworkers on smaller farms are excluded from the act altogether. The federal minimum wage law does not apply to any farm that did not use more than five hundred "man-days" of labor in at least one calendar quarter the prior year—the equivalent of seven full-time employees. By its peculiar focus on the prior rather than current year, this exception allows any new agricultural employer a full year free from the worries of the minimum wage, since a first-time employer by definition will not have used any man-days the prior year. Second, because the exemption is based on calendar quarters, many labor-intensive activities of relatively short duration fall outside the law's coverage, particularly when the harvest season straddles two calendar quarters. For example, a harvest that runs from June through July crosses two calendar quarters—the second (April, May, and June) and third (July, August, and September). A farmer who uses a crew of twenty-five workers for six weeks from early June through late July still is likely to be exempt from the law, even though the total man-days used approaches nine hundred.

In addition, farmworkers remain exempt from the law's overtime provisions. Thus, while the worker at a fast-food restaurant who places tomatoes and lettuce on a hamburger receives overtime pay after forty hours, the farmworker who picked the tomatoes or cut the lettuce may work upwards of eighty hours per week without ever receiving a cent of overtime pay, unless he or she is employed in one of the few states that has enacted its own special overtime law for agricultural workers, as Oregon and New Jersey have. Even in these states, the overtime coverage for farmworkers tends to be more stingy than that paid to other employees. For example, while Maryland overtime law does not exempt agriculture, it only applies to farmworkers who work more than sixty hours in a week, while other workers receive overtime pay after forty hours in a week.

The arbitrary nature of the overtime exemption is striking. For example, while workers employed in planting, cultivating, or harvesting fruits and vegetables are not covered by the overtime provisions of the Fair Labor Standards Act, workers who plant, cultivate, or harvest trees are entitled to overtime pay. Tree farming is not generally considered to be agriculture and thus does not have agriculture's exemption from overtime pay. Similarly, overtime payments to workers employed in packing and processing plants depend on seemingly arbitrary distinctions. If the packinghouse or processing plant handles only the produce of the owner of the facility, the workers are considered engaged in agricultural labor, with no right to overtime pay. Once the packinghouse or plant handles as much as a single box of produce from a farmer other than the facility owner, the workers are considered nonagricultural workers, with full rights to overtime pay.

Child labor Besides establishing minimum wages and requiring overtime pay in most industries, the Fair Labor Standards Act prohibits full-time employment of those under sixteen years of age. Employment in certain jobs determined to be "particularly hazardous" is off-limits for children between sixteen and eighteen years of age. Prior to 1966, no federal child labor laws covered agriculture. However, when farmworkers were incorporated under the minimum wage provisions of the Fair Labor Standards Act in 1966, Congress was faced with the issue of whether to apply the law's child labor provisions to agriculture.

As is the norm, a separate set of rules was created for agriculture. Children under sixteen may not work during school hours, but after school and during vacations, children may perform a wide range of farm labor tasks. Children fourteen and older may routinely perform most agricultural tasks outside of school hours. Children as young as twelve may work under certain conditions, provided that they receive parental permission or work alongside their parents. Children as young as ten may apply for waivers to allow them to harvest crops. In addition, children between sixteen and eighteen are permitted to perform "particularly hazardous" tasks, provided these tasks are in agriculture. Despite renewed interest in child labor laws since 1990, efforts to apply the same child labor standards to agriculture as are in place in other industries have so far proven unsuccessful.

Unemployment compensation   The Social Security Act was passed in 1935 as one of the foremost pieces of New Deal legislation. As part of the Social Security system, the law included a system of providing income to workers who experienced an involuntary loss of employment. This system of unemployment compensation is funded principally through a tax on employers' payrolls. Not surprisingly, agricultural workers initially were exempted from the unemployment compensation system.

The unavailability of unemployment compensation benefits condemns most farmworkers to a life of migrancy. In very few areas is sufficient farm labor employment available on a year-round basis to support a worker and his or her family. Once work ends in an area, many workers have no choice but to travel to another area or state to find agricultural work.

Unemployment compensation is operated jointly by the federal and state governments. A minimum level of benefits and coverage is established under federal law, with the states allowed to adopt more generous programs if they choose. Early efforts to include farmworkers primarily came at the state level. However, except for a few small jurisdictions, the states declined to include farmworkers in their unemployment compensation laws, capitulating to claims by farmers that such coverage would put them at a competitive disadvantage as compared to farmers in other states who were not required to pay unemployment compensation taxes.

Finally, in 1978 Congress amended the Social Security Act to include certain farmworkers under the unemployment compensation program. A sizable exemption remains for agricultural employers who do not hire large numbers of workers for an extended period of time. Nonetheless, for those farmworkers covered by the law, unemployment compensation has offered a means of escaping the seemingly endless migrant stream.

Sanitation at the workplace   With the passage of the federal Occupational Safety and Health Act in 1971, the federal government became deeply involved in issues of workplace safety. The federal Department of Labor, through its Occupational Safety and Health Administration (OSHA), has issued detailed regulations specifying standards for workplace safety for hundreds of industries. However, the push for workplace safety has stalled whenever farmworkers are involved. The Department of Labor has refused to issue specific standards for most agricultural jobs. For example, while OSHA has published detailed standards for ladders and scaffolding used in the construction industry, it has not issued standards for ladders used by fruit pickers.

OSHA has promulgated regulations relating to sanitation facilities at agricultural worksites. These regulations require that toilet facilities and drinking water and hand-washing facilities be provided by any employer of more than eleven farmworkers. However, the evolution of these regulations underscores the difficulty in persuading federal agencies to undertake action on behalf of farmworkers.

Beginning in the early 1970s, farmworker advocates formally approached OSHA regarding the need for basic sanitation facilities to be provided for agricultural workers. It was believed that there would be relatively little resistance to this proposal within the agency because the public health benefits of proper sanitation are well established. The proponents of field sanitation had not anticipated the strong opposition from agricultural interests. Farm organizations objected to the cost of providing facilities, remarking on the cost of providing toilet facilities at various fields and job sites.

OSHA deferred action on the field sanitation issue, contending that it had matters of greater importance on its agenda. Frustrated with OSHA's inaction, several farmworker organizations and a handful of individual farmworkers sued OSHA, asking the court to direct the agency to issue field sanitation regulations. It was only in 1987, after eleven years of litigation in the federal courts, that OSHA reluctantly acquiesced and required agricultural employers to provide toilets and other basic sanitation facilities for their workers.

Organizational rights   Federal laws specify low minimal levels for wages and outlaw only the most abusive working conditions. A worker earning the federal minimum wage falls below the government poverty line, particularly if the employee is a family's sole support.

Throughout the nineteenth century and well into the twentieth century, employers of large numbers of industrial workers dictated most wage and job terms to their employees. While disgruntled workers were free to quit a job with poor wages or working conditions, such individual actions mattered little to employers. Because immigration to the United States continued at a high rate throughout the period, employers experienced little difficulty in replacing departing workers with new arrivals to the country.

Pre–New Deal efforts at collective action by industrial workers were largely ineffectual. Employers discharged with impunity employees suspected of leading organizing drives. When work stoppages occurred, employers could usually crush any rallies or picketing activity with the assistance of local law enforcement agencies or private security officers. As a result, prior to the labor reforms of the New Deal, labor organizers made few inroads toward unionizing industrial workers.

One of the most far-reaching statutes adopted as part of the New Deal was the National Labor Relations Act (NLRA). Often referred to as the Wagner Act after its principal Senate sponsor, the NLRA revolutionized the U.S. industrial workplace. Because of the NLRA's provisions, unions found themselves on a far more sound footing when negotiating with employers. Once a designated proportion of the workforce gave its assent, a union gained the right to bargain with the employer on behalf of the employees. Employers who refused to bargain in good faith with such a union faced potentially severe legal sanctions. With the NLRA in place, thousands of workplaces became unionized. Progress toward unionization was less pronounced in the South, where "right to work" provisions were included in several state constitutions that prohibited mandatory union membership at work sites where union contracts were in place.

The NLRA provided critical protections for employees who engaged in collective action. Workers involved in organizing efforts aimed at improving wages and working conditions were no longer left without a legal remedy if their employers retaliated. The NLRA deemed retaliation against workers for participating in collective actions an unfair labor practice and entitled workers discharged for engaging in these activities to reinstatement and back pay.

It is no accident that the wave of unionization that swept through U.S. factories following passage of the NLRA did not extend into the nation's fields, orchards, and groves. The NLRA excludes agricultural workers from its protections. Efforts to remove this exclusion have not achieved much success. Farm interests have persuaded Congress that providing farmworkers with a meaningful right to collective action, including the right to strike, is inappropriate when perishable commodities are involved, despite the fact that there are few examples of labor unrest ever resulting in a grower being unable to harvest his or her crop. A few states, notably California, have passed state laws providing farmworkers with protections similar to those offered industrial workers under the NLRA, and not surprisingly, the modest number of union contracts won by farmworkers are concentrated in these states. However, in most areas of the country, including all of the southeastern states, farmworkers who undertake collective action against their employers have little legal protection against retaliatory actions by their employers. Thus, the vast majority of farmworkers today remain in the same position that industrial workers were in prior to passage of the NLRA—disorganized and fearful of undertaking concerted action to demand better wages and working conditions.

B. STATE LAW

Under federal law, farmworkers have struggled to secure the basic rights enjoyed by virtually all other workers in this country. They have been even less successful at the state level. Every state has laws that treat farmworkers less favorably than other employees. Only a few states have laws that guarantee the minimum wage to farmworkers excluded from the federal minimum wage law (e.g., farmworkers employed on small farms), and none of these states is in the Southeast. Some states, including South Carolina, expressly exempt

residents of migrant labor camps from their landlord and tenant statutes, leaving camp owners free to evict camp residents without any judi-
cial process. In several states, including Mississippi, compulsory education laws do not apply to farmworker children.

Because corporate and large-scale agricultural groups are disproportionately influential in state capitals, none of this is surprising. On the
federal level, farm interests represent only one of thousands of organized
groups trying to press their agendas on Congress. While agribusiness
is well represented in Washington, D.C., so are many other interest
groups. Agribusiness initiatives must compete for Congress's attention
with those proposed by other groups. Furthermore, in many matters
such as environmental and trade questions, agribusiness faces opposition from equally well-organized interests. However, by contrast, farm
interests often are among the well-heeled and influential lobbies at the
state level, particularly in rural states. In major farm states, agricultural
groups have few peers in terms of influence. The longstanding exclusion of farmworkers from workers' compensation coverage in more than
half the states bears witness to the enormous power of agribusiness over
state legislative bodies.

Workers' compensation is one of the major achievements of the Progressive Era. As the United States was transformed from an agrarian
to an industrial society, an increasing number of workers suffered debilitating injuries in the workplace. Injured workers could seek damages from their employers through negligence suits, though such cases
proved extremely difficult to win. Injured employees had to demonstrate
that their employers were negligent in maintaining the workplace. Employers could raise a wide range of defenses to such claims. If the employee contributed to his or her injury, even to a small extent, his or her
claim was likely to be barred. If the employee was aware that the working conditions were dangerous and nonetheless continued in his or her
job, a subsequent case for negligence would be dismissed.

Workers' compensation laws sought to replace the system of negligence suits, which required showing fault on the part of the employer,
with a no-fault system. Under workers' compensation, most workplace
injuries are considered compensable, regardless of whether the employer was negligent, the employee contributed to the accident, or the
employee knowingly assumed the risks associated with the job. Through
a system of insurance, workers' compensation is structured to ensure
that injured workers receive necessary medical care and monetary payments for a proportion of their lost wages while convalescing.

There is no federal workers' compensation law applicable to most employees, and, accordingly, workers' compensation is peculiarly a matter of state law. Each state decides which workers are covered and the amount of benefits to be paid.

Even though statistics routinely show agriculture as one of the most dangerous occupations in the country, a large proportion of farmworkers in the United States are not covered by workers' compensation. In half of the states, if a farmworker falls out of a fruit tree at work, he or she is not guaranteed that medical care payment or lost wages will be provided.

In 1972 a federal commission evaluating the workers' compensation systems nationwide recommended that farmworkers be included in each state's workers' compensation system (Report of National Commission on State Workmen's Compensation Laws 1972). Implementation of this objective has proven problematic. Only a few of the largest farming states provide workers' compensation coverage for farmworkers equal to that given to other workers. Many states, including the southeastern states except Florida and Virginia, make workers' compensation optional rather than mandatory. In some of these states, the vast majority of farmers have chosen to forgo purchase of costly workers' compensation insurance policies.

A Strategy of Amelioration

Because of the abject failure by policymakers to end farmworker exceptionalism, advocates have redirected reform efforts toward passage of laws designed to treat some of the most serious symptoms of farmworker exclusion from the economic and political mainstream. Many advocates for farmworkers have concentrated on laws to reduce or eliminate the worst features of farm labor. Under this strategy, the emphasis is on passage of specific laws to protect farmworkers rather than to remove the myriad exemptions that have denied them the basic rights enjoyed by most other employees. While there have been some notable successes, the overall effect of this strategy has been to perpetuate farmworker exceptionalism.

In campaigning for farmworker protective laws, advocates for farmworkers sought federal action to overcome seemingly intractable resistance in many states. Initial efforts at federal regulation to protect farmworkers proved no more successful than the efforts in most state legislatures. Although various presidential commissions and special congressional committees were established in the 1950s to study the abuses suffered by farmworkers, the recommendations of these bodies regarding farmworker housing, labor conditions, health, and education attracted little interest in Congress.

An unexpected turn of events finally prodded Congress into action. On Thanksgiving Day 1960, many U.S. citizens came face to face for the first time with the horrid conditions migrant workers experienced when CBS network televised the groundbreaking documentary "Harvest of Shame." Legendary newsman Edward R. Murrow narrated the program, which presented the lives of individual migrant farmworkers, including many children. "Harvest of Shame" brought into American homes a visual image of the unsanitary housing in which migrant farmworkers resided and the unsafe and overcrowded vehicles that transported the workers thousands of miles. The documentary also highlighted the conditions of migrant children, showing many of them suffering from hunger and malnutrition, with virtually none of them completing high school. In the closing minutes of the program, narrator Murrow urged U.S. citizens to support proposals to ameliorate the shocking conditions faced by farmworkers.

"Harvest of Shame" prompted a relative frenzy of federal legislative activity on behalf of the long-forgotten farmworkers. Most of the major federal social service programs directed at farmworkers, such as migrant health, education, housing, and job training programs, trace their origins to the broadcast.

The program graphically depicted the failure of the limited state laws in protecting migrant farmworkers and the need for federal intervention. In this atmosphere of heightened public concern for farmworkers, Congress in 1963 passed the Farm Labor Contractor Registration Act (FLCRA), the first federal law regulating the working and living conditions of farmworkers. Although modest in its scope, the FLCRA was a landmark piece of legislation for farmworkers because it established federal primacy over the regulation of farm labor matters. Farm groups had long opposed federal intervention on issues involving migrant workers, believing correctly that legislation at the state level was far more susceptible to control and influence by agricultural interests. In particular, farm organizations feared the role of federal agencies that would be assigned the task of drafting regulations to implement the FLCRA and subsequent federal farm labor laws. Agricultural interests worried that federal bureaucrats, protected by civil service laws, would adopt a wide

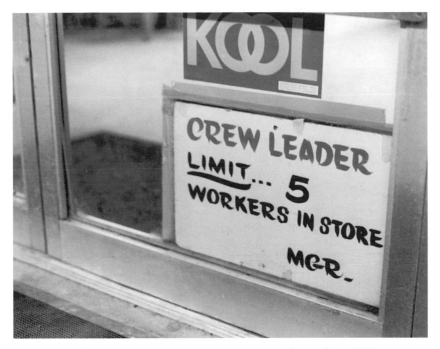

FIGURE 5.2. *Sign in a store in Sampson County, North Carolina, 1994. Photograph by Christopher Sims.*

range of regulations governing farm labor with little attention to growers' concerns.

The FLCRA itself was a very small step toward curbing abuse of migrant workers. It imposed no obligations on farmers but instead directed its requirements exclusively at farm labor contractors or "crew leaders," intermediaries who recruit, transport, and pay migrant workers.

The crew leader system had become widespread following World War II. Prior to that time, most fruit and vegetable farms were fairly small, serving only local geographic areas. Because their crops were highly perishable, most of these truck farmers could only ship their fresh produce to markets within a few hundred miles of the farm. The truck farms needed only a small number of workers, most of whom could be recruited locally.

The fruit and vegetable industry changed dramatically with technological advances in the 1940s and 1950s. With improvements in transportation and refrigeration, fruit and vegetable growers were able to ship their produce much greater distances to market. The development of citrus concentrate made it possible to deliver orange juice to millions of new customers. Because they were able to sell fruits and vegetables to markets far beyond their local areas, many growers sharply increased the size of their farms.

These expanded farms required larger numbers of pickers during the relatively short periods for harvest. Local labor proved insufficient to meet these needs, in part because of the burgeoning opportunities for unskilled workers in industry. To fill the need, farm labor contractors emerged as the primary source of harvest labor for larger farms. Farm labor contractors recruited pickers for a job, transported them to the job site, supervised their work, and paid them their wages. Most farm labor contractors were former migrant workers themselves and relied on their contacts in the farmworker community to recruit and hire large groups of migrants. By stringing together a series of jobs following the successive harvests around the country, farm labor contractors provided their crews with work throughout the year, albeit irregular and sporadic.

Farmers did not view farmworkers furnished by labor contractors as farm employees; they treated the crew leaders as independent contractors and thus considered pickers the crew leaders' employees. While national farm groups opposed the passage of the FLCRA, their opposition was largely prompted by fears that excessive federal regulation would possibly interfere with crew leaders' capacity to furnish harvest labor on a timely basis.

The growers' fears regarding the impact of the FLCRA proved baseless. The FLCRA required labor contractors to obtain a certificate of registration, make disclosures in writing to workers regarding the wages and conditions of work, keep basic payroll records, and provide written earnings statements to farmworkers on payday. Despite these minimal requirements, noncompliance with the FLCRA proved the norm rather than the exception. By the time Congress reviewed the FLCRA again in 1974, it found that only one-third of the identified farm labor contractors had applied for certificates of registration, even though there was no charge for registration. According to a 1974 congressional report accompanying amendments to the FLCRA, 73 percent of crew leaders were found to be violating the act's requirements. This was not surprising, given the lax enforcement by the U.S. Department of Labor. In the first decade after the FLCRA was passed, the Department of Labor referred only four cases to the Justice Department for prosecution, and only one contractor in the nation had been tried and convicted.

In an effort to strengthen the law, Congress amended the FLCRA in

1974. The 1974 amendments, regarded at the time as relatively modest, ultimately proved pivotal in expanding the role of the federal government and the federal courts in curbing migrant worker abuses. For the first time, federal standards were imposed nationwide regulating the housing and transportation of farmworkers. In addition, the amendments included the first obligations under federal law imposed on farmers with respect to the use of migrant workers. Finally, farmworkers themselves were authorized to enforce the law through lawsuits in the federal courts.

Under the 1974 FLCRA amendments, crew leaders were required to meet federal safety standards with respect to vehicles used to transport workers. These standards outlawed the transport of farmworkers in truck beds and in other vehicles in which individual seats were not provided. Crew leaders were required to insure these vehicles at the same coverage levels required of common carriers under the Interstate Commerce Act. Previously, the insurance levels were set by state law. Housing provided to farmworkers by crew leaders was required to meet federal safety and health standards. Since many states had not issued standards for migrant housing, this represented the first application of public health standards to much of the farmworker housing in the nation.

Under the FLCRA as originally passed in 1963, growers had no obligations with respect to migrant workers. The 1974 amendments required farmers to obtain copies of crew leaders' payroll records, making it easier for the Department of Labor to conduct payroll audits. The amendments also prohibited farmers from using crew leaders who were not properly registered. The registration process requires that potential crew leaders be screened to eliminate persons convicted of serious crimes or who repeatedly have violated farmworker protective laws. It requires crew leaders who house migrant workers to provide facilities that meet federal standards and requires that vehicles that transport migrant workers meet safety standards and are properly insured.

Frustrated with the Department of Labor's dismal record of enforcement of the FLCRA, Congress used the 1974 amendments to bring new partners into enforcing the law—farmers and farmworkers themselves. Farmworkers were deputized as enforcers of the federal law through the 1974 amendments' inclusion of a provision allowing farmworkers denied the protections of the FLCRA the right to bring suit in federal court. Farmworkers could recover damages resulting from violations of the law. The amendments further provided that in cases where the precise monetary value of the damages was difficult to prove, courts could simply award farmworkers damages of up to $500 for each violation of the law. By allowing farmworkers to sue in federal court, Congress allowed farmworkers to bypass local and state courts, which in rural areas often had proved to be extremely hostile to farmworker claims. Federal courts were situated in major cities, where judges were more insulated from the influence of local farmers.

The addition of this private right of action for farmworkers coincided with the advent of a nationwide system of federally funded legal services for migrant workers. In the late 1960s the federal Office of Economic Opportunity funded several pilot projects to provide free assistance in legal matters to migrant workers. In the early 1970s Congress established and funded an independent Legal Services Corporation, which undertook a study of the needs of underserved indigent populations, including farmworkers. The study concluded that specialized legal services projects were needed to meet the unique legal problems faced by migrant workers. By 1974 migrant legal services projects were in place in most of the largest agricultural states. Through the creation of a private right of action, the 1974 amendments handed migrant legal services lawyers a powerful tool with which to represent farmworkers.

The 1974 amendments to the FLCRA produced more controversy. Stung by the criticism of its enforcement efforts, the Department of Labor undertook an aggressive campaign to improve the registration numbers in the wake of the 1974 amendments. In its zeal, the Department of Labor did not limit its registration efforts to traditional itinerant crew leaders: it also required registration of a wide range of agricultural cooperatives and associations—very common in California and the Midwest—as well as individual farmers. Under the FLCRA, a farm labor contractor included anyone who furnished farm labor to another for a fee. The Labor Department reasoned that since many cooperatives and grower associations routinely referred migrant workers to their members, these groups were required to register as labor contractors as well.

The farm groups protested that they received no fees for such referrals and thereby were exempted from registration. However, a series of court rulings found that all sorts of compensation, including membership dues, were "fees" under the act, backing the Labor Department's position. The growers' groups were troubled by the result. Some farmers complained that the registration process itself, which required submission of a set of fingerprints, was demeaning and insulting.

At the same time, migrant legal services advocates were using the new private right of action in a number of cases against crew leaders and growers. Some of the legal services cases pressed arguments regarding registration similar to those advanced by the Labor Department. For example, legal services advocates in Illinois filed a series of FLCRA lawsuits against Stokely-Van Camp, one of the nation's largest vegetable growers, arguing that Stokely-Van Camp was subject to the FLCRA's registration requirements because it dispatched workers to various small growers who produced vegetables for the Stokely-Van Camp cannery. Once the courts determined that Stokely-Van Camp was a labor contractor, they found it liable for failure to comply with the FLCRA's requirements relating to disclosure and record-keeping. Migrant legal services lawyers also sued individual growers, charging the growers with the use of unregistered crew leaders and failure to obtain payroll records from the crew leaders.

Between the actions of the Labor Department and the legal services projects, an unprecedented flurry of enforcement activity occurred in the years following the 1974 FLCRA amendments. Farm groups such as the American Farm Bureau Federation that had been relatively restrained in their opposition to the FLCRA and the 1974 amendments, mobilized to reverse the perceived onslaught of federal regulation of agricultural labor. By 1980 agricultural lobbyists had persuaded more than half the Senate to cosponsor a rewrite of the FLCRA that promised to reduce drastically the law's coverage. However, the farm organizations faced a tougher battle in the House of Representatives, where supporters of farmworker rights chaired critical committees and subcommittees with jurisdiction over the bill.

In an effort to avoid the potential roadblocks in the House, agribusiness lobbyists approached farmworker advocates about a consensus bill that could easily pass both houses of Congress. They found a ready audience in farmworker advocates who feared that the growers' amendments would gut the essential protections of the law.

The erstwhile opponents ultimately settled on a new scheme that addressed both sides' concerns. The new law, the Migrant and Seasonal Agricultural Worker Protection Act (AWPA), restructured the registration requirements, relieving all farmers and agricultural associations from the need to register as farm labor contractors. At the same time, the new statute broadened the class of persons responsible for complying with the law's disclosure, record-keeping, payment, housing, and transportation requirements.

Under the FLCRA, farm labor contractors alone were responsible for ensuring compliance. The AWPA also placed responsibility on a new class of regulated parties—"agricultural employers." Under the law, agricultural employers included all persons operating farms that recruited, transported, or "employed" farmworkers.

Early on, a battle began between growers and farmworker advocates over the meaning of "employ" in the new law. Powerful farm organizations argued that the term was a fairly narrow one and only covered those farmers who directly supervised or paid the farmworkers employed on their farms. The growers' position was buttressed by the Department of Labor's regulatory definition of "employ," which concentrated on direct supervision of the workers, a task only rarely performed by farmers who relied on farm labor contractors. On the other hand, farmworker advocates contended that "employ" was an expansive term intended to cover many farmers who had little direct contact with the farmworkers on their property. To support their view, farmworker supporters pointed to the official report of the House committee that drafted the AWPA, which discussed at length the extraordinary breadth of the term "employ."

It was left to the courts to sort out the definition. While the first two federal appeals courts to review the question adopted the narrow position urged by agribusiness, a noticeable shift began in 1996. That year, federal appeals courts in Atlanta and San Francisco concluded that the AWPA applied to growers who relied on crew leaders to recruit, transport, supervise, and pay vegetable pickers. Also in 1996 the Department of Labor revised its regulatory definition of "employ," replacing the narrower version first published in 1983.

As a result of these changes, a number of growers around the country took over payroll and transportation responsibilities from labor contractors. This trend was counterbalanced in California by an increasing reliance on farm labor contractors there. The crew leader system formerly had been primarily an East Coast phenomenon; however, since 1990, California has experienced an exponential increase in the use of farm labor contractors. Despite the court decisions under the AWPA, many growers place all hiring, transportation, and payroll responsibilities on farm labor contractors.

In part, growers' resistance to formally adopting the mantle of "employer" and their reliance on farm labor contractors is based on fears of liability under other laws, including those relating to minimum wages, child labor, and workers' compensation. The growers' concerns were heightened by the enactment of the Immigration Reform and Control

Act (IRCA) in 1986 that for the first time authorized stiff sanctions on employers of undocumented workers. The Immigration and Naturalization Service has generally concentrated its enforcement efforts on the individuals who hire and pay undocumented workers. If a grower delegates these tasks to a farm labor contractor, it is likely that any adverse consequences from use of undocumented aliens will be borne by the crew leader rather than the grower. After an initial flurry of activity, the employer sanction provisions of IRCA have become practically a dead letter in agriculture, with no meaningful enforcement.

Besides placing obligations on growers who are legal employers of farmworkers, the AWPA's principal innovation was the application of federal housing standards to virtually all migrant housing, whether provided by a labor contractor, grower, or private landlord. By contrast, under the FLCRA, the only farmworker housing regulated under federal law was that provided to workers by farm labor contractors. Because many states have failed to regulate farmworker housing, the AWPA represented the most comprehensive effort yet to establish minimum standards for migrant farmworker housing.

The standards incorporated by the AWPA are fairly minimal and apply only to units occupied by migrant (as opposed to seasonal) farmworkers. Minimum square footage limits are established for units based on the number of occupants and the use of the room. Housing providers must furnish beds, blankets, cooking facilities, refrigerators, and heat when appropriate. Toilets and bathing facilities must be provided in a designated ratio based on the number of occupants.

Despite these limited requirements, many housing providers have reacted angrily to the AWPA standards and have ceased offering housing to migrant farmworkers. Critics of the law contend that federal involvement in housing has simply led to a reduction in the housing stock available to migrant workers.

Similar arguments have been raised by agribusiness interests with regard to the AWPA's vehicle insurance requirements. The AWPA requires persons who transport farmworkers, as well as those who "cause" the transportation, to provide insurance roughly equivalent to that carried by bus lines and other common carriers. In recent years, regulations under the AWPA have mandated one hundred thousand dollars in insurance for each seat in the vehicle, resulting in a four-million-dollar liability insurance requirement for a forty-passenger bus.

Because of their low profit margins, many farm labor contractors have found it impossible to maintain the required levels of insurance.

Some labor contractors continue to transport workers in uninsured vehicles, hoping that no accidents will happen and that Labor Department investigators will not discover the unlawful transportation. A growing number of farm labor contractors have parked their buses in favor of an informal system of transportation. These labor contractors pay other workers, commonly referred to as *raiteros* (a Spanish adaptation of the English word "ride"), to drive employees to the job site. In exchange, the labor contractor pays the driver a fee for his or her services, occasionally based on the volume of work performed by the passengers. If apprehended, the *raitero* insists that the transportation is a carpool arrangement, exempt from the AWPA. Critics of the AWPA lay the blame at the law's drafters for enacting draconian insurance requirements and therefore creating an extensive underground network of farm labor transportation.

Shortcomings of the Amelioration Strategy

Two decades after its enactment, the AWPA illustrates both the strengths and limits of legislation directed at amelioration of the most severe abuses suffered by farmworkers. Certainly, as a result of the shift of responsibility to growers, many farmworkers are now paid in a more formal manner, with proper records maintained on their work and all requisite taxes paid on their behalf to the government. Some farmworker housing has been dramatically upgraded, and a number of employers now transport farmworkers in safe and properly insured vehicles.

On the other hand, there has been considerable resistance to the federal law. This resistance has manifested itself in two major ways. First, many growers and farm labor contractors continue to ignore the law, although some have gone to great lengths to establish legal buffers between themselves and the workers. The *raitero* system is but one example of growers' and farm labor contractors' efforts to shield themselves from liability.

Second, as enforcement of the AWPA is strengthened by the Labor Department and through legal services programs, there has been a corresponding increase in efforts to weaken the law through congressional action. For example, in 1990 the U.S. Supreme Court heard its first case under the AWPA. In a unanimous opinion, the Supreme Court affirmed farmworkers' position, holding that growers and labor contractors could be held liable for the full damages suffered by farmworkers transported in unsafe vehicles, even if the injured workers also received workers' compensation benefits for the same accident. Fearing that this would greatly increase their potential liability, growers immediately pressed Congress for reform. In 1995, under enormous pressure from agricultural interests, Congress passed an amendment to the AWPA that essentially reversed the Supreme Court's ruling.

Similarly, the efficacy of protective statutes such as the AWPA depends on the degree to which they are enforced. Under the AWPA and the Fair Labor Standards Act, enforcement occurs in two ways. First, the U.S. Department of Labor is charged with administrative enforcement of these laws. The Labor Department is authorized to investigate farm labor contractors, employers, and housing providers regarding their compliance, and if violations are uncovered, the agency may issue administrative fines or file legal action against the wrongdoer. Like most federal agencies, the Labor Department is susceptible to political pressures. Numerous opportunities arise for disgruntled members of Congress to curb perceived improprieties by the Labor Department. Members of Congress on the appropriations committee are able to propose that the agency's funding in future fiscal years be based upon changing certain policies. Disgruntled growers frequently contact members of Congress and their staffs when the Labor Department undertakes a major AWPA investigation. Regardless of the validity of the underlying investigation, congressional pressure is often directed toward the executive branch. A clear message is conveyed that if the Labor Department continues in its actions against the grower, the member of Congress will withhold his or her support on future initiatives favored by the president. While this sort of pressure is applied in countless other circumstances, it is particularly effective with regard to farm labor issues because only rarely is countervailing political pressure asserted in the interest of farmworkers.

A vivid example of this sort of pressure is found buried in a Labor Department investigative narrative of the actions of farm labor contractor Jack Simmons, one of the most notorious farm labor contractors in the country. In the mid-1970s Simmons was convicted of holding farmworkers in debt slavery, in violation of the federal peonage statutes.

The Labor Department was contacted by an angry South Carolina peach grower who lived in the home county of longtime U.S. Senator Strom Thurmond in the summer of 1981. The grower had advanced funds to Simmons while his crew was picking the grower's crop, only to have

Simmons leave for his next job in North Carolina without repaying the debt. The Labor Department promptly located Simmons in North Carolina and arranged for the South Carolina grower to be reimbursed. However, as the Labor Department investigator's report reveals, many other problems were discovered:

There appear to be substantial minimum wage liabilities to the employees while they were working in South Carolina. In consultation with the [Department of Labor assistant area director], it was decided that this should not be pursued. Considerations in this decision were . . . the close joint employment questions that would be involved and the extremely sensitive political climate in the South Carolina area (U.S. Department of Labor 1981).

Similar pressures have forced the Labor Department to adopt relatively cautious positions on a number of enforcement questions under the AWPA. Although the AWPA placed responsibility for compliance with the law on many farmers as well as farm labor contractors, the Labor Department oftentimes shies away from directing its enforcement actions at growers. Many times, the Labor Department enforces the law against only the workers' "primary employer," usually the farm labor contractor who directly supervises and pays the workers their wages. Thus, even though the AWPA's expansive definition of employment extends to most farmers, much of the Labor Department's enforcement remains unchanged since the days of the FLCRA—focused on the farm labor contractor, with little or no effort made to require compliance by the farmer. Virtually all of the efforts—largely successful—to enforce the AWPA's provisions against growers who rely on farm labor contractors have come through private actions brought on behalf of individual farmworkers, rather than in suits instituted by the Labor Department.

The AWPA provides an alternative means of enforcing the law's provisions. The AWPA incorporated the private right of action added to the FLCRA by the 1974 amendments. Using this section of the law, a farmworker who has been denied the rights and protections guaranteed him or her by the statute may file suit in federal court to recover either his or her actual damages or up to five hundred dollars in statutory damages.

As was the case with the private right of action under the FLCRA, almost all of the cases filed by farmworkers under the AWPA have been brought by attorneys with federally funded legal services. Growers have relentlessly sought to restrict the activities of these lawyers, particularly their efforts on behalf of farmworkers.

Although federal legal services agencies were intended to be independent of the political process, political pressures have been placed on the programs. During the Reagan Administration, for example, the president's annual budget proposed elimination of all funding for the Legal Services Corporation. When Congress continued to fund the agency, the White House appointed members to the agency's board who were far from supportive of its work. After a more sympathetic administration took office, opponents of legal services directed their attention to Congress, which reduced funding for the programs and, beginning in 1996, placed a number of stringent restrictions on legal services grantees. Among the restrictions that most seriously impacted the representation of farmworkers was a ban on class action lawsuits and a prohibition of using any funds (including funds from sources other than the federal government) to represent undocumented individuals. These limitations substantially reduced the potential liability of unscrupulous growers and farm labor contractors. Class action lawsuits had permitted a few farmworkers to sue on behalf of all their coworkers, leading to large judgments in a number of cases. Without the threat of class actions, growers and crew leaders face only the claims of those workers able to bring suit themselves. Coupled with the prohibition on representation of undocumented workers, these changes translate into a free pass for many violators of the AWPA and the Fair Labor Standards Act, because at many farms, either the workers will be ineligible for legal assistance because of their immigration status or none of the workers will be willing to formally complain.

An End to Farmworker Exceptionalism?

More than a half-century has passed since the reforms of the New Deal vaulted industrial workers in the United States out of the worst abuses of nineteenth-century commerce. The New Deal succeeded in opening the door to middle-class living standards for millions of unskilled workers and imposed governmental limits on the actions of employers.

Farmworkers have not shared in the great advancements experienced by industrial workers. They remain mired in conditions reminiscent of the nineteenth century rather than reflective of the twenty-first. Employers have few obligations to farmworkers, and those that exist are oftentimes ignored. Workers who complain have little protection against retaliation. A chronic oversupply of labor has led to stagnant wage levels and has discouraged collective action by disgruntled workers.

Since farmworkers were first included in the unemployment compensation system in 1978, the policies of agricultural exceptionalism have not changed appreciably. Indeed, most farmworker advocates have tacitly forsaken as futile any frontal attacks on exclusionary policies. Instead, the emphasis has been on specialized programs and statutes designed to address symptoms resulting from agricultural exceptionalism. Ultimately, these programs and laws are bound to fall short as they become subject to the same political forces that created agricultural exceptionalism in the first place.

Wells Farms

Rachel Avery,
1997 SAF intern

Bob and I are going out East to do some pre-occupancy inspections, make sure the housing meets the minimum standards before the workers get there. A couple of brothers, farming forty-eight acres of tobacco, beans, and corn, want to hire four migrant workers to help out on the farm. Carl and David Wells have never used migrant labor before; probably aren't enough kids around to pitch in anymore. So we're going to check out an old farmhouse they've been doing some work on. "How long has it been since anyone lived here?" "Oh, probably about ten years now, but my brothers and sisters, or my mama and daddy stay here sometimes when they come to visit." The two of them have been farming all their lives, probably all they have ever done, come from generations of farmers, farming the same land for just as long. Truthfully, they probably don't live anywhere much fancier than the place they were fixing up for their workers . . .

Carl, a forty-five-, maybe fifty-year-old man wearing a baseball hat, square, metal-rimmed glasses, a short-sleeved blue work shirt with his name monogrammed above the pocket, light-weight denim pants with a black belt pulled tightly across his waist making his pants a little short. His brother David, probably five to ten years younger, is a good bit shorter, barrel-chested, his arms, neck, and face tanned by the sun, wearing a sleeveless work shirt, his name too sewn above the pocket, blue Sears work pants and work boots, dirty and worn . . . [David says], "I am new at this, I ain't never had no migrants before. I tried to do what you told me" [in a phone conversation . . . with Bob to arrange the date and time of the inspection] . . . Bob gets up and begins to check everything out—"Is the fridge grounded? Is there enough hot water? Has the county checked your water and sewage? . . ."

He gives them the rundown on what needs to be fixed, how to report repairs to the Department of Labor. We make our exit, get into the conspicuous state car, and drive away. I breathe a sigh of relief. They probably did too.

————

The Conditions at the Camp Are Not Great

Vanessa, farmworker and daughter of crew leader

Interview by Kris Adams, 1997 SAF intern

Regarding their own camp, Vanessa confesses, "The conditions at the camp are not great." Even though the inspectors wanted the camp to have inside bathrooms, they continue to use the outhouses. Unlike other crew leaders' families who live separately from the crew and are unaffected by the conditions, Vanessa's family participates in every aspect of the crew's camp life. Vanessa's family and crew live together in a two-story building with sixteen rooms. She says the rooms are sufficient size because the camp is not that large. There are usually one or two guys to a room.

CHAPTER 6

Bitter Harvest

Housing Conditions of Migrant and Seasonal Farmworkers

Christopher Holden

Coming Home from the Fields

Farmworkers are among the worst-housed groups in the United States. After long hours toiling in the fields, few farmworkers can look forward to a warm shower, clean laundry, or a room to call their own. Even a decent supper is difficult to come by if the stove is broken, the refrigerator does not work, or the place lacks a kitchen altogether. The deplorable housing conditions experienced by many of the nation's migrant and seasonal farmworkers have been described in journalistic accounts, but little effort has been made to document systematically the nature and prevalence of housing problems farmworkers and their families face. Without adequate data, policymakers and project funders cannot make informed decisions about how to use limited public resources to improve the housing in which farmworkers live.

Addressing the Lack of Housing Information

Organizations that wish to improve farmworker housing conditions are hampered by a lack of reliable data. Only one national survey of farmworker housing conditions has been done, *Final Report: National Farmworker Housing Survey.* Mandated by Congress during the Carter Administration and completed in 1980 during the Reagan Administration, it was never published and is now out of date. The study includes interviews with government officials and field investigations of more than twelve hundred farm labor camp and private rental housing sites in sixty-three counties out of the total nine hundred counties nationwide that had seasonal and migrant farmworkers (Housing Assistance Council 1996, 16).

The study documented a prevalence of older camps with just a few buildings; about one-fourth of the camps lacked heat and plumbing. Laundry facilities were found in only about 20 percent of the camps. Migrant housing was more likely to lack plumbing and heat than the year-round seasonal housing that was studied. Crowded quarters were common, with 62 percent of camps exceeding their legal capacity. Structural problems were also common, with almost half the camps having at least one building where residents were exposed to the elements through structural damage or deterioration.

Responding to the need for housing information, the Housing Assistance Council (HAC) began an effort in 1997 to collect and analyze farmworker housing data in the eastern migrant stream. Starting in the summer of 1999, HAC began conducting surveys of farmworker housing conditions in the midwestern and western migrant streams, resulting in a national survey of farmworker housing conditions. HAC is a nonprofit corporation that supports the development of rural low-income housing nationwide through loans from a revolving fund, technical assistance to local organizations, and research. HAC also has extensive experience assisting local nonprofit housing groups to improve the housing available to farmworkers.

To conduct the survey, HAC developed a partnership with Farmworker Health Services, Inc. (FHSI), an organization that provides outreach workers on a contract basis to clinics that serve farmworkers in the Eastern migrant stream. Members of the FHSI staff are placed primarily in Florida during the winter season and relocate to agricultural areas northward in the migrant stream for the summer and fall. Working together, HAC and FHSI developed a survey form for FHSI outreach workers to use when they visited farmworkers in their homes, apartments, mobile homes, and at farm labor camps. The survey form was designed so that a great deal of housing information could be collected without disrupting the health care work of FHSI staff.

Like the 1980 study of farmworker housing, this research included FHSI staff's visual observations about the condition of farmworker housing units. Staff members also asked questions of farmworkers living in the units to determine the number of occupants, the cost of the housing, the burden of that housing cost on their incomes, and other relevant information.

In the 1980 study, information provided by farmworkers was not available because that study was conducted in the off-season in many locations when camp and private rental housing was not occupied by farmworkers. Also, because of the pending 1980 Census, survey workers for the 1980 farmworker housing study were not allowed to conduct interviews with farmworkers in the housing that was occupied. Finally, in many areas it was very difficult to determine when farmworkers were living in private rental housing, and so the 1980 study had only a limited sample of housing in the rural rental markets (Housing Assistance Council 1996, 16).

In its study, HAC gathered a wealth of housing information not available in the 1980 data because of the FHSI staff members' knowledge of the counties and communities in which they worked, the fact that they conducted the survey in both the winter and summer harvests, and their ability to gather information directly from farmworkers. HAC limited the interviews to a few questions to keep to a minimum the time commitment from farmworkers in each housing survey.

The eastern stream survey of farmworker housing was conducted from December 1997 through October 1998 and was funded by the U.S. Department of Housing and Urban Development (HUD) and the Rural Housing Service at the U.S. Department of Agriculture (RHS, formerly the Farmers Home Administration). Unless otherwise noted, the farmworker housing data presented in this chapter are from HAC's 2000 report, *Abundant Fields, Meager Shelter: Findings from a Survey of Farmworker Housing in the Eastern Migrant Stream.*

Key Findings from the
Eastern Stream Survey

HAC and FHSI collected information on 1,566 housing units in sixty-seven counties in the eastern migrant stream, including 605 units in eleven counties in Florida. The other states in the survey are Connecticut, Kentucky, Massachusetts, Maryland, North Carolina, New Jersey, New York, South Carolina, and Virginia. Each survey provided information on a single housing unit. Single-family homes, duplex units, mobile homes, apartments, and dormitory and motel rooms are examples of single housing units. In total, the units surveyed housed 8,965 people, of whom 1,584 were children. Children lived in 36 percent of the households surveyed.

Of all the farmworker housing examined, the most common types were mobile homes, which made up 32 percent of the units. Dormitories or barracks were the next most common types of units surveyed, making up 30 percent. Single-family homes, duplexes, apartments, and motel rooms made up the remaining units surveyed.

Housing at farm labor camps accounted for 60 percent of all the units examined and employer-owned housing for 55 percent. These percentages overlap because farm labor camps may be owned or managed by a growers' association, public agency, or nonprofit organization rather than by a single grower. Farmworkers living in housing not located at a farm labor camp or not owned by an employer were renting housing in the private rental market. The large proportion of units at farm labor camps in the HAC sample is consistent with findings from the National Agricultural Workers Survey (NAWS), an annual survey of crop-worker demographics. The NAWS found that farmworkers in the eastern states were most likely to have housing provided by their employers (U.S. Department of Labor 1993, 35).

Among only the units examined at the farm labor camps, dormitories and barracks were the most common types of housing, accounting for almost half the units at these sites. Mobile homes were also commonly used to house workers and were almost one-fourth of farm labor camp units. The reliance on mobile homes among growers is a concern, since mobile homes had the highest incidence of housing quality problems of all the types of housing surveyed.

HAC's survey documented that overcrowding was both common and severe. An overcrowded housing unit is defined by HUD as one with an average of more than one person per room. Almost 85 percent of the units were overcrowded. Despite the large number of occupants, more than 40 percent of the units had one or no bedrooms, meaning farmworkers had to sleep in living rooms or even on kitchen floors. Farmworker children were not exempt from living in overcrowded conditions. Among the overcrowded housing units, more than 50 percent had children present.

These findings reinforce popular accounts of severe overcrowding among farmworkers, where ten or twelve people may be packed into a trailer, a rented room, or even a garage or tool shed. Gloria Hernandez, a farmworker testifying before the National Advisory Council on Migrant Health, described how many farmworkers she knew lived in poor-quality, crowded housing. She told the council that "people began to tell us . . . how much they have suffered because they are sent to one house, crowded. They have to work hard. They don't have a good mattress to sleep on, and they are mistreated" (U.S. Department of Health and Human Services 1999). In some parts of the country, particularly in California, farmworkers who cannot find housing to share may become homeless, living in campgrounds, under bridges, or in their cars (Greenhouse 1998).

Overcrowding is not a new phenomenon for farmworker families. The 1980 farmworker housing study found that 62 percent of farm labor camps nationally were occupied beyond capacity. Although this measure of overcrowding is not directly comparable to that used in HAC's survey, it suggests that crowded conditions remain a persistent problem for farmworkers and their families. The persistence of overcrowding among farmworkers is troubling because it can contribute to a variety of health problems, including the spread of infectious diseases such as hepatitis and tuberculosis. A farmworker quoted in a report prepared by the Migrant Health Program asked ironically, "If we go to a field, we can see a cabin with eight or nine men living together, and these people have to cook and sleep in one single place, do you think that makes us susceptible to illness or not?" (U.S. Bureau of Primary Health Care 1995).

The median monthly income for individual wage earners in HAC's survey was $850, and the median unit cost was $200 per month. These figures represent in-season income and housing cost. Mobile homes and duplexes were the most expensive types of units, with median costs of $440 and $425, respectively. The high cost for mobile homes was particularly significant, given their prevalence among the units surveyed and because low cost is one of the features that is supposed to make mobile homes an attractive housing choice. In fact, mobile homes were among the most costly housing options for farmworkers and their families.

Paying too much for housing is a growing problem for low-income households throughout the United States, with rents and home prices rising faster than the rate of inflation in most areas of the country during the economic expansion of the past decade. As defined by HUD, having "housing cost burden" means a household pays more than 30 percent of its monthly income for housing costs, which includes paying rent or a mortgage plus utilities such as electricity and water. At first glance, housing cost burden did not appear to be a significant problem for the farmworker households in the HAC survey, but this was because of overcrowding, with many wage earners sharing the cost of rent. On average, households paid 16 percent of their monthly income for rent. However, 14 percent of the units surveyed had households where paying the rent was a burden on their incomes. Half of these had severe burdens, paying more than half their monthly income on housing. Not only were children living in a large percentage of overcrowded units, but 66 percent of households paying too much for housing had children living in the units.

Households that pay so much for their housing are very likely to be financially distressed and have difficulty paying for such basic necessities as food, clothing, and health care. Housing cost burden also has other consequences for farmworkers, especially those caring for children. If they choose to buy food or take children to the doctor, they run the risk of not paying the rent and being evicted. Children in these households are much more likely to go without some meals or necessary medications than are children in households paying more affordable rents. The problems of high housing costs and low incomes are compounded by the additional work-related expenses many farmworkers must pay, such as for transportation or use of tools. It is worth quoting Hernandez at length about the kinds of charges employers or crew leaders impose that make it difficult for farmworkers to cover their expenses, including housing costs:

[T]hey are charged 20 dollars a week for giving them work or 10 dollars for taking them to work, or 5 dollars a head when they want to go shopping for food or washing clothes because that day the chauffeur or driver doesn't work and they have to have a driver to take them to wash clothes and then to buy food. We are talking about an entire day, depending on the amount of workers that you have. So, you have to pay the driver to take them (U.S. Department of Health and Human Services 1999).

The percentage of households with housing cost burden would be much higher if not for overcrowding and rent-sharing. Not only were units generally overcrowded, but they also tended to have large numbers of wage earners living together. There was an average of 4.5 wage earners per housing unit. An individual farmworker would have a hard time paying the rent without the help of other wage earners sharing the same unit.

Telephones and laundry equipment were the appliances most often lacking in farmworker housing. Only 41 percent of the housing surveyed had access to a telephone, either in the unit or somewhere on the property. Only 25 percent of the housing units had access to laundry machines. The 1980 farmworker housing study noted similar problems, with only one-fifth of all farm labor camps examined having laundry facilities (Cavenaugh 1980, 20–21). Given the great risk of pesticide exposure that most farmworkers face, HAC's survey suggests a significant need for more and better laundry facilities at farmworker housing sites.

From the time of Edward R. Murrow's "Harvest of Shame" documentary to news reports today, journalists have described horrendous living conditions experienced by many farmworkers, particularly the poor state of sanitary facilities. For example, in 1998 a Florida newspaper provided this description of the bathroom and kitchen a Haitian farmworker shared with the occupants of four other dormitory-style rooms:

The shower has filthy, crumbling concrete walls—the kind that won't come clean. There is a metal sink held by a rotting plywood counter, and the toilet often backs up, so the tiny room reeks of sewage. At six feet tall, Etienne nearly bumps against the sagging ceiling of the narrow community kitchen, where days before a leak had puddled more than an inch of water (Edwards 1998).

Such vivid portraits of unsafe, filthy housing are borne out in HAC's survey results. Among the 1,566 units surveyed, 110 lacked access to toilets in the units or elsewhere on the property. In many units that had stoves and toilets, these appliances and fixtures were broken. Broken stoves were found in 110 units, and 126 units had broken toilets. More than 250 units surveyed had at least one major appliance broken—a stove, refrigerator, bathtub or shower, or a toilet. Mobile homes generally had the largest proportion of broken appliances. More than 16 percent of mobile homes had broken toilets, almost 10 percent had broken bathtubs or showers, and 12 percent had broken stoves. Among mobile homes, 30 percent had at least one major appliance or fixture broken. Under these conditions, many farmworkers are unable to store food safely, prepare a warm meal, have adequate sanitation, or take a shower after a hard day in the fields.

HAC's survey also tried to determine how significant a risk pesticide exposure posed in farmworkers' living quarters. Almost 40 percent of all the units surveyed bordered fields where pesticides are applied. More than one-fourth of these units had children present in the household. These trends are particularly disturbing given the lack of laundry machines and the prevalence of broken showers, thus preventing farmworkers and their families from cleaning pesticide residue from themselves or their clothing.

FIGURE 6.1. *A farmworker "neighborhood," 1998. Photograph by Esteban Echeverria.*

Reinforcing disturbing images of run-down and unsafe housing occupied by farmworkers, the survey results indicated that the quality problems associated with dilapidated housing were both common and severe. FHSI staff had a checklist of twelve exterior and eight interior problems. Some problems were very serious and posed immediate hazards, such as sagging structural features. These included noticeably unstable or sagging roofs, porches, house frames, or walls. Damaged windows and window screens and peeling paint were also common. A large percentage of the housing surveyed was in serious disrepair and likely posed health and safety risks, either because of one or more severe problems or because of the combination of many exterior and interior problems present.

Of the exterior problems examined, dilapidated structural features such as roofs and walls posed the most immediate and significant hazard to health and safety. Among the units surveyed, 27 percent had sagging structural features, and one-third had structural problems, holes in the roof, or both. Children lived in 34 percent of these units. The prevalence of housing in serious disrepair is consistent with findings from the 1980 survey, which found that 38 percent of camp buildings and 41 percent of non-camp buildings exposed their occupants to the elements through holes in walls and roofs or structural deficiencies (Cavenaugh 1980, 42).

The most commonly reported exterior problems in HAC's survey involved the condition of windows and exterior paint. More than 40 percent of the survey units had broken windows or damaged screens, and more than 40 percent had peeling exterior paint. More than 80 percent of the units had at least one exterior problem.

In many cases, growers and private landlords make efforts to improve the appearance of their properties without repairing serious hazards inside the units. *The New York Times* described a typical mobile home park in Immokalee, Florida, a town that boasts of being the winter vegetable capital of the East Coast.

Outside, many trailers are painted a crisp white that masks the conditions inside. Because the trailers have few electrical outlets, wires crisscross bedroom ceilings so the workers can plug in fans and radios. To protect their food supplies from rats, migrants hang bags of flour and cornmeal, piñata-like, from strings nailed to the ceiling (Greenhouse 1998).

The most common interior problems found in the HAC survey were peeling paint, broken plaster, and water leakage, each present in 35 percent of the units. Most old housing has problems with lead paint, which is a particularly serious hazard in the 35 percent of housing that had peeling paint where children lived. More than 62 percent of the units had at least one interior problem.

A large proportion of the units had substantial numbers of both exterior and interior problems. Almost one-fifth of the housing surveyed had four or more exterior problems and three or more interior problems. Housing with problems of this magnitude almost certainly poses a serious health and safety hazard to the farmworkers living there.

Although HAC's survey provides detailed documentation of specific housing problems, the true magnitude of substandard farmworker housing can best be shown using an overall measure of housing quality. The American Housing Survey (AHS) is conducted every two years by HUD and the U.S. Census Bureau and is the most detailed regular source of housing data. The AHS uses a formula to rate the physical condition of housing units as "adequate," "moderately inadequate," or "severely inadequate." Severely inadequate housing has serious plumbing problems (lacks indoor plumbing or has broken sinks, toilets, or showers), broken heating elements, damaged electrical systems, and structural damage inside and outside. Housing units in this condition are seriously distressed and not fit for human habitation.

The housing problems examined in HAC's survey correspond closely to the items used in the AHS formula, and among all the units covered in HAC's survey, 38 percent would be classified as severely inadequate by the AHS. As for the different types of structures, mobile homes were most likely to be substandard. More than 53 percent of the mobile homes were in severe condition. By comparison, the 1995 AHS found only 2 percent of all housing in the United States severely inadequate (Housing Assistance Council 2000).

Farmworkers often find themselves paying high rents for very poor-quality housing. The primary reason for the high rents charged for substandard housing is simply supply and demand. Some growers have ceased providing free housing to their employees, citing its high cost and the difficulty they have complying with state and federal inspections. With less on-farm housing provided free, farmworkers are forced to seek housing in the private market. Rural agricultural areas usually have a very limited amount of rental housing. Also, few landlords are willing to rent on the short-term basis required by migrant farmworkers who may move into an area to pick crops for a short harvest season.

Discrimination against farmworkers and local "not in my back yard" opposition to farmworkers as neighbors also limits the housing available to them. In Immokalee, farmworkers often pay more monthly rent for trailers than renters pay for condominiums in the nearby vacation resort of Naples, Florida. A lawyer with Florida Legal Services notes how the crush of farmworkers moving into a rural area for the harvest encourages landlords with poorly maintained rentals to charge high rents: "[Landlords] can afford to keep these trailers in terrible condition and charge abominable rents because [farmworkers] have no choice" (Greenhouse 1998). The limited supply of decent rentals affordable on farmworker incomes not only supports high rents for substandard housing, it also often forces farmworkers and their families to choose between overcrowded, dilapidated housing and homelessness.

Not only did HAC's survey gather quantitative data on the poor quality of farmworker housing, but qualitative information about the units and their occupants also was collected. As a part of the survey, FHSI staff were asked to note positive and negative features of the housing and sites they visited. Of the comments associated with one hundred units occupied by children, about half noted significant problems. While some comments described how well maintained the housing was, that the occupants owned the home, or that the unit had a public subsidy, most of the comments by FHSI survey workers documented deplorable living conditions, especially where children lived. Many noted that sites were very isolated. Others noted that many houses had privies and portable toilets instead of indoor plumbing. Still others described extreme overcrowding, dilapidated structures, or lack of heat and other amenities. In some cases, children were living in barracks made by converting old chicken coops. A number of units in colder "upstream" states lacked heat, and in at least one case the landlord refused to fix the refrigerator without raising the rent by seventy-five dollars.

HAC's survey highlights the often-overlooked fact that poverty and its negative impacts are not confined to U.S. inner cities. In addition, it makes clear that children are vulnerable to poverty's ill effects as much in rural areas as in urban ones.

Federal Housing Standards

According to the NAWS, in 1997–1998, only 28 percent of all farmworkers lived in housing provided by their agricultural employers. Of this, 21 percent received the housing free of charge. Farmworkers who had an arrangement with a crew leader and those who lived on the East Coast were more likely to live in grower-owned housing. Fifty-five percent of the housing HAC surveyed was provided by the employer. Yet many growers who once provided housing no longer do so, citing as disincentives the expense of maintaining housing and the trouble of regulatory compliance.

The Migrant and Seasonal Agricultural Workers Protection Act of 1983 established basic housing standards for the Occupational Safety and Health Administration (OSHA) to follow in regulating housing provided for farmworkers. AWPA requires those who own or control facilities used for housing farmworkers to ensure that it meets federal and state health and safety standards. Furthermore, AWPA specifies that a state or local health authority or other agency must inspect the facility and certify that it meets basic health and safety codes before farmworkers may occupy it and that owners must post the certification at the site.

If owners request an inspection forty-five days before farmworkers arrive and the inspection agencies fail to inspect a site within this time period, farmworkers may occupy the facility. This is extremely important considering that most states have very limited inspection and enforcement resources and rarely are able to inspect each camp in their state once every few years, let alone annually. States have some latitude in how they interpret and implement AWPA's standards, and many states have codes that are less strict than OSHA's. In 1997 the North Carolina Department of Labor, which is responsible for inspecting farmworker housing in North Carolina, reported that during a five-year period beginning in 1992, it had located only 55 percent of the grower-owned housing. Furthermore, it only conducted a pre-occupancy inspection in 28 percent of the housing facilities and found only 1 percent in full compliance (North Carolina Department of Labor 1997).

The U.S. Department of Labor (DOL) administers a program known as H-2A that allows growers to recruit foreign agricultural workers, or guestworkers, to work in agriculture on a temporary basis. Growers who use guestworkers must provide them with housing, and this housing must pass inspection under standards established by OSHA. Thus, some states have prioritized inspecting housing owned by growers participating in the H-2A program. Without the inspection certification, growers are not eligible to receive H-2A workers. Though H-2A employers must meet these basic housing standards, other growers have little incentive to do so. Many simply risk not getting inspected or being fined the moderate penalties.

Resources to Improve Farmworker Housing

Despite the prevalence of problems in farmworker housing, many local nonprofit organizations around the country have struggled for years to develop new housing affordable to farmworkers and their families. These groups have managed to build or rehabilitate thousands of apartments and houses. However, despite their many successes, local farmworker housing organizations still must contend with a variety of challenges. Their chief obstacles are limited federal and state program funding, delays receiving project funding, difficulties developing housing affordable to very poor migrant farmworkers who will only occupy the units part of the year, local opposition to farmworker housing projects, and the unavailability of federal funds to provide housing for undocumented workers.

Of life's basic necessities—food, clothing, and shelter—the most expensive is shelter. Producing housing is a complex endeavor involving financing, construction, and public relations. In fact, construction is probably the least complex aspect of producing new housing for farmworkers. Building housing affordable to people with the very low incomes typical of most farmworkers is an even more complex undertaking. Not only must the housing be of sound quality, but its development costs also must be contained so that the rent required from tenants is low enough to be affordable while generating enough income for the owner to make the mortgage payments on the property. The primary means for reducing tenant rents are development subsidies that provide grants or low interest loans for financing a project or rental assistance, which allows a tenant to pay a small portion of his or her monthly income for rent while compensating the project owner for the difference between the tenant's contribution and the market rental rate.

The U.S. Department of Agriculture's Rural Housing Service (RHS) administers the only federal programs providing development funding for safe, decent rental housing specifically for farmworkers. One is called Section 514, named for the section of the Housing Act of 1949 as amended in 1963, that authorized the program. Section 514 provides loans at 1 percent interest to growers and nonprofit housing developers. Its companion program, Section 516, provides grants to nonprofit organizations for off-farm housing development. Nonprofit housing developers sponsoring farmworker housing projects may receive up to 90 percent of the development costs as a Section 516 grant, with the remainder covered by a Section 514 loan. A project financed this way creates very little debt, so the nonprofit owner can charge very low rents that farmworkers can afford.

In addition, nonprofit project owners may receive rental assistance from RHS. This means that the farmworker tenant only has to pay 30 percent of his or her monthly income for rent, with the federal government providing the balance. The substantial subsidies associated with the Section 514/516 and rental assistance programs make it possible to provide quality housing to farmworkers with the lowest incomes. Since the Section 514/516 programs' inception in 1962, approximately 17,000 units have been constructed (Housing Assistance Council 1997b). Although these programs produce an average of 506 apartments and houses per year, this pace of housing development cannot keep up with the overwhelming demand. The 1980 survey of farmworker housing estimated a national need for an additional 800,000 camp units alone to meet demand. Furthermore, farmworkers who are undocumented are excluded from participating in any housing program funded by the federal or state governments. This is a serious problem, considering that more than half of farmworkers today do not have legal documents.

Even though the Section 514/516 programs have seen small funding increases in recent years, the funding does not reflect the overwhelming need for decent-quality housing that farmworker advocates see every day. In 1997 and 1998, HAC surveyed nonprofit housing developers that serve farmworkers in order to estimate the potential demand for the Section 514/516 programs. The more than thirty nonprofit developers surveyed were preparing over $134 million in Section 514/516 applications. However, the combined appropriation for the two programs was only $28 million. The programs received $34 million in funding in 1999 and $43 million in fiscal year 2000. A tremendous discrepancy remains between the demand and supply of these funds. Given the relatively limited resources that have been available for Section 514/516, substantial increases in program funding are needed to make a serious dent in the housing need among farmworkers.

The lack of resources to develop affordable farmworker housing reflects a general trend in housing markets in the United States, where the cost of housing has risen much faster than incomes during the nation's long economic expansion. In addition, hundreds of thousands of units affordable to low-income people have been lost during the economic expansion, either through rent increases or by being taken out of service because it is not cost-effective for owners to repair and rehabilitate them. This means fewer affordable apartments and homes are available for low-income families.

HUD determined that in 1997 there were 5.4 million renter households with "worst-case housing needs," a record high. These are households that do not receive government housing assistance, have very low incomes (less than half the median income in their areas), and pay more than half their incomes for rent or live in severely inadequate housing. Between 1991 and 1997 there was a decline of more than 370,000 units affordable to renters with very low incomes. In addition, federal assistance has not kept pace with the need. For example, in the four years before 1999 federal rental assistance did not expand and in 1999 and 2000 expanded only modestly (U.S. Department of Housing and Urban Development 2000).

Legislation passed in 1998 provided a new source of financing for farmworker housing by making Section 514/516 projects eligible for low-income housing tax credits (LIHTC). LIHTCs allow private investors to receive tax credits for investing in affordable housing projects, thereby offering them an incentive to help fund housing for low-income households. Allowing this sort of development capital to be used in farmworker housing projects should bring more private financing to address farmworker housing problems. Also, if more proposed Section 514/516 projects have tax credits, they will require fewer Section 514/516 dollars, which should allow the farm labor housing programs to fund a larger number of projects.

The process for awarding and disbursing Section 514/516 funding itself has posed an obstacle to nonprofit farmworker housing developers. Until 1999, applications for funding from Section 514/516 were taken on a first-come, first-served basis. If an application for a farmworker housing project was sound and met all program criteria, RHS approved it and placed the project on a waiting list until funds became available. Because of great demand, applicants often had to wait three to five years before receiving their funding. This means it took nonprofit housing developers a very long time to build new affordable housing for farmworkers. Often, this is too long for families to wait to move into new housing. While they are on the waiting list for affordable apartments, they must continue living for years in housing that is often substandard and very expensive.

Funding delays can have a negative impact on farmworker housing projects. An organization proposing a project must first obtain land on which to build. Loans to purchase land are generally considered risky by banks and carry very high interest rates. This is because land purchase occurs early in the development process, and many variables along the way can derail a project before it is completed. The longer a farmworker housing developer must make land payments before receiving low-interest development financing through Section 514/516 or other sources, the more it will cost to build the project because the group must pay high interest rates for a longer period of time. The increased project cost must then be passed on to the tenants in the form of increased rent or to the government in the form of increased subsidy. If the government must pay more subsidies for each individual project, there are fewer dollars to help additional projects. Therefore, delays in financing and building a project can undermine the purpose of the housing.

In 1999 RHS changed the way it allocates Section 514/516 funding. Instead of awarding funds on a first-come, first-served basis, RHS awards funds on a competitive basis. RHS publishes a notice announcing the availability of funds, nonprofit housing developers submit applications for project funding, and the funds are allocated to projects with the highest scores on their applications. This speeds the development process, because successful applicants receive their funding the year in which they apply. An annual, competitive process for awarding Section 514/516 funding should reduce delays and therefore make it easier for nonprofit housing developers to build decent, affordable farmworker housing in a timely manner.

The DOL also contributes to farmworker housing development, but its programs are very limited. Under the Workforce Investment Act (WIA, formerly the Jobs Training Partnership Act, or JTPA), DOL administers a job training program to retrain farmworkers for higher-paying occupations. One component of this program provides funds to farmworker service organizations that want to build housing for farmworkers. The technical assistance includes help in securing land, preparing project designs, obtaining permits, and drafting applications for project financing. This money cannot be used to purchase land, construct the housing, or provide long-term financing. Less than $3 million was allocated to this program in 2000.

The U.S. Department of Housing and Urban Development (HUD) administers housing and community development programs for low-income people generally that also may be used to assist farmworkers. Section 8 tenant-based rental assistance provides vouchers for people with low and very low incomes to use in renting apartments in the private market. Recipients pay 30 percent of their monthly income for rent, with the federal government paying the landlord the difference. This program is administered by state and local housing authorities, which are public agencies established to own and operate public housing in local communities or in rural areas not served by a city housing authority.

In many areas the waiting list for Section 8 rental assistance is so long that it can take two or three years for an applicant to receive Section 8 assistance. In the past, housing authorities used preferences established by the federal government to give priority to families on Section 8 waiting lists. For example, families who were homeless or lived in housing that posed an immediate hazard to health and safety would be moved to the top of the list. However, the 1999 public housing reform made changes to the Section 8 program so that housing authorities can establish their own local preferences. HUD and farmworker advocacy organizations could encourage housing authorities to give priority to farmworkers for Section 8 vouchers or to set aside vouchers for farmworkers. This would be especially effective because these vouchers are "portable," which means that once a farmworker has received a voucher he or she may use it anywhere else in the country where a housing authority administers a Section 8 program.

HUD also has two large block grant programs that provide flexible housing and community development funding administered through state and city governments. The Community Development Block Grant (CDBG) program provides funds to states and large towns and cities for housing, economic development, and community development initiatives. Small rural towns must access this program through the state government agency administering the program. Nonprofit housing developers have cooperated successfully with local governments to use CDBG for such projects as extending water and sewer lines or access roads onto sites proposed for farmworker housing projects. Because only town or city governments may apply to the state for these funds, it offers nonprofit farmworker housing developers a chance to work more closely with town officials and gain their support for farmworker housing projects.

For example, the Idaho Migrant Council, a nonprofit group that owns farmworker housing projects throughout Idaho, wanted to build more housing at a farmworker housing project in Twin Falls, Idaho. However, the group needed to extend water and sewer lines out to the site in order to build the additional apartments. The city of Twin Falls was considering a commercial development on vacant land near the property, but the site did not have access to utilities. So the organization worked with the city to get CDBG funds from the state to extend water and sewer lines through the Idaho Migrant Council farmworker housing site and out to the parcel slated for commercial development (Housing Assistance Council 1997a).

Although local governments often oppose farmworker housing projects in response to the fears of local residents, farmworker housing advocates can tailor their housing proposals to mesh with other local needs. By using programs like CDBG, advocates can work more closely with local governments and improve farmworker housing at the same time.

The other federal block grant program is called the Home Improvement Program, or HOME. It provides block grants to larger local governments and to states for a variety of housing development purposes. To access these funds, rural nonprofit organizations apply directly to the state agencies that administer the program. However, in many cases state administrators have not made farmworker housing a priority in the plans that are supposed to outline the state's most important housing needs. These plans, called consolidated plans, determine the most pressing housing needs and document which regions or population groups have been underserved by housing programs. Sometimes because of vocal local opposition to farmworker housing and sometimes merely through a lack of awareness of the scope of the problem, farmworkers are excluded from consolidated plans as a group whose housing needs should receive priority when HOME funds are disbursed. Farmworker advocates can improve this situation since states must update their consolidated plans every two years and are required to seek public input when making changes. Advocates can contact local nonprofit housing organizations or state housing agencies and get information on how to participate in the process of revising their state's consolidated plan.

Sometimes even when farmworkers are included in consolidated plans, state HOME program administrators do not prioritize farmworker housing proposals, often ceding to local opposition. One way this problem could be remedied is to have a national set-aside of HOME and CDBG funds for farmworker housing projects that would guarantee that these funds be used even in states with recalcitrant administrators.

Challenges to Developing Housing for Migrant Farmworkers

Migrant farmworkers often send a portion of their wages back home to support their families, and since most have very low incomes, they have little money leftover to pay for their housing in the United States. Despite the substantial subsidies attached to Section 514/516 housing, it has been difficult for nonprofit housing developers using these loans and grants to bring their rents low enough to serve migrant farmworkers while still making their mortgage payments on the property. In order for a project owner to receive rental assistance on a housing unit, the apartment must be occupied. This means that in upstream states with shorter growing seasons, apartments will be vacant for much of the year and the nonprofit owner will not receive enough subsidy through rental assistance to make mortgage payments on the project. In the long run, temporary occupancy discourages sponsors from building housing for migrant farmworkers.

Delmarva Rural Ministries, a nonprofit organization based in Maryland, has addressed the problems of housing migrant farmworkers by developing rental properties that have units reserved for migrant and

FIGURE 6.2. *Farmworker relaxes after a hard day's work in his bedroom in a labor camp, 1990. Photograph by Jeff Whetstone.*

seasonal farmworkers. With technical assistance from the National Council on Agricultural Life and Labor Research, Inc. (NCALL), Delmarva Rural Ministries has developed at least three such projects on the Delmarva Peninsula in Maryland and Delaware. Having farmworkers who live year-round in the area as tenants means that Delmarva Rural Ministries collects rent from some of the apartments all year. In effect, the year-round apartments cover the lack of income from the migrant units when they are vacant in the off-season. The migrant units are fully furnished, and Delmarva Rural Ministries is considering using these apartments in the off-season to provide shelter to local people experiencing homelessness, a further contribution to the communities where these projects are located.

Other resources are needed, though, if more nonprofit organizations are to sponsor affordable housing projects for migrant farmworkers. A measure was included in the same 1998 legislation that allowed nonprofit housing developers to use tax credits in Section 514/516 projects to help farmworker housing groups better serve migrant farmworkers. The legislation allows Section 514/516 projects that serve migrant farmworkers to receive their rental assistance in the form of a year-round operating subsidy. This means that nonprofit developers can maintain cash flow and make their mortgage payments even when the apartments are vacant in the off-season.

No matter how creative farmworker housing developers are in obtaining the necessary financing for a project or designing projects to meet migrant housing needs, local residents often fear farmworkers moving into their communities. These fears frequently are expressed in opposition to proposed farmworker housing projects, and local opposition can derail proposed projects by denying requests for rezoning or building permits or by increasing the cost of projects so much that they are no longer feasible and affordable to farmworkers. Although projects serving low-income people generally may encounter opposition from local residents, projects serving farmworkers seem to receive particularly strong opposition.

Although much of the violent reactions against racial and ethnic minorities has subsided since the turbulent civil rights era, in some communities the fear of different people still leads to ugly, discriminatory actions. Farmworkers often have difficulty finding places to rent because of prejudice, and advocates who are building new housing or community centers for farmworker services still sometimes encounter violent resistance from local residents. In the summer of 1999, Telamon Corporation, a multistate nonprofit organization serving farmworkers in the Southeast, proposed a new migrant Head Start center in the eastern Tennessee town of Bybee. A week before a meeting Telamon scheduled to announce its plans to the community, local people opposed to the project organized a protest march with more than one hundred people and gathered almost four hundred signatures against the project. They criticized the project as being too far away from emergency services to assist the children attending Head Start, even though the site is right next door to the local fire station. They also feared that the Head Start center would bring a wave of crime and rape into the community, despite the fact that the center serves toddlers!

Soon the hateful rhetoric turned to violence. The man who had leased the land for the Head Start center found a stuffed dummy with ketchup all over it left on the property, and his barn was burned down. Two of the Head Start buses were run off the road. The FBI staked out the bus routes to protect the children, to apprehend those threatening them, and to provide security to Telamon staff who needed to be alone at work early in the mornings. With this kind of hatred and extreme prejudice directed against a Head Start center for farmworker children, it is not surprising that some local people in rural communities resist new farmworker housing projects that will make migrant and seasonal farmworkers their neighbors.

Not-in-my-back-yard sentiments often are expressed when organizations that sponsor farmworker housing projects make a proposal. Local critics of farmworker housing development use public forums such as community group meetings or zoning hearings to voice their fears about the negative impact of a project on their community. If a farmworker housing developer needs to obtain rezoning or other land use permits, opponents can slow or halt that process by pressuring public officials to deny permits or zoning requests. Restrictive zoning laws are a powerful tool that local opponents of farmworker housing have used on numerous occasions to make it difficult for growers and nonprofits to provide decent housing.

An example of restrictive zoning can be found in Accomack County, Virginia, where farmworker housing projects must receive a special use permit requiring the project to meet a number of cost-inflating provisions and to undergo public hearings for approval. The county's comprehensive plan provides criteria for building permits and notes that while migrant labor is needed for county agricultural activities, "farm labor housing is perceived as being undesirable due to its general appearance, its association with crime, the number of persons per location, and general apprehension of the seasonal worker." The comprehensive plan also confines farmworker housing to agricultural zoning districts, lots at least five acres in size, and buildings set back two hundred feet from all property lines (Carter and Rosenthal 1996, 791). Agricultural land often lacks necessary infrastructure such as water and sewer service, and extending these services or adding a well and septic tank raises the cost of building a project in these zones. Altogether, these requirements have effectively stopped most efforts to build new housing for farmworkers in the county.

Even if a project succeeds in obtaining the necessary zoning and permits, this kind of opposition can drive up the cost also by forcing a farmworker housing sponsor to redesign a project to comply with conditional use provisions, which means that the project will be approved only on the condition that the developer makes the requested changes. In one Florida case, a group had to create an additional landscaping barrier between the proposed housing site and a neighboring mobile home park, even though the properties already were separated by a canal (Housing Assistance Council 1998b, 27). Unless public funding covers the added project costs from delays, the increased costs have to be passed on to either the tenants or the owner.

One final important farmworker housing challenge should be noted. Undocumented workers are not eligible to reside in housing developed using federal funds and except for emergency shelter are prohibited from living in housing developed through various states' programs. It is estimated that more than 50 percent of farmworkers in the United States are undocumented, and this large segment of the farmworker population has few affordable housing options apart from crowding together to reduce the burden of high rents or living in housing provided by growers or by organizations that do not receive government housing funds.

Working Together

In addition to their difficult working conditions and low incomes, many farmworkers in the United States have little choice but to live in overcrowded, substandard housing. HAC's survey provides one of the only systematic, regionwide assessments of the quality of farmworker housing to date, and its results suggest that farmworkers are among the country's worst-housed groups. Developing decent-quality housing affordable to farmworkers is a monumental undertaking, complicated by many factors. Local opposition to farmworker housing projects, lack of subsidized project financing, undocumented farmworkers' lack of eligibility for government-funded housing, and other housing development challenges make it difficult for farmworker service organizations to improve housing conditions.

HAC's approach to collecting farmworker housing information—using outreach workers who are familiar with the farmworker community—not only resulted in significant housing information but also provided a unique opportunity for various farmworker service organizations to collaborate with one another. Numerous service networks are working to address farmworkers' various needs, including health care, education, employment training, occupational safety, and housing. Farmworker organizations often work in isolation from each other, thus collaborative projects enable them to learn who is doing what and to better coordinate their efforts.

Projects like HAC's survey benefit greatly from combining a number of organizations' resources. Designing a survey with input from different service providers helps produce a resource that can serve a wide range of needs. Having input from a health care organization like FHSI helped HAC design a survey that would document the kinds of housing problems most likely to contribute to health problems. In turn, the survey can provide valuable information to health care groups concerned about the effects that poor housing and unsanitary living conditions have on disease and injury. Pesticide safety advocates have access to detailed information about farmworker housing sites adjacent to fields where pesticides are applied. And because the survey asks about the presence of children in the household, education and training organizations can use the information to examine the link between unstable housing situations and poor school performance by children.

A number of measures could promote development of farmworker housing or at least help farmworkers pay for housing in the communities where they work. Chief among these is for Congress to budget substantially greater funding for the Section 514/516 farm labor housing programs. Subsidies for nonprofit developers, rental assistance, and recent reforms in assistance for migrant farmworkers make these programs the most effective vehicles for improving the housing options available to documented farmworkers nationwide.

As noted earlier, HUD programs can play a larger role in improving farmworker housing conditions. Individuals and organizations concerned with farmworkers' quality of life need to work at the local and state levels to target more of these resources for farmworker housing. Local housing authorities must hear from farmworkers and their advocates before they institute farmworker preferences for Section 8 rental assistance. State housing agencies must respond to public input on their consolidated plans every two years, and this provides an opportunity to ensure that more HOME and CDBG funding supports new housing for farmworkers.

States with large farmworker populations also should be encouraged to develop their own farmworker housing financing programs, and advocates certainly can play a vital role by informing state legislators and program administrators about the need to invest more state resources to improve farmworker housing. Some states, most notably California, already have a number of programs to assist nonprofit farmworker housing developers and growers in building or rehabilitating affordable farmworker housing. Many other agricultural states, however, have very limited programs or none at all. Even in states that provide substantial support for farmworker housing development, program requirements and regulations may conflict with federal guidelines, making it difficult for advocates to use state resources in projects financed through Section 514/516 (Housing Assistance Council 1998a).

Federally funded nonprofit farmworker housing must meet high-quality standards, and in many cases, such as Delmarva Rural Ministries' projects in rural Maryland and Delaware, local growers have expressed an appreciation that good housing is available in their communities so that workers and their families will return each harvest season. New mechanisms need to be developed to encourage growers to contribute to farmworker housing developments sponsored by non-profit organizations; an example would be tax credits for grower contributions to nonprofit projects to improve the housing they provide for workers. Advocates could help support this kind of effort by volunteering with local nonprofit housing organizations that have good ties with local growers and by lobbying state officials to provide additional incentives for growers to assist nonprofit farmworker housing developers with cash contributions or donated land for projects. Advocates also can encourage growers to maintain safe and sanitary housing for workers who live in their facilities and hold their peers accountable to the federal and/or state housing codes.

Although there is a long way to go before farmworkers routinely live in decent, affordable housing, programs and a network of farmworker housing advocates exist that can provide the foundation for future development work and improved farmworker living conditions. Greater coordination of efforts between various farmworker service networks can improve the level of program funding for farmworker housing improvements. Advocates should share their resources and expertise to improve the effectiveness of the programs that currently exist or undertake initiatives like HAC's survey that could not readily be accomplished by a single organization or service network. Despite the hardships faced by those who harvest the nation's crops, the efforts of farmworker housing developers and other advocates offer hope that most farmworkers may in time fully participate in the American Dream of a safe, decent, and affordable place to call home.

The History We Wrote This Summer

Jenny Carroll

Cecilia kills turkeys,
dipping their beaks into the cold water,
she feels the volt in her own hands.
Cutting carrots for her daughter,
"No meat tonight, Mija."
No meat for $5.75 an hour,
six turkeys a minute,
three hundred and sixty an hour,
to stand in a trailer
in the middle of the summer
and feed your family carrots.

Trisha bends her back all day to the sun.
Bow down before the tobacco, Trisha,
kneel before the altar
of wage slavery,
$60.00 a barn,
$30.00 a bottle,
in the one room home
of the goddess of tobacco croppers.

Jessica,
with Jesus tattooed between her breasts.
Jessica moves from mission to mission.
In the hot shed where they grade cucumbers,
six fingers smashed,
broken
before she was sixteen in the fast wooded slots
where the cucumbers vanish.
"If you wore your sweat as a gown,
your blood as your crown,

you would tattoo
his name too,
just to feel his presence
when the night was too long."
Jessica sleeps with her God each night
beneath the stars
in a lonely room behind the cucumber shed.

Margarita,
fifteen years old,
carries her child
into the pepper fields
so he will learn at a young age
what is good and what is bad.
Margarita, bending under the weight of her own
    offspring,
works all day
to bend another.
What must she think
of her baby on the cot beside her
praying her husband will not come home.
When the door opens,
praying his hands will not fly.
What must she think
when her baby,
too tired to cry,
lays and stares at the ceiling of the room.
She tells me one day she will buy a house.
One day her son will sleep in a bed.
(Close your eyes, Margarita,
somewhere the darkness will buy you
a castle better than any on earth.
Somewhere a child rolls in the swells of a bed,
somewhere a husband does not return,
somewhere your night is silent.)
One of these days
I will leave, she says,
through the trap door of night
and the bottom of empty bottles.
I will climb from my bed,

count the stars on my back,
the steps down the road.
I will rise like the myrtle,
green vines and orange blossoms
lining endless rows of melon,
cracked in the sun.
And I want you to know,
if he loved you with his words,
and saved you with his hands,
and tamed you with his belt,
and broke you with his heart,
would you expect to stay
one moment longer?

Cecilia, Trisha, Jessica, Margarita,
all day under the sun.
Cecilia, Trisha, Jessica, Margarita,
all day in the white man's tobacco shed,
pepper,
cucumber,
turkey plant.
Cecilia, Trisha, Jessica, Margarita,
I close my eyes
to see
my hands vanish beneath their brown
sun-kissed skin.
I pass
them to you in a glance
and a handful of the earth they breath.
Cecilia, Trisha, Jessica, Margarita.

CHAPTER 7

The Struggle for Health in Times of Plenty

Colin Austin

Esperanza Martinez lives in a trailer on the outskirts of a rural town in North Carolina. Even though the trailer is small, she tries to make it a nice place to live for her family. She hangs pictures over cracks in the walls and places hand-crocheted doilies on the television and the secondhand sofa. There is a small garden in front of the trailer where Esperanza grows a few fresh vegetables. Every day she tries to do the best with what she has. These patterns she weaves in her life help make her family feel stable, yet one issue is a constant challenge: she is almost always worried about her family's health.

A central reason Esperanza's family experiences health problems is because they are migrant farmworkers. Since coming from Mexico several years ago, Esperanza and her family have traveled to many states as they follow the harvesting seasons. The crops they have worked the most are tobacco and oranges. The work is difficult, but the family labors to make ends meet.

Esperanza understands the health problems that farm work causes her family. Still, she and her husband keep working because they have the dream of finding a good place to live and more stable jobs. Esperanza's youngest daughter is continually sick and irritable. Esperanza takes her to a clinic where there is usually an interpreter. On the weekends when the clinic is closed she ends up going to the emergency room. Esperanza receives bills in the mail that she does not understand and often cannot pay. She tries to go to the hospital to work out an arrangement for paying in installments, but her English is not very good and the staff people at the claims office are impatient with her. Meanwhile, her husband complains about pain in his back and a leg injury he got at work. Esperanza thinks she may be getting sick from harvesting the tobacco. She is always tired and finds herself crying a lot.

Esperanza is not alone. Farm work consistently ranks as one of the most dangerous occupations in the United States. Many health risks have to do with farm work—the strain of labor, accidents, and exposure to toxic substances. Other health problems result from surrounding conditions, such as unsafe housing, physical isolation, and lack of access to primary and preventive care. When farmworkers do receive health care, they often present physicians with multiple and chronic health problems. Some of the most common problems seen at migrant health clinics are injuries, respiratory infections, dermatitis, gastrointestinal problems, hypertension, and diabetes (Wilk 1986). But very often the toll of migration and below-poverty wages causes farmworkers to try to get by without formal medical treatment. Like Esperanza and her family, going to a doctor to seek care may be the last option:

What I do is I wait, and if I don't feel really bad, then I keep going to work. And if I can't take the sickness any more, then I will have to stop working and go see a doctor. But that's when I REALLY don't feel well. That's the last step I take. And the same with the girls. If they have a cough or fever, I'll wait a day or two. Three at tops (Hemming 1996).

At Risk in the Fields

Health studies show just how dangerous farm work is. For example, the Hispanic Health and Nutrition Examination Survey (HHANES), an extensive study conducted between 1982 and 1984, found that Hispanic farmworkers reported significantly more work-related injuries than workers in other industries (Guarnaccia, Angel, and Angel 1992, 121). And the injuries suffered are often very severe. Many of the problems are musculoskeletal conditions due to stoop labor that causes chronic back injury (Meister 1991, 510). Other dangerous work activity includes carrying large loads, climbing ladders, and riding on and working around heavy machinery. The disability rate for farmworkers is up to three times the rate for the general U.S. population (Wilk 1986).

Plenty of minor scrapes, abrasions, and sprains go along with everyday labor in the fields. If untreated, such injuries can worsen over time and cause infection, debilitating pain, and even permanent disabilities.

While most other occupations have standards about safe and healthy work practices, farm work is still largely unregulated. Farmworkers often must accept these risks or face the risk of being fired. Esperanza spent several seasons in Florida and describes her work environment:

There the work was really tough as well because you have to go to the
trees and work on a ladder to get the oranges. And the trees are full of
thorns. And it scratches you all over your arms—or your body—if you're
not careful (Hemming 1996, 3).

Esperanza is only one of thousands of farmworkers who routinely
face danger in their workplaces. In many crops, such as oranges and
apples, in which farmworkers use ladders, they must be careful about
falls and accidents. They often receive scrapes and scratches that can
lead to chronic sores and infections. And they have constant contact
with the leaves of the trees that may be covered with recently applied
agrochemical residues.

Pesticides routinely used in commercial agriculture generally are insecticides to control insects and worms, herbicides to kill weeds, and
fungicides to halt diseases that affect plant growth. As a critical element
of the "Green Revolution" that modernized agriculture in the 1950s and
1960s, the application of pesticides enabled farmers to produce greater
yields on larger acreages with less labor input and to avoid major losses
to their crops. While pesticides have allowed for short-term gains in agricultural production, their effect on nature, the land, and humans continues to be a concern.

Pesticides adversely affect farmworkers laboring in areas that are
sprayed by hand, by self-propelled machinery, and from aerial appli-
cators. Farmworkers come in contact with pesticides by breathing them
in the air, spraying them, getting spilled or sprayed pesticides on themselves, or simply by touching plants with pesticide residues. A study
in North Carolina found that one-half of farmworker participants reported being sprayed and noticing a strong chemical smell in the fields
where they worked (Ciesielski et al. 1994, 448). Pesticide exposure can
cause acute and immediate reactions such as nausea, vomiting, dizziness, headaches, rashes, and burns. In some cases the exposure can be
deadly. Even small amounts of contact over time can cause severe health
problems. Long-term effects of exposure include cancer and sterility. For
pregnant women, pesticides may cause reproductive risks and birth de-
formities (Meister 1991, 508).

Pesticide exposure is difficult to detect and prove and therefore difficult to remedy. Most agricultural employers do not believe that farmworkers are exposed, especially if the workers do not apply the chemicals (Quandt et al. 1998, 364). But farmworkers often are exposed in other

ways, such as through drift or contact with recently sprayed plants. As one farmworker states:

I have worked many times after they have sprayed—here as well as in another place. They would spray and the spraying machine would go, and they'd bring in a crew leader and they would tell us that we were going to pick. And we would start to pick. Sometimes the boss tells us that he wants to finish filling up the barns, and sometimes they spray and we are behind picking (Quandt et al. 1998, 363).

Pesticide residues, often undetectable and invisible, can remain at dangerous levels on plants while they are being harvested. Yet many farmworkers lack knowledge and awareness of the dangers of their workplace. They often are not told what kind of chemicals are being used and when they are applied. As Esperanza relates from her experience in North Carolina, it is difficult for field laborers to know when to be careful and what may be causing dangerous symptoms or reactions:

The work was very heavy, hard. And there were a lot of complications involved, like if you started getting a headache, other people were vomiting a lot. On others, they would get a lot of rashes. Different kinds of skin rashes or allergic reactions. I don't know if it's because of the plant itself or because of the chemicals that they use on the plants. Or the two things. But all the time that we worked in tobacco, everybody seemed to either have a headache or a rash. You know, on top of being tired. You were always scratching yourself or taking something for the headache (Hemming 1996, 3).

The U.S. Environmental Protection Agency (EPA) was given the responsibility of enforcing the Worker Protection Standards in 1992 to protect farmworkers from potentially dangerous exposure. Resistance from growers and the agricultural industry delayed EPA's implementation of the standards until 1995. Now that they are in place, these regulations require that employers train farmworkers in pesticide safety and inform them about chemical applications. The EPA and other agencies have developed various health education materials for farmworkers in booklets, posters, flip charts, and videos.

However, studies have indicated that most farmworkers receive no training in the use of pesticides or protection from them (Arcury et al.

FIGURE 7.1. *Worker without protective gear spraying Christmas trees in the North Carolina Appalachian Mountains, 1996. Photograph by Chris Johnson.*

1999b, 463). Even when they do receive materials and education, they continue to face grower resistance and work conditions that are out of their control. Growers may be reluctant to provide information because they want to guard against the workers being overcautious or thinking that protective equipment is necessary.

When farmworkers feel that they have some control over pesticide exposure levels in their work situations, they are more likely to change their behavior by taking precautions and implementing safety measures (Austin et al. 2001). While training increases knowledge, the knowledge alone does not necessarily increase farmworkers' ability to change their work conditions. Even when educated about pesticides, farmworkers are forced to work quickly and have little or no time to take precautions. Many do not complain because they fear losing their jobs. Few farmworkers ask questions or refuse to work in a recently sprayed field even if they do not have the right protective equipment because of fear of being perceived as lazy or as troublemakers. Since farmworkers need their jobs and have few alternatives, they usually put aside their health concerns.

Poor hygienic conditions can contribute to the danger of pesticide exposure. For example, farmworkers may not have access to water where they are working or a place to wash their clothes at home. By not changing their work clothes every day or washing the residues off at work, the workers can experience pesticide buildup that the skin and lungs absorb.

Simple problems of field sanitation and work hygiene likewise cause and spread disease. While field sanitation laws were passed in 1987 requiring employers to provide water and bathrooms near the fields, many farms remain noncompliant with these regulations. In 1990 the Occupational Safety and Health Administration (OSHA), the agency responsible for implementing these laws, found that 69 percent of field workplaces were in violation (U.S. Bureau of Primary Health Care 1995, 28). The lack of these basic sanitation facilities can cause communicable diseases, parasitic infections, hepatitis, and a host of other sicknesses.

In addition to these hazards, farmworkers work directly in adverse climatic conditions. Laboring outdoors in hot weather subjects them to heat exhaustion, with symptoms including dizziness, cramping, heavy sweating, fast pulse, and rapid breathing. If untreated, heat exhaustion can lead to heat stroke, a life-threatening medical emergency. Severe dehydration can occur along with loss of consciousness and possible fatal damage to the vital organs (U.S. Environmental Protection Agency 1993).

Other common work-related injuries include back and muscle strains, sprains, cuts, broken bones, severe skin rashes, and even snake bites. Serious injuries occur on the job from such accidents as falling from ladders and getting caught in machinery. Getting to and from the job site also poses hazards, as farmworkers are often transported in the backs of pickup trucks or in crowded vans. In August 1999 a van carrying farmworkers collided with a tractor-trailer on a farming road in California. Thirteen of the workers in the van were killed, and several others were injured (Associated Press 1999b).

While similar injuries occur in other types of work such as construction, farmworkers encounter barriers to getting care that others do not face. For instance, most farmworkers are not covered by workers' compensation. No state in the Southeast covers agricultural workers the same as all other employees. Many southern states determine coverage based on the number of employees growers hire or the amount farmworkers earn, or they allow employers to secure coverage voluntarily. For instance, in Florida, farms that employ fewer than five full-time and twelve part-time workers are not required to carry coverage. In Louisiana, farmworkers must earn at least $2,500 to be covered. And in Alabama, Arkansas, Kentucky, Mississippi, South Carolina, and Tennessee,

coverage for farmworkers is voluntary (Commission for Labor Cooperation 2000, 65). Growers rarely provide any form of health insurance for
farmworkers, and some growers and crew leaders have refused to allow
farmworkers to leave their farms to seek treatment.

Like Esperanza, most farmworkers need their wages to survive and
are reluctant to take time off from work to seek medical care. This
means that farmworkers will often try to work through an injury and
say nothing about their sickness. It is ironic that while the heavy labor
of farm work requires strength and endurance, those who work in the
fields can rarely afford to keep themselves healthy and treat their own
illnesses and injuries. And in many ways farmworkers do not get to leave
their dangerous work environment—the hazards that they encounter
are brought home to their families and are aggravated by a lifestyle of
migration.

Health at Home

Adequate housing for farmworkers continues
to be a major problem impacting health. For migrant farmworkers in the
Southeast, housing is usually provided on the farm or in rental units.
Housing provided by growers is usually an old house, a barracks facility,
or a collection of trailers. While some housing may be in good condition, a significant percentage is old, run-down, and potentially dangerous. The water supply often is contaminated, and toilet facilities are not
available. Special federal government programs target farmworker housing, but they only provide housing for a small fraction of the farmworker
population (U.S. Bureau of Primary Health Care 1995, 43).

Overcrowded housing can lead to the transmission of diseases such
as tuberculosis. Because tuberculosis can spread through the air, people
can be exposed by being in the same area and especially by sleeping in
the same room with someone with an active infection. Farmworkers
often sleep on mattresses on the floor in cramped labor camps. In barracks, large numbers of farmworkers sleep in lines of bunk beds. Often
eight to twelve farmworkers share small trailers for a couple of months.
The Centers for Disease Control and Prevention determined that farmworkers are six times more likely to be infected by tuberculosis than the
general population of employed adults. A skin testing of 470 farmworkers in California found that 17 percent of the participants reacted posi-
tively and were potential carriers for tuberculosis (Migrant Clinicians
Network 1997, 1).

Many labor camps are located down dirt roads on farms in rural areas, physically isolating workers from others. Without their own transportation, farmworkers only leave the labor camp when the employer drives them to the store or the laundry.

Even farmworkers who live in rental housing closer to town face language and cultural barriers when relating to the larger community. In the evenings after work or during long stretches without work, farmworkers may be stuck in their housing with little to do. This type of isolation can lead to high rates of depression and substance abuse. When combined with the stress of work and the unstable nature of migrant farm work, you have a group at risk of depression and self-destructive behavior. Yet very few mental health services are available for farmworkers (U.S. Bureau of Primary Health Care 1995, 23).

Depression and substance abuse can lead to HIV infection and other sexually transmitted diseases. Though HIV often spreads by sharing needles for narcotics and other hard drugs, for Latino migrant farmworkers it is common to use a needle repeatedly to self-inject vitamins and antibiotics (McVea 1997, 91). Many Latin Americans believe that injections are much more effective than taking pills. This cultural belief is an example of why it is important for health providers to understand the context and background of the farmworker patients they serve.

Farmworkers also risk contracting sexually transmitted diseases when they participate in sexual activity with prostitutes or strangers. In situations where people are lonely, and especially if affected by drugs or alcohol, they forget to practice safe sex. While different health surveys indicate a wide range of possible rates of HIV infection among farmworkers, they agree that it is well above the national average. One estimate of the rate of HIV infection among farmworkers in the Delaware, Maryland, and Virginia (Delmarva) peninsula found that 6 percent of farmworker respondents were HIV positive (Inciardi et al. 1999, 653). Farmworkers are particularly vulnerable to AIDS because if they are HIV-positive they tend to seek care only when they are so sick they can no longer work. By the time they are diagnosed, the virus may be so far advanced that the available medical treatments have limited effects, even if they can afford them, and many cannot.

Beyond the particular risks associated with farm labor, farmworkers suffer from the same health problems of the general populace and especially those shared by people with limited financial resources. Studies indicate that the most prevalent conditions are common diseases like diabetes and hypertension (Rust 1990, 1216). The most acute health issue for farmworkers is the lack of access to treatment for ailments and injuries. Because they are often new to their communities, farmworkers may not know the location of clinics, pharmacies, or dental offices. When they do learn where these facilities are, farmworkers have difficulty arranging for transportation to these services. Once they get to a health facility, it may not have an interpreter on staff or they may be told that they have to set an appointment by phone.

Due to many obstacles to basic care, farmworkers often do not seek care until their health condition is an emergency or the injury or sickness prevents them from working. Even though it is much more costly to treat common illnesses and injuries in emergency rooms, these are often the only places that will see patients without an appointment and during hours that farmworkers are off work. The majority of these serious health problems could be prevented by regular medical visits.

Immigrant farmworkers may bring with them a cultural system of health and healing different from a western medical institutional model. While away from their communities of origin, farmworkers still may practice home-based and traditional types of care such as using herbal remedies and visiting *curanderos* (traditional healers) (Meister 1991, 506). Some Mexican farmworkers interpret sicknesses as folk illnesses. In one study in Florida it was found that many Latina farmworkers treated their children for *susto* and *mal de ojo*. *Susto* is defined as a fright or something startling that causes the soul to separate from the body. Some believe *mal de ojo* is caused by an adult from outside the family, perhaps someone who is envious of the mother, looking at a child. The look creates a charm that causes the child to be sick. The treatment usually involves prayer and a purification ritual, such as passing an egg over the body. This can be done by the parent or with the help of a *curandero*. While farmworkers need to be educated about clinical treatments, health care providers also should be aware of farmworker health beliefs and respect their responses to serious medical problems (Baer and Bustillo 1993, 90).

Cultural experiences combine with work and financial pressures, causing farmworkers to self-medicate and to use alternative therapies. Beliefs and practices based on traditional remedies enter strongly into their use of health care, particularly when medical options are limited. It is important for farmworker health care providers to understand these differences and recognize the perspectives and realities that farmworkers face.

Children at Risk

The children of farmworkers face many potential health risks. Some children work in the fields alongside their parents, filling their mothers' and fathers' bags and buckets so that the family can earn more money. Children may also play in the fields because no child care is available or parents may not want to leave their children with strangers. Babies and very small children may be placed in parked cars alongside the fields. Increasingly, teenage Latinos are entering farm work. Many travel without their parents, either on their own or with uncles and cousins. Often farmworker children and teenagers are outside for long periods of time during extreme weather conditions and subject to the dangers of machinery and the pace of hard labor.

Particular harm can occur to children that come into contact with pesticides, by accidentally being sprayed, by playing with empty containers, or touching residues on plants or contaminated work clothing. A simple hug from Mom or Dad coming home from work may result in sickness and hospitalization. It is important that the effects of low-level and long-term pesticide exposure be studied in children. Children may come into greater contact with pesticides and other dangerous chemicals at home, and because their bodies are smaller the chemicals are of greater harm to their system (Zahm, Ward, and Blair 1997, 281).

As with farmworker adults, farmworker children spend long days in crowded, unsanitary conditions where water may be contaminated by pesticide runoff. In some cases indoor plumbing is not available and heating and air conditioning systems are broken or not installed. Families may live in old houses and thus be exposed to high levels of lead resulting from chipped paint. And because farmworker housing is often located near the fields, children eat, sleep, and play in an industrial agricultural environment rather than in safer neighborhoods, playgrounds, or yards.

Another issue that disproportionately affects farmworker children and women is domestic violence. In 1995 the Migrant Clinicians Network (MCN) interviewed 520 farmworker women and found that 20 percent reported physical abuse within the past year from their intimate partners, husbands, or boyfriends (Migrant Clinicians Network 1996). While domestic violence exists in all cultures and communities, farmworkers are particularly vulnerable because of barriers to assistance and their lack of access to education concerning prevention. Factors that prevent farmworker women from getting help for themselves and their children include the isolation of migrant work camps, constant moving from place to place, language and cultural barriers, lack of transportation, and the need to maintain employment in order to have access to grower-provided housing. An intern with SAF describes the difficulties of helping a family in an abusive situation:

When I first found out about the abuse in the household, I immediately wanted to tell Rita to leave her husband. However, this might not be the best thing for Rita or her kids. There is nowhere for her to go if she does leave her husband. She might be able to stay in a shelter for a month, maybe two, but what is she going to do after that? She is not legal—that means she cannot qualify for any social services and she cannot get a job. She has already lost one job because she does not have any papers and she is afraid to find another one (Risteen 1998, 99).

Health care resources for farmworker families are very limited. Most have no health insurance or even the money to pay for simple checkups. Farmworker children are often untreated until they are severely ill. This is not because their parents are inattentive or do not care; it is just a daily reality that farmworkers like Esperanza face:

If we get sick, I try to cure them, the girls, with some remedies I've learned at home or some kind of medicine I can get at the pharmacy that I understand a little bit about how it helps to cure. Sometimes it works and sometimes it doesn't. One time I tried to cure myself of something and I ended up having to go to the emergency room at the hospital. Well the first thing, I don't know where to go. I mean, which doctor to go to, or what kind of service to get, because we don't have any money. And it was very, very hard for us just to decide to take Cynthia to the doctor. I was afraid that we have to pay much money (Hemming 1996, 3).

Like all children, farmworker children need immunizations, periodic health exams, and dental checkups. When they do not receive this preventive care, they fall further behind the level of care needed to maintain good health and protection against diseases and serious harm.

Many poor children in the United States receive government assistance to help pay doctor bills. The Medicaid program, for example, allows children from low-income families to receive a variety of services. However, farmworker children are often ineligible for such programs because they require U.S. residency status. This requirement disqualifies children of immigrants who are undocumented or new arrivals who have not received their residency or citizenship status (most applications take several years to be processed). Medicaid and newer government initiatives such as CHIP (Children's Health Insurance Program), which is supposed to cover children of the working poor, also demand residency status in order to provide primary care.

On top of financial barriers, farmworker parents are often unable to transport their children to seek medical care. As is often the case with adult health care, local public health departments or hospitals may not have interpreters, classes, or materials available in Spanish. All of these factors combine to create a complicated set of barriers and require health responses that go beyond single programs. And while we await these programs, farmworker children pay the price by suffering deteriorating personal health.

Responding to the Need

During the 1960s, when the U.S. government increased its involvement in many social and economic issues, the Migrant Health Program was created to improve the health status of farmworkers. Documentary and news stories' presentation of the difficult life of farmworkers was particularly poignant and led to public support for improving the lives of those who provide food for the supermarkets and the tables of consumers. The images and descriptions of farm work became a national issue. The continuation of migrant health as a federal program, as opposed to just a local service, is in part due to the fact that farmworkers operate in a national (and international) context and that responses need to go beyond state boundaries.

The Migrant Health Act was enacted in 1962 to provide farmworkers and their families with comprehensive medical care services. Most of the federal migrant health funding goes to community health centers and clinics that serve large farmworker populations. Migrant health programs are often expected to provide a range of services for farmworker clients, including primary care, dental services, maternal and child care, and assistance in obtaining benefits such as Medicaid and the Women and Infant Children coupon program (WIC).

Outreach programs are a vital component of migrant health care; in these programs, providers and health educators visit farmworkers in their homes. Migrant health programs also promote the use of bilin-

gual and bicultural health personnel and culturally appropriate proto-
cols. While the federal migrant health program has played a major role
in establishing health services for some farmworker families, they can
meet the needs of less than 20 percent of the migrant farmworker population (National Migrant Resource Program 1990, 2).

Programs that are locally based are an important component of migrant health care. These programs vary considerably, with some having
migrant councils that coordinate services and care between the various local agencies. County health departments often provide substantial
care to farmworkers, especially to women and children. Health departments also provide testing and treatment for diseases like tuberculosis
and HIV/AIDS. Social service agencies also can have a significant health
impact by enrolling farmworkers in programs like WIC, Medicaid, and
child care programs. However, the desire and the capacity of local health
agency personnel to help farmworkers varies greatly. Without strong advocates or farmworker involvement at the local level, many needed services, even those provided for by federal funds, are undelivered.

Local churches and ministry organizations also play an important
role in health care. Many churches with migrant ministries coordinate
health fairs and distribute medical information, first aid kits, clothing,
and blankets to farmworkers. And some churches have taken charge of
major efforts, such as creating a mobile dental unit or conducting health
screenings. Though churches are limited in the kind of services they
can provide, they do play an important role in delivering comprehensive
care.

One problem that farmworker health programs face is the difficulty
of evaluating the extent to which they improve health status. Baseline
data are insufficient about farmworker health needs and even about the
general demographics of farmworkers at any given time in an area. An
important objective of health programs continues to be obtaining more
information on their potential clientele, particularly from farmworkers
themselves (National Migrant Resource Program 1990, 1). Clinics and
other groups do what they can to identify needs of farmworkers in their
communities. Some outreach programs have had success not only in
advertising services but also in obtaining input and involvement from
farmworkers through special focus groups, advisory committees, and
patient surveys.

In some cases farmworkers are trained to become health promoters
or lay health advisors who can serve as a resource for their peers. The
Camp Health Aide Program based in Michigan is a model program in

FIGURE 7.2. *Student activist provides HIV information to a farmworker in a rural health clinic, 1996. Photograph by Chris Johnson.*

which farmworkers are recruited to provide preventive care within their own communities and work groups (U.S. Bureau of Primary Health Care 1995, 11). An assessment of a lay health advisor program in North Carolina found that mothers who had contact with a lay health advisor were more likely to bring their sick children to clinics for care. Women contacted by lay health advisors also demonstrated greater knowledge and practice of health care, such as prenatal visits (Watkins et al. 1994, 85).

The current health care climate for farmworkers is one of dramatic shifts and changes. One of the threats to health care includes rising anti-immigrant sentiment. The passage by California voters of Proposition 187, which attempted to limit state services only to citizens, had a direct impact on health access. Even though Proposition 187 was later declared unconstitutional by the California Supreme Court, undocumented immigrants remained afraid that if they went to the hospital or clinic they would be reported to the Immigration and Naturalization Service (INS). At the same time, federal funding for migrant health programs has remained inadequate, creating the potential for local health resources to be overburdened. The experience and knowledge gained by specialized migrant programs must be used to help current and future health providers to adjust to changes, responding in ways that are effective and that build on strengths within the farmworker community.

Organizing around Health Issues

Health and safety issues provide incentives for farmworkers to join together to address their own problems. At one level, farmworkers can advocate for better health access and identify and even develop their own specific health services. For example, a group of farmworkers might meet informally to arrange for a mobile dentist unit to visit their area or even to demand prenatal care from the local health department. As part of the Lideres Campesinas program in California, women farmworkers organize a series of dinners, or *cenas*, in their homes to talk about domestic violence and other health issues and to exchange information about local support services. Lideres Campesinas has reached 17,000 women. Due to this success, they are now providing training and consulting with women's groups nationwide ("Breaking the Silence" 1997, 3).

At another level, health issues have proven to be effective platforms from which to organize farmworkers to address related problems such as poor pay, inadequate housing, and lack of educational opportunities. While government officials and consumers may not be directly involved in wage disputes, there is general support for good health.

Farmworker unions have a history of advocating for health care on and off the job. For example, back problems caused by stoop labor were a rallying cry for the United Farm Workers (UFW) in its campaign against the short-handled hoe. In recent years unions have invested their resources in documenting and publicizing the effects of pesticide exposure on farmworkers and their families. By highlighting these health problems, unions appeal to the sympathies of consumers as well as to the self-interest of farmworkers. To address broader issues of health, some unions set up their own primary care clinics for members.

During the 1960s the UFW began to establish clinics in many areas of California. By providing health care to farmworkers, the UFW engaged the community, delivered needed services, and demonstrated the value of their union. Medical clinics for undocumented workers were established and also viewed as organizing centers (Griswold del Castillo and Garcia 1995, 81). Membership in the union provided many health benefits including low-cost medical treatment, dentistry, and even a retirement home (Griswold del Castillo and Garcia 1995, 126). In addition, unions like the UFW operate service centers where farmworkers can receive assistance such as workers' compensation and food stamps.

Community organizations that work with farmworkers also are responding to health care issues. Although not acting as official labor unions, many farmworker-based organizations bring farmworkers together in committees, conduct trainings, and offer social services. These groups are involved with health education on topics such as HIV/AIDS, tuberculosis, substance abuse, and pesticide exposure. They help farmworkers access health services in their local areas.

One community-based organization (CBO) that advocates within the farmworker community is the Farmworker Health and Safety Institute (FHSI) located in New Jersey. With networks and partnerships along the East Coast, the FHSI has developed training programs on pesticide poisoning and other health issues. The FHSI teaches farmworkers how to document health and safety problems as well as monitor agencies and regulations at the state and the federal levels (Grimes 1998, 33).

A strong health care program and network of services can provide ways for farmworkers to organize. In particular, programs that encourage farmworkers' participation in health care decisions and delivery create opportunities for farmworkers to address problems. Participation may include holding community forums, training farmworkers as lay health advisors, and partnering with grassroots farmworker organizations (Arcury et al. 1999a, 563).

At a very basic level farmworkers should be consulted about their own health and about their perspectives on health services. Farmworkers can be involved in planning health programs and take part in identifying priorities and strategies for implementing them. Community participation at a deep level involves actual implementation of a health care program in which farmworkers take ownership by helping to deliver health services (Cornwall and Jewkes 1995, 1667).

Challenges for the Future

In 1995 the CBS News Special Reports revisited the famous documentary "Harvest of Shame" that CBS produced more than thirty years ago. One theme of the "Legacy of Shame" update was that the living and working conditions farmworkers endure remain virtually unchanged after three decades. However, while many of the issues remain the same, the labor and migration patterns of farm work are in constant flux. These changing migrancy patterns of farmworker populations must inform health care providers and advocates as they develop new and appropriate solutions and policies.

The changing demographic trends of farm labor have an impact in the design and delivery of health programs. Farmworkers today are increasingly male, Mexican, and young. These trends have important implications such as the degree to which maternal and child care will be emphasized and what kinds of health education are most needed. Young men are probably the least likely to seek out medical services. A greater percentage of farmworkers are now undocumented: the proportion of unauthorized farmworkers is estimated to have grown from 7 percent in the 1980s to 37 percent in the early 1990s and now to more than 50 percent as workers with other options leave agriculture and as economic and political crises in Latin America have pushed people from their native countries (Mines, Gabbard, and Steirman 1997).

In an attempt to reduce the use of undocumented labor, the federal government allows foreign nationals to obtain temporary worker visas, called H-2A visas, to work under limited contracts with farm employers in the United States. At present, farmworkers in the H-2A program are usually from Mexico and are almost exclusively male.

Though a small percentage of the total agricultural workforce, the H-2A program is growing rapidly. Employers use the program because they like the guaranteed workforce and are applying pressure to Congress to issue more temporary work visas. Not only are large numbers of laborers made available on a short-term basis, but also participating farmworkers are prohibited from working for any other employer. If farmworkers fail to perform a task according to specifications, if they complain too much, or if they do not like the work, their only option is to return to their home country. One farmworker said:

Sometimes the contractor or the boss wants us to fill three or four barns, that's where we put the tobacco, and he says, "hurry, hurry, he is no good because he is too slow," and with the gloves we would be slow. And the boss will say, "I don't want him," and we think, he might fire us because we are slow, what we always do is try to hurry, hurry to do everything, and not just me, but everyone has gone through this. I have seen it in some fields with some people that were slow, they were fired. But [the bosses] don't care. They just say: "Come on, hurry, hurry or I'll send you to Mexico" and they just threaten us and that's what we don't agree with (Austin et al. 2001).

While farmworker advocates struggle against this large-scale revival of the federal Bracero program of temporary workers, health providers must meet these challenges by providing services at the ground level for those in their clinical service area. This situation has led clinicians and others to consider farmworker health in the context of international economics. The policies made in Congress and the trade negotiations with foreign countries have a direct impact on who may obtain care and what health problems they experience.

Farmworker health is not just an issue within the United States. The men and women who harvest the food we eat are largely a binational population. The emergence of the North America Free Trade Agreement (NAFTA) and other trade agreements with Mexico continue to have far-reaching effects on labor in both countries. As immigrant farmworkers travel between their home villages and their places of work, they experience health problems on both sides of the border. Pesticide poisoning, for example, is common in Mexico, where chemicals that were banned in the United States still are used and farmworkers receive little help in avoiding exposure (Barry 1995, 214–216). Responding to the health needs of farmworkers will require expanded efforts and transnational labor organizing, education, and health policies.

Some recent efforts to coordinate health activities across the border include TBNet and the exchange of health professionals. In 1994 the U.S.-Mexico Border Health Association identified the need to control tuberculosis infection and track patients who were taking medication to ensure that they completed their treatment. For migrant farmworkers, moving to and from many locations in the United States and other countries, the usual interstate referral tracking process proved to be inadequate. To meet this challenge, the Migrant Clinicians Network, a national organization of health service providers, worked with agencies in the United States and Mexico to create TBNet. As a tracking and referral system, TBNet enrolls and issues farmworker patients a portable treatment record and a toll-free telephone number that can be used by clinics for referral and followup. A TBNet project team updates the database for the binational system, which includes monthly treatment plans, clinical contacts for each patient, and demographic information. Binational medical consultation is available for each specific case.

The goal of TBNet is to increase the proportion of farmworkers who finish their regimen of medication and are cured. In the first year of the project, 68 percent of the patients completed at least six months of active treatment. By the second year this percentage had increased to 80 percent, and in 1999, the third year, more than 90 percent of patients enrolled had positive treatment outcomes (Migrant Clinicians Network

1999). This program is a good example of how responding to the changes in farmworker populations can lead to successful interventions.

As a group contributing invaluable labor to U.S. agricultural industries, farmworkers pay a high price as displaced binational laborers. As they work in dangerous environments with little compensation, they face substantial obstacles in maintaining a level of health and well-being that most U.S. citizens would consider fundamental. With the continuing dependence of agricultural production on a steady flow of Latino immigrants, it is essential that we learn about and respond to health needs among farmworkers.

For farmworkers, developing binational systems of health care delivery can be lifesaving. But the ability to remain healthy also depends on having work that provides a living wage and health benefits. In some respects, the health care system operates as a subsidy to agricultural employers, the growers. If low-cost primary care is available to farmworkers through the federal migrant health program or other public or private sources, then employers do not have to pay for medical treatment or health insurance. A 1992 survey in Florida found that only 6 percent of farmworkers had employer-provided health insurance (Arrieta, Walker, and Mason 1998, 39). Health providers and advocates should encourage growers to provide health care insurance and workers' compensation for their employees. In the absence of these, farmworkers will continue to live at the margins of the U.S. health care system. As Jill Hemming notes, farmworkers like Esperanza Martinez consider conventional U.S. health care a last resort.

Esperanza has followed many avenues of treatment in her life. She trusts and seeks out conventional medical help from doctors and clinics. In Mexico, she used doctors, in addition to self-diagnosing and self-medicating with easy access to Mexico's unrestricted pharmaceuticals market. She also grew up in the household with a traditional healer mother who relied on herbal remedies, massage and other techniques to heal her family and neighbors. Finally, she has always sought divine intervention and help through prayer when there is illness in her home. Here she can no longer buy the medications available to her in Mexico and she has only minor familiarity with her mother's healing methods. This limits her choices to over-the-counter medications, a few herbal remedies, prayer, and visits to the doctor. There are enough obstacles to seeking the help of a doctor to keep her away until all her other resources are exhausted (Hemming 1996).

Farmworker health advocacy means struggling for farmworker access to and input into the health system and for cultural sensitivity when treating people born outside the United States. Thousands of farmworkers experience preventable injuries and sicknesses annually, even as they bear the burdens of U.S. consumers' groceries on their backs. Because she is a farmworker, Esperanza Martinez constantly worries about where to find basic health care for her family and about the conditions her children will face in coming years.

That Summer

Marcella Hurtado
Gomez, farmworker
and 1997 SAF
intern

"Mommy, can I wear my blue dress, the one that has those pretty bows?"

"Well, I don't know, it is the only good dress that you have and I don't want you to get it dirty. Here, you better wear this purple one, it's pretty too. And hurry up and fix your hair."

When the bus arrived, my mother took me by the hand and helped me on the bus. I was a little scared, but I saw my cousins and friends on the bus and I went to sit down with them. It wasn't until I got off the bus that I really felt scared. I had to leave my cousins and I came into a class of strangers and a "gringa" teacher that didn't even greet me, on the contrary, it seemed that my presence bothered her.

"Look Gladys, another one! . . ."

I didn't understand what the teacher was saying, but it was obvious that she was angry and that made me cry. All the excitement that I had felt that morning disappeared at that moment.

"Well don't just stand there crying, come in and play with the toys or something . . ."

That same day I met my other two teachers. One was a black woman that liked to hug the kids. She gave me a lot of hugs but I didn't like that at all. The other one was a young [white] woman who was very concerned about [me]. Neither of the three teachers spoke Spanish and I didn't speak English.

Bella Juventud/ Wonderful Youth

Gloria Velásquez

*Pregúntame qué aprendí en
la escuela
ese tiempo feliz
en mi niñez y juventud,
en los fifties y los
sixties.*

*Aprendí que Columbus
descubrió la América,
y que mis forefathers
fueron Washington y
Roosevelt.*

*Aprendí que mi "cultura"
consistía en Dick y Jane,
con comidas americanas
de hot dogs y mustard.*

*Aprendí de prejudice
a los morenos y los spics
porque los demás
con sus P.T.A. mothers
se olvidaron de nosotros.*

*Aprendí del sportsmanship
de anglo football players,
de anglo cheerleaders;
ignoraban a los morenos
que eran tontos y muy slow.*

*Aprendí de summer
vacations, swimming pools
and suntans
hincada en los files de
betabel
con el azadón en las manos,
aguantando el calor.*

*Ay, qué bellos recuerdos
de ese tiempo feliz
de mi niñez y juventud,
en los fifties y los
sixties.*

Ask me what I learned in
school,
those joyful days
of my childhood and youth
in the Fifties and the Sixties.

I learned that Columbus
discovered America
and that my forefathers
were Washington and Roosevelt.

I learned that my "culture"
consisted of Dick and Jane
with American meals
of hot dogs and mustard.

I learned about prejudice
toward morenos and spics
because all the others
who had P.T.A. mothers,
forgot all about us.

I learned about sportsmanship
from Anglo football players,
from Anglo cheerleaders.
They avoided the greasers,
who were stupid and very slow.

I learned about summer vacations,
swimming pools and suntans,
stooped down in the beetfields
with a hoe in my hand
suffering the sun's heat.

Oh, what wonderful memories
of those joyful days
of my childhood and youth
in the Fifties and Sixties.

CHAPTER 8

Understanding the Challenges and Potential of Migrant Students

Ramiro Arceo, Joy Kusserow, and Al Wright

Though nearly 80 percent of the three million to five million migrant and seasonal farmworkers in the United States are men, at least a quarter-million children travel with their families as they follow the harvests (Leon 1996, 1). Almost three-fourths of these children who are under the age of fourteen live in poverty (Davis 1997). Many children whose families migrate to work in U.S. agriculture stay with relatives in their home countries instead of traveling with their families. Two in five migrant farmworkers live away from their children while doing farm work (Mines, Gabbard, and Steirman 1997). Many minors travel alone or with family members to do farm work themselves. Approximately 8 percent (200,000–800,000) of farmworkers in the United States are minors (Mines, Gabbard, and Steirman 1997). Most young farmworkers or children of farmworkers in the United States are Mexican, while others are from Guatemala and El Salvador and a small proportion from Haiti.

Educators classify school-age farmworker children as "migrant students," thereby defining them by their parents' occupation. Their parents' constant movement impedes children's ability to succeed in school. Migrant students attend two, three, or more schools each year in as many states, encountering different curricula, textbooks, educational standards, and policies each time they move. Because their education is interrupted, disjointed, and often sporadic, migrant students lack continuity in their coursework. In addition to the challenge of constant mobility, other factors such as limited English proficiency, low self-esteem, poor housing, and economic pressures affect migrant students' ability to succeed in school. By the time a migrant child is twelve, he or she may be working between sixteen and eighteen hours per week (Bell, Roach, and Sheets 1994). As one Guatemalan youth in Morganton, North Carolina, said, "If we don't work, we don't eat. That's why we don't go to school" (Hernandez 1994).

While none of the disadvantages migrant children face are unique to their population, they experience the challenges in greater concentration than do other groups. It is therefore not surprising that "school enrollment for migrant children is lower than that of any other population group, and their high school dropout rate is twice the national average" (Davis 1997). Latinos continue to spend fewer years in school than their African American or Anglo counterparts—entering school later and leaving school earlier (de la Rosa and Maw 1990).

These statistics reflect the negative impact of factors such as poverty, mobility, the hardships of farm work, and language difficulties on migrant students' education; combined, these factors amount to much greater challenges, especially for those migrant children who move frequently and over long distances. In this chapter, we will address each of these issues, as well as how various agencies such as the Migrant Education Program deal with these challenges.

Who Are Migrant Children?

If it takes a village to raise a child, how much more does it take to raise those children whose "village" may spread across a broad mosaic of cities and towns, fertile fields, and remote rural landscapes. At the very least, a migrant child's village may revolve around two widely separated poles: one a more or less permanent home, probably in Florida, Texas, or Mexico, and the other a migrant camp or temporary residence that serves as a second home for two, three, even six months out of the year. Often the village is a bewildering succession of temporary homes in as many as five or six states each year. Migrant families in Florida who follow the harvest may travel through the Carolinas on their way to Virginia and Maryland and from there northward through Pennsylvania and New York and on to Michigan, Ohio, Illinois, and Indiana.

How can a village that is distributed across a thousand miles of landscape raise a migrant child? How can even the most willing of villagers reach out to help children who are here today and gone tomorrow, whose parents often speak an unfamiliar language, and whose customs are easily misunderstood? Willing villagers are not the norm. Migrant families typically are strangers in whatever village they inhabit, tolerated because of the economic significance of their work but only infrequently welcomed into the civic and social fabric of a community.

For the children of migrant workers, the village schoolhouse is a confusing collage of different buildings, English-speaking teachers, strange curricula, and conflicting rules. The succession of school buildings in which migrant students are enrolled is probably the least daunting aspect of transience. While school buildings tend to look alike, teachers speak with different accents as one moves south to north or east to west. Classrooms may be comparable to those at the children's previous school, but textbooks will probably be different, and the entire scope and sequence of various curricula will be different. Each successive school in which children are enrolled is often on a slightly different calendar and daily schedule.

And those are only the superficial differences. Mobile students in general, and migrant students in particular, confound conventional educational planning. The buzzwords of educational reform—site-based management, local development of academic standards—focus on the school as the medium. But THE school, standing true as a star fixed in the firmament, is a comfort that migrant children do not have; their education depends upon ALL of the schools in which they enroll.

A central issue in educating migrant children, then, is making a whole out of the disparate parts of a frequently interrupted education. It is not a goal that can be accomplished simply by making each enrollment as academically productive and beneficial as possible. It depends instead on making each enrollment, each course of study, relevant to the one that preceded it and the one that will follow it. Even more, it means having an overall vision of where students are heading and what it will take to get them there.

Overview of the Migrant Education Program

The Migrant Education Program (MEP) was enacted by Congress and signed into law by President Lyndon Johnson in late 1966, and the first nine million dollars for the program was appropriated the following fall. Since the beginning, the MEP has required all states receiving funds to coordinate with other states in educating migrant children. Next to the infusion of federal dollars, this requirement probably has made the biggest difference in the lives of migrant children. Since the implementation of the Migrant Education Program, the graduation rate for migrant students has improved from an estimated

FIGURE 8.1. *Migrant students participating in SAF's school success project, 1996. Photograph by Chris Johnson.*

11 percent to better than 50 percent (National Program for Secondary Credit Exchange and Accrual 1994, 41).

There were some educational and support programs for migrant children prior to the MEP—a patchwork of church-sponsored efforts and some other federal programs. But the new education program greatly expanded states' capacity to provide more and better services while altering the focus of the services as well. Instead of concentrating on services addressing needs that existed during children's limited residency in a single location, the clear implication of the legislation was to put all programs and services into the larger context of a continuum of services that would follow migrant children as they moved.

Interstate coordination is the single most important characteristic of the federally funded MEP for these children who move often. Migrant Education is also concerned with the coordination of migrant students who move within a state (intrastate coordination), but it is in the area of interstate coordination that the program has accomplished its most distinctive successes and experienced its greatest frustrations. States that receive children from their home-base states are called receiving states. Michigan is the largest receiving state, schooling children primarily from Florida and Texas. In the West, California has the largest number of migrant children, which is directly related to the year-round work that migrant farmworkers perform. Texas has the next-largest population of migrant students, followed by Florida.

The fact that the MEP legislation placed the burden on the states was significant. Michigan congressman William D. Ford, who authored the Migrant Education Program as an amendment to the Elementary and Secondary Education Act, was convinced that many school districts would not be responsive to the needs of migrant children. He wanted the state departments of education to be responsible for ensuring that programs were established to meet the needs of migrant children, and thus the Migrant Education Program was created as a state grant program. The legislation, even in its beginning, permitted the states to bypass local school districts and give the funds to community agencies if necessary to ensure that services were delivered. Although the bulk of MEP funds do flow to school districts, many programs are operated by combinations of districts, regional entities, nonprofit agencies, and even state education departments.

The nature of MEP as a grant program tended to channel the interstate coordination requirement to the state level. While coordination of educational services for migrant children ostensibly depended on school-to-school coordination for appropriate placement and courses of instruction, state agency officials began from the outset to establish linkages with their counterparts in other states. Thus, a primary thrust of interstate coordination lay in initiatives that originated in planning among state rather than local educators. The emphasis on state-level programs and projects was not intended to obscure the continuing role of school-to-school coordination by the practitioners who actually dealt with the children. Indeed, state-initiated projects like the Migrant Student Record Transfer System were designed to streamline coordination at the local level.

Eligibility for the Migrant Education Program

Historically, the federally funded Migrant Education Program has determined which children are eligible for this spe-

cial educational assistance. At the outset of the MEP, children who migrated from one state to another were almost the total focus, sharing
the spotlight only with children who migrated within a state. But as the
MEP evolved over the years, it was extended to additional categories of
children.

Barely a year after the program was created, it became possible to
use MEP funds to continue serving migrant children for up to six years
after they stopped migrating. In 1974, these formerly migratory children
were included in the official count on which funding was based. In that
same year, the category of migrant fishing was added, along with an expanded range of agricultural work, including dairy, livestock, and timber
harvesting.

As eligibility categories expanded, children who had "settled out" of
the migrant cycle represented a substantial percentage of "migrants" for
whom coordinated educational experience was a concern. Additional
categories of migrant work increasingly eschewed traditional patterns of
migration. While such newly minted migrants may have traveled a long
distance to obtain work, it was more likely to be a one-way move. In
almost no case was it a matter of a regular migratory cycle.

By the early 1990s the number of children who actually migrated from
state to state on some kind of a regular cycle accounted for less than one-
fourth of all children enrolled in the Migrant Education Program. Over
the years, a kind of schism developed in the Migrant Education community between those who wanted migratory children to remain a top priority and those for whom it was essentially irrelevant. Yet the image of
migrant children trudging thousands of miles with hard-working, crop-
picking parents continued to be the favored depiction of what Migrant
Education was supposed to be about.

The legislation that created the Migrant Education Program defined it
as "Education of Migratory Children." This is preserved even in the 1994
MEP reauthorization, which underscores the point by citing the word
"migratory" four times in the Statement of Purpose while only citing
"migrant" once. It is expected that "migration" will appear six times in
the 2001 Statement of Purpose. While not apparent at first, it became
clear as the program evolved that "migratory" and "migrant" were not
the same thing. Migratory children are migrant children, to be sure, but
not all children now defined as migrant are migratory.

The meaning of migratory is fairly clear. It refers to a regular pattern
of back-and-forth travel between two points, keyed to seasonal changes,
north in the spring, south in the fall—the familiar pattern of migra-

tory waterfowl. The same is true for the most classic pattern of migratory farmworkers. Former Arizona state director J. O. "Rocky" Maynes complained in the mid-1960s, before the MEP was created, that the federal government spent more on migratory waterfowl than on migratory children! Wintering in warmer climates for economic reasons, migrant workers move northward as the crops ripen. They either go from site to site in a generally northward path as crops come in or go to a single destination where the work will last throughout the warm months. Then they return to their homes in Texas, Florida, or elsewhere along the southern border or back to Mexico. Then it is a matter of finding whatever work they can find until it is time to start the northward swing again.

It is this cyclical migration, the rhythmic, somewhat predictable pattern of movement between a home place and a seasonal workplace far from that home, that calls out clearly for interstate coordination. And the most significant efforts in Migrant Education are largely based on this migratory pattern. From it derives a small lexicon of terms widely, though sometimes inappropriately, used among migrant educators.

First, there is the concept of the sending state and the receiving state. The former is the state where migrant workers can be found during the winter, the location from which they set forth on their search for seasonal farm work. The receiving states are migrant workers' destinations, the places they go to find work picking crops or working in seasonally operated canneries. The sending states are migrant workers' home bases, and the schools their children attend in the sending states are their home-base schools.

It was once common in the Migrant Education Program to characterize each state as either a sending state or a receiving state, depending on the net outflow or influx of migrant children. Some of those distinctions have blurred over time, both because of changing migration patterns and because of more expansive definitions. Only two states have been consistently identified as sending states by the MEP—Texas and Florida. Each spring about forty thousand students who attend Texas schools depart with their families for agricultural work in one or more of about forty other states, from Washington on the West Coast to New York on the East. About half that many students leave Florida to travel up the eastern seaboard and to the Midwest. Some even travel between Texas and Florida. Because Texas and Florida schools enroll these thousands of migrant students as they trickle back home in October, November, and December, these two states have been especially active in promoting interstate coordination with the states that educate the same children. Some of the receiving states have made extensive efforts to become active partners with one or both of these sending states.

For many years migrant educators characterized California as a sending state, but this was a misperception. As the nation's leading producer of fruits and vegetables, California is a magnet for farmworkers, attracting both migrant and seasonal workers who make a more or less permanent residence there. About five thousand Texas students migrate to California each year, plus thousands of students from Arizona, Oregon, Washington, and other states. Just about as many migrate annually within the state. An even larger number (nearly sixty thousand) come to California from Mexico. Recently California began a binational program that became the basis for a broader effort for about fifteen states to participate in records exchange, teacher exchange, and other linkages with Mexico. In some states the binational program has replaced interstate coordination as a priority.

Some students migrate from California to other states, mostly in the Pacific Northwest, but not enough to change the basic nature of California as a receiver rather than a provider of migrant labor. Characterizations of other states are not always easily made. Washington state, for example, is a major destination for migrant families from Texas, but many such families have settled in the Yakima Valley. Many of these families continue to migrate, with Washington now their home-base, traveling to the Midwest in the summer months.

If the classic back-and-forth migratory patterns were the only difficulty affecting Migrant Education, the challenge of coordinating services to children and making smooth transitions from one school to another would be complex enough. However, things are not that simple. Some migrant workers escape the migrant stream at the earliest opportunity. Many decide that almost anything is better than the backbreaking toil in the fields. For others, migrating is an intermittent activity. If the family can earn enough to survive for another year without migrating, they stay in an area, only to have to move the following year. Some families find permanent work and new homes in the receiving states where they had been working or start making enough money at their home bases to satisfy their needs. Still others get locked into the pattern of migrating year after year. Consequently, the hundreds of thousands of children who migrate in any given year are not all the same children as those who moved the previous year. The annual turnover rate is probably no less than 30 or 40 percent.

The turnover in the ranks of migrant students is a minor coordination problem compared to that of children whose families migrate irregularly and unpredictably. Students who migrate to one state in one year and to another state the next or who are shunted from place to place as work opportunities for their parents fail to materialize are the students who are most educationally disadvantaged. It is hard to prepare for students whose moves are so sporadic. With students whose moves are fairly predictable, it is possible to do realistic planning for the transitions faced in the recurrent moves.

Other migrant students clearly are not migratory. These are students who have relocated with their families for reasons that qualify them for Migrant Education. The anomaly in a program entitled "Education of Migratory Children" is that the statute confers eligibility based upon a single move. In some cases, this single move results in conditions commonly associated with "migrant" farm work, such as the Mexican family who moves to California, works the fields, and then settles in California. In other cases, being identified as a "migrant" student can be almost arbitrary. For example, children of workers in poultry-processing and meat-packing plants can be certified as migrants if a survey shows that 60 percent of those jobs turn over within a year, satisfying the Department of Education's guidance on what constitutes "temporary" employment. The only consistent pattern associated with work in southern animal food production is that the unpleasant, low-paying jobs attract an influx of immigrant workers. Some of them are former fieldworkers who see the jobs as a step up from the fields; many are recruited directly from Mexico.

Inclusion of meat-packing and poultry-processing plants as qualifying work arenas separates Migrant Education from other federal programs for migrant farmworkers that generally limit eligibility to persons working row crops or picking in orchards. Additionally, persons involved in reforestation efforts or in logging can qualify as migrants for the MEP when they move into a new school district to pursue the job on a temporary or seasonal basis. Migratory dairy workers are specified in the legislation, even though the typical pattern of the mobile dairy worker is to move from farm to farm based on opportunity. The broad category of migratory fisher accounts for about 5 percent of all children in the Migrant Education Program, but almost all live in Alaska and in smaller numbers in Massachusetts and Louisiana. Few reside in more than one state. The commercial fisher who sets out to sea from a home port and returns home with his or her catch could arguably be called "migratory," but his or her children qualify for the MEP only if they accompany him and they change residence somewhere along the way. There are Native Alaskans who each summer conduct a traditional migration to catch fish for winter food; their children qualify as migrants under a special dispensation.

The distinction between "migratory" and "nonmigratory" migrant children is significant for understanding interstate coordination as an emphasis within the Migrant Education Program. Simply stated, interstate coordination is an imperative in the effort to help migratory children, who have a unique set of needs derived from their cyclical movements and educational disruptions. For these most vulnerable of students, coordination is virtually a matter of continuing with their education or dropping out of school. Efforts that began when the MEP served only highly mobile migrants continued through the years, producing marked improvements in structures to assist the students who traveled the migrant streams. For children who are not clearly migratory but who do move frequently if unpredictably from state to state, interstate coordination is an ideal that is extremely difficult to carry out. And for those children who qualify as migrants without being migratory, interstate coordination is essentially irrelevant.

Poverty's Effects on Farmworker Children

While "farmworker," "migratory," and "migrant" children pose difficult classification problems for educators, many of these children share a common thread: poverty. As mentioned earlier, nearly seventy-five percent of migrant children live below the poverty line. For these children, economic marginality is a major barrier to attaining an education. Poor housing conditions, lack of health and nutrition, work in the fields, and the inability to afford school supplies drastically affect these students' chances of achieving in school.

When students' families are poor, this often means they do not have adequate nutrition or enough to eat. "Even when farmworker children attend school, they are often tired, irritable, or unable to concentrate due to hunger, illness, or fatigue" (Davis 1997). Poverty also affects their ability to seek medical care, as does the location of migrant camps, which are often situated in rural, isolated areas. Making the journey to a health practitioner is difficult due to the family's lack of health insurance, money, and/or transportation.

Migrant housing is often substandard: poor heating systems, lack of air-conditioning, overcrowding, inadequate lighting, and lack of toilets and running water are just a few of the detrimental living conditions in which these children live. Fifty-four percent of overcrowded farm-worker housing has children present. And children live in more than one-third of the housing with structural problems such as holes in the roof and sagging structural features. All these factors make it difficult for students to concentrate and study. In addition, poor housing causes such illnesses as respiratory disease due to lack of ventilation, parasitic conditions resulting from stagnant water and overcrowding, and skin infections and diarrhea caused by unsanitary toilet and bathing facilities. Lack of adequate housing therefore influences migrant children's ability to attend school regularly and reduces their motivation and ability to learn efficiently.

Many migrant students have to compete with siblings and other adults for space to do their schoolwork because usually the house or trailer is home for more than one family. This environment makes it difficult for students who may already be lagging behind in school to concentrate on their studies. A student simply may not have space to study without disruptions. There is usually no established area for studying, leaving places also used by everyone else, like the kitchen table, as the only alternative. Since many migratory families do not stay long enough in one place, many families are unable to provide students with a specific area or an allotted time for their schoolwork.

Adults in the home often interrupt students while they are in the middle of their schoolwork, requesting their assistance with chores around the house. This is common in households where one person, often the mother, is responsible for all the chores. In order for her to get everything accomplished, she delegates daily chores such as washing the dishes, making the beds, and doing the laundry to children. This atmosphere makes it difficult for children to keep up with their schoolwork, resulting in students turning in incomplete homework or none at all. This in turn embarrasses the children and can lead to lower self-esteem. Ramiro Arceo, a former farmworker and child of farmworker parents, relates his experiences of trying to study in an overcrowded housing situation.

We moved to Riverbank, California, in early 1981 when my father was following the peach and apricot harvest. We lived in a small two-bedroom apartment across the street from the town's movie theater. I lived with my

parents, three sisters, three brothers, a cousin, and my uncle in that apart-
ment. After coming home from school we had to help my mother clean up
the apartment. Usually my younger sister and I would sweep and mop,
while my older sisters would run errands and help my mother make the
beds, clean the bathroom, and cook before my father, brothers, uncle, and
cousin would come from work. We didn't like doing homework, so even
though it might have been just filling out lines with letters of the alphabet,
my mother was too busy to tell us to do it. And if we were doing it at the
living room coffee table, when the "workers" got home they would lie on
the couch to rest and watch television. They would ask us to bring them
a soda, or water, or, in my dad and uncle's case, a beer from the kitchen.
They would talk about how their day went. Sometimes they were mad and
cussing about their contractor. So, instead of doing homework we would
just listen to their stories. They would not tell us to do our homework.
My older sisters would go in the bedroom to do their homework. But my
mother would be calling after them to help her heat up the tortillas or to
clean up the table and do the dishes after dinner (Arceo 1999).

To survive economic hardship, farmworker families need extra income from every source possible. So children often feel compelled or
are required to help their parents in the fields. Most farmworker children directly contribute to the household income through farm labor at
a young age, and this work usually adversely affects their school performance. "[One] study found that students who work more than 20 hours a
week were less likely to do homework, earn A's, or take college prepara-
tory courses" (Nixon 1995, 26). Farmworker families frequently have to
face the agonizing choice between allowing older students to continue
their education and asking them to work full-time to provide desperately
needed income. Though Latino farmworker families highly value education for their children, when faced with matters of survival, encouraging their children to remain in school becomes increasingly complicated. Even though dropping out may not be the best long-term decision
for the children, farmworker families' choices are limited. While most
farmworker parents value their children's education, short-term needs
of income for food and rent outweigh the long-term benefits of formal
education.

Because child labor laws are less restrictive in agriculture than in
other industries, some farmworker children assist their parents in the
fields. Child labor on farms is only minimally regulated, even for dangerous work such as pruning trees or using farm machinery. Children

as young as sixteen can perform hazardous work in agriculture without penalty to growers (Nixon 1995, 23). Even when child labor laws are broken, weak enforcement and skimpy fines do little to punish violators. Few states in the Southeast assess strict fines for child labor violations in agriculture or have child labor inspectors. For example, employers who violate the child labor laws in Florida receive only a warning for the first violation, while violators in South Carolina receive a minimal fine of fifty dollars (Nixon 1995, 22).

Numerous health risks are associated with farm work including chemical exposure and work-related injuries. Farm equipment and pesticides make farm work one of the most dangerous jobs in the United States. In fact, farmworkers suffer from the highest rate of toxic chemical injuries of any U.S. workers. And as Davis points out, "Children are more likely to be harmed by pesticide exposures than are adults because children have lower body weight, higher metabolism, and immature immune and neurological systems" (Davis 1997, 15). According to Nixon, many children suffer tremendous damage from farm work:

23,500 children are injured and another 300 die on the farm each year. According to studies, children are more susceptible than adults to the effects of pesticides. Children absorb more than adults per pound of body weight, but the EPA standards for protecting workers from exposure to pesticides are based on adults only (Nixon 1995, 21).

While farm work is often debilitating for adults, its effects on children are even worse.

It is not difficult to understand why farmworker students drop out of school if one understands the hardships they face. Often, students are not motivated to go to school. At other times they find it difficult because they are so far behind other students of their same age or even younger. In this environment, their self-esteem suffers and going to school seems like a waste of time. The value of an education means little to a family needing income to pay for basic food and clothing. Many children trudge through school until they are old enough to begin working the fields full-time. This pattern repeats itself in many, if not most, farmworker families.

At the same time, most migratory students are highly motivated to escape the migrant lifestyle. Education provides a chance for these students to do so. With a high school and/or postsecondary education, students have the choice to pursue careers other than farm work. Yet this does not solve the problems faced by their families or other farmworkers who are unable to receive an education. While it is certainly an achievement for each student who escapes the migrant stream, it does not alter the system that keeps migrant farmworkers economically marginalized. If farm work itself is ever to be an economically viable and respectable job to which young people can aspire, the social structures that sustain farmworkers' poor housing conditions, lack of health care and nutrition, racial prejudice, and political marginality must be changed.

Isolation from the School Community

Lack of proficient English affects migrant students' ability to achieve in school. The first language of 75 percent of migrant students today is a language other than English, and often students are illiterate in their own languages (GEMS 1997, 95–96). These children may have moved away from their home countries at an early age, thereby not learning grammar and reading in their native languages. Arriving in the United States, the children's past challenges are compounded by new environments. While attempting to deal with the multitude of obstacles, migrant students have to adjust to learning English in order to succeed in school. Not only does lack of English proficiency affect migrant students' ability to learn in the classroom, but it also hampers students' ability to make friends and to participate in the school community, ultimately harming students' self-esteem and confidence.

Many migrant students' parents lack English proficiency. This makes it difficult for families to communicate with teachers or school administrators about problems concerning children, to attend parents' meetings, and to read and understand notes sent home about school events and reports on their children's progress. As Chavkin and Gonzalez explain, Mexican Americans clearly differentiate between the roles of home and school in a child's education:

Mexican American parents see their role as being responsible for providing basic needs as well as instilling respect and proper behavior. They see the school's role as instilling knowledge. They believe that one should not interfere with the job of the other . . . Other barriers to parental involvement include a negative view of the school system, past negative experiences with education, and language barriers. Often parents view the school as a bureaucracy controlled by non-Hispanics. The school often

*reminds Mexican American parents of their own educational experiences
including discrimination and humiliation for speaking Spanish. Many
times the lack of bilingual staff can make parents feel powerless when they
are attempting to resolve problems or advocate for their children (Chavkin
and Gonzalez 1995).*

Migrant families' work schedules likewise make it difficult for parents to get involved even when they are willing to participate. Parents'
isolation from the school system and lack of English proficiency creates a bifurcation between students' primarily English-speaking classroom setting and Spanish-speaking home life. Problems between children and parents often occur when students become stronger in English
and choose no longer to speak Spanish.

These factors contribute to a general feeling of social isolation and
marginality, particularly between farmworker students' school and
home communities. When Spanish-speaking students attend schools
where they are in the minority, they rarely interact with the rest of the
student body. The problems with peers can range from other students
not wanting to interact with the "new" students to overt discrimination.
New immigrant students may even face rejection by Latino youth who
already are acculturated and do not want to be reminded of their past
uneasiness in a new school or community. This can lead to withdrawal
of new immigrants from other classmates (Saragoza 1994, 15).

Migrant students often feel unwanted and resented in the towns in
which they live; often they are teased and even ostracized because of
their differences in appearance, socioeconomic class, and ethnicity. A
generalized exclusion of migrant children and their families often pervades the local communities in which they live. For example, non-
migrant students might refuse to sit next to migrant students on the
school bus. Again, Ramiro Arceo describes his personal experience with
differences of identity:

*When we lived in Manteca, [California], around 1981, my two older sisters
and I were the last ones to be picked up by the bus in front of our house in
the grape orchard where my father worked. The only seats available were
beside other kids. When we would sit next to them for the ten-minute ride
to the school, they would frown and get up to sit next to another white kid.
Then they would start complaining about how dirty we were and laughing
at our clothes. At the time I didn't understand why they were saying that
because my mom would make us take a bath every night before going to*

*bed. She would also wash all of our clothes by hand behind the house be-
cause she said that the Laundromat in town was too expensive. I told her
many times to just wash them in the washer in town because our clothes
would stay dirty even after she had washed them. When we had to sit in
the long back seat of the bus, some kids would switch to sit next to me,
because I had lighter skin than my sisters. My older sister would always
get in trouble in school. She would get into fights because other girls would
make fun of her, the way she looked, and the clothes she was wearing.
Some kids would make fun of my clothes, but I didn't care. I would still
beat them running in track, even though I was running in cowboy boots
that my mom had bought me at K-mart. I wanted to get new clothes and
tennis shoes, but my mom said that we didn't have the money. She would
always say, "When you can work and have your own money you can buy
as many pairs of tennis shoes as you want." So I couldn't wait until I could
go to work so I could buy a pair of tennis shoes and get my sisters Barbie
stuff like the other girls (Arceo 1999).*

Students who are permanent residents in an area have built-in advantages: their teachers know them better and may know their parents, and
the students are more likely to share a common sense of belonging. Migratory students, by contrast, are "strangers," demanding of teachers a
greater level of effort to know them, to relate to them, and to find appropriate strategies for teaching them. Even teachers with the best intentions have difficulties working effectively with migratory students.
Many times, as migratory students become familiar with a particular
school system, the harvest season ends and they move to another town
or state with their parents and start over in another school. They do
not get to know their teachers well enough to consult them about their
troubles in school. At the same time, teachers do not get to know these
students enough to notice when there is a problem or to know how to
assist them. Though teachers may realize that these students need additional help, they may not know how to provide it or might decide it is
not worth spending the time since the students will be moving soon.

All these factors combine to make school a difficult and even dreadful
place for migrant farmworker students. Lack of peer and teacher support
makes school tiring. Farmworker students often lose motivation to continue their studies and look forward to being old enough to join their
parents in the fields.

Mobility and Education

Significant institutional barriers deter migrant students' success. Graduation requirements vary from state to state as well as among districts within a state. Scheduling classes for migratory high school students may prove pointless unless they are enrolled in courses that count toward graduation in the state where they intend to receive their diplomas. Furthermore, required courses vary widely from state to state. A notorious example within the Migrant Education Program is the Texas requirement that a student must pass a unit in Texas history to graduate from a Texas school, regardless of the length of time a student spends in schools in other states.

Inherent difficulties arise in transferring credits, especially partial credits, from one school to another. One of the disadvantages of locally autonomous schools for any mobile student is the prerogative of local administrators to accept or reject credits earned elsewhere. Students' lack of protection is compounded by state-to-state and even school-to-school differences in course descriptions so that, for example, an English course taken in Michigan may not meet expectations of a counselor in Texas. Many migratory students fail to receive credit for partial work that is interrupted by a move to another school.

School schedules differ as well. Southern schools commonly start earlier than northern schools. Some start at least two weeks before Labor Day and complete the school year before the end of May, while northern schools typically start after Labor Day and continue until mid-June. Many migratory students who stay in their home-base schools until almost the end of the spring term find themselves in limbo in a northern school only to repeat work already done, yet where the summer migrant program still is four to six weeks away. Worse, migratory students who start school after Labor Day in the North and then return to Texas or Florida six weeks later may find that even though they were out of school only three days in the northern school, they are already three weeks behind in the southern system.

When families move from one place to another it is usually because the parents have a job or know that one will be available immediately after arriving. As soon as they arrive in the new location they start working. Meanwhile, the children are left at home waiting for someone to enroll them in school. As a result, children often miss weeks of school when they first arrive in a new community. Parents who do not speak English and do not know of anyone in the school who speaks their language find it extremely difficult to enroll their children ahead of time. Again, Ramiro Arceo speaks from experience:

I always wondered why my sisters were the oldest ones in their classes. They would just be one grade behind each other in school. But one of my sisters is five years older than the other one. My sisters would say that they were like that in school because they didn't know very much. "Besides," they would tell me, "we are going to get out of school soon to work" (Arceo 1999).

At the very least, any interruption in a student's education means instructional time lost, both in the time consumed in moving from one site to another—which for migratory families can be more than two thousand miles—and in the time spent in becoming acclimated to the new school environment. Educational disruption was a principal reason for a categorical program for migrant children, but it was only in the 1994 reauthorization of the Migrant Education Program that Congress specified that children whose education was interrupted would receive a priority for services. However, under the impact of the MEP, some migrant families had delayed migrations long enough for children to complete school or made arrangements for children to stay with relatives through the end of the year or during the opening months of school in the fall.

Strategies for Addressing Barriers

Despite such horrific experiences, it is possible for schools with migrant students to provide an environment in which these students are more confident. By identifying with schoolmates from the same ethnic background and who speak their language, regardless of whether they are children of migrant farmworkers, students can fit in more easily and find their "voices." Peer support for students is important in combating isolation and creating an environment in which they feel confident that they can fit in and succeed in school.

Schools have attempted to deal with the special educational needs of migrant students in a multitude of ways. Many models and strategies have proven helpful to these students and have been creatively employed by schools.

One such method is the transitional model. The Madera Unified

School District in California has developed a transitional center that migrant students attend for nine months before joining a regular school. These Newcomer Assessment Centers familiarize youths with the school, develop basic reading and writing skills, and establish an individual learning plan for each student (Morse 1997). This model attempts to make the transition to a school environment less difficult for students who have not attended a U.S. school before. Other schools offer a supplementary model, providing after-school tutorial support, literacy, and English as a Second Language (ESL) classes in addition to school. This is a useful model particularly for immigrant students who need help in learning English, which in many cases is their biggest obstacle to migrant students reaching their full potential.

Numerous school-based strategies attempt to provide an atmosphere that will reduce anxiety and cultivate respect for diversity. Susan Morse suggests that bilingual staff members and student ambassadors can help students become acclimated to new schools (Morse 1997). Schools that attempt to address students' apprehensions and fears through school-based strategies are making important advances in migrant education. Providing students with language instruction is another essential strategy if students are to stay in school.

However, providing students with bilingual teachers has proven to be more of a challenge than imagined, mainly due to the scarcity of bilingual teachers. LeBlanc, citing Fleishman and Hopstock, says, "There are more than 360,000 teachers providing instruction to these students, but only 10 percent are credentialed bilingual teachers, and only 33 percent have ever taken a college course on culture, language acquisition, or teaching English to limited-English-proficient (LEP) pupils. To further aggravate the problem, the majority of these teachers are not proficient in Spanish" (LeBlanc 1996, 154). In light of these findings, a binational initiative between the United States and Mexico has been developed to increase the number of qualified bilingual teachers and to increase teachers' awareness of Mexican history and culture.

The Binational Initiative for Educational Development was established by the Office of Bilingual Education and Minority Language Affairs (OBEMLA) and the University of Texas at El Paso to enhance education in the El Paso/Ciudad Juarez region. The binational approach strives to develop educational ideas using the extensive knowledge of educators in both Mexico and the United States. It is a collaboration between the two nations that aims to develop effective strategies that will serve as a model for all schools with migrant students throughout the United

States. The initiative aims to develop essential models for U.S. educators by investigating issues of mutual interest and concern through collaborative projects and a sharing of ideas on bilingual and binational education. Importantly, this collaboration has developed effective classroom strategies for teachers with migrant students that focus on the inclusion of cultural material from both nations.

The binational initiative has found that classroom strategies need to be creative if migrant students are going to remain engaged in the classroom and retain feelings of cultural pride. It is in the classroom that a student's perception of school and education will be shaped. Teachers must utilize strategies that are culturally sensitive and interesting to the student and that value the student's ethnicity and culture. Morse suggests the following classroom strategies: providing activities that appeal to all modes of learning (art, music, verbal, mathematical, logic, inter/intrapersonal skills, physical); having students work in cooperative learning groups that offer opportunities to interact successfully with their peers; using constructive strategies to develop thinking skills and the ability to access information; and drawing upon students' previous learning and experiences (Morse 1997).

Other successful classroom strategies developed by the binational initiative include using multicultural children's literature and focusing on national celebrations of different cultures. For example, by celebrating Mexico's Day of the Dead, comparing it to Halloween, and examining the specific customs of these similar celebrations, all the students can learn. Other ideas include having students make artwork and discuss it with the class or having students write histories of their own immigration to the United States. There are also opportunities to relate Latino experiences to those of other ethnic groups in the United States (LeBlanc 1996, 235).

According to Chavkin and Gonzalez, "One of the most promising ways to increase students' achievements is to involve their families" (Chavkin and Gonzalez 1995). Parental involvement is essential to migrant students remaining in school. Effective strategies for parental involvement must take into account access to the school by parents, their limited English, and their perceptions of educators and school institutions. Schools must be creative and sensitive in the methods they employ to involve parents. Sending written letters home should be avoided, as parents might not be able to read Spanish or English. Home visits to parents conducted in a culturally sensitive manner by a bilingual school representative will increase parents' involvement and communication.

Parents can become directly involved in their child's school; one means of encouraging this is asking active parents to invite other parents of migrant students to get involved in the school community.

Interstate coordination of migratory students' education must be a priority. Educators from a number of states met in 1968 to establish a process for exchanging student records across state lines. Two years of planning led to the creation of a national database, the Migrant Student Record Transfer System (MSRTS), which represented one of the earliest successes in a broad-based harnessing of technology to an educational need. MSRTS was for many years the cement that held the Migrant Education Program together, and it was through the planning and early implementation of the system that state officials coalesced into the National Association of State Directors of Migrant Education (NASDME). NASDME provided a vehicle through which educators addressed interstate coordination problems and priorities.

Either directly through NASDME or through the state-to-state linkages fostered by NASDME, migrant educators developed an array of services, structures, and mechanisms to address particular challenges such as teacher exchanges. Early in the history of Migrant Education, educators began to address the issue of credit transfer and accrual for migrant students. Because of established programs like the Texas Migrant Interstate Program and its more recent counterpart in Florida, the task is more manageable now. These programs ensure that transcripts are forwarded to the appropriate schools and advocate on behalf of students to see that credits are awarded properly.

Other Programs Supporting Farmworker Children

The East Coast Migrant Head Start Program (ECMHSP) is an educational assistance program that focuses specifically on infants, toddlers, and preschoolers who fall within the poverty guidelines and have moved or traveled with their families within the previous twelve months for the families' agricultural work. ECMHSP works with existing agencies that are capable of carrying out its goals and services. The six components of this program are education, health information and services, nutrition, social services providing information on community services and resources available to migrant parents, parental involvement in the development of their own children, and a special effort to recruit and serve children with disabilities.

Portable Assisted Study Sequence (PASS), a series of packaged semi-independent study courses, was developed to provide alternative means for earning high school credit. The High School Equivalency Program (HEP) is one such program that aids migrant and seasonal farmworkers in their pursuit of the General Educational Development test (GED) diploma or the HSED (High School Equivalency Diploma). The goal of the HEP program is to assist students in the successful completion of these certificates through preparation, classroom instruction, and tutorial assistance. HEP also provides transportation to and from class, a weekly stipend, housing for those in residential programs, and academic and vocational training.

With help from these and other programs, many farmworker students do succeed in school. Yet many are not well informed about college. After struggling to make it through school, they may face a dead end. However, the federal government has funded programs in some colleges and universities to help children of farmworkers continue their education. One of these is the College Assistance Migrant Program (CAMP), which operates at twenty colleges and universities around the country in states where large concentrations of farmworkers live. This program provides computer labs, counselors, tutors, and stipends to migrant students during their first year in college, the most difficult stage for students at this level of their education. It has proven successful; its participants have one of the highest retention rates of college freshmen. According to Marcos Sánchez, director of the CAMP at California State University at Sacramento, nearly 100 percent of the CAMP students complete their first year, about 90 percent continue on to their second year, and approximately 70 percent graduate after five years in college. The CSU-Sacramento CAMP is one of the largest, with an incoming class of about eighty-five to ninety students each year.

This program's success is due in part to the personalized attention and support that students receive from CAMP peers. Since most of the CAMP staff and tutors come from similar backgrounds, they understand the difficulties that students experience and how best to support them. Even though in theory CAMP only provides aid for the students their first year, alumni come back year after year to give and receive tutorial assistance, speak with counselors, use computer labs, or provide help to CAMP freshmen. Programs like CAMP make a difference in farmworker students' lives by specifically recruiting students from high schools in agricultural communities, encouraging younger students to attend college, and informing them of the many career and academic options available to them.

FIGURE 8.2. *Ramiro Arceo speaks to migrant students about staying in school, 1996. Photograph by Chris Johnson.*

Other programs motivate migrant students to stay in school and graduate as well. One is Project Levante (meaning "raise up" in Spanish), coordinated by Student Action with Farmworkers (SAF) with support from the Migrant Education Program in North Carolina. Project Levante reaches out to middle and high school migrant farmworker students. This program uses various methods to motivate migrant students to stay in school, from leadership retreats, conferences, and workshops to art programs for photography and theater.

SAF staff members have found that the theater component is one of the most successful ways to get students, parents, and educators talking about the barriers students face in schools. Student interns from SAF's Into the Fields summer program perform plays about the importance of staying in school and how educators and parents can support students. After the performances, the interns facilitate a discussion about how the issues in the play affect them.

At Levante leadership development conferences and retreats, students and Migrant Education staff share ideas and concerns with their peers about better ways to serve the migrant student population. Migrant students have the opportunity to learn from their peers about how to make school a supportive place for them. SAF college interns also serve as mentors for younger migrant farmworker students. Those SAF interns who are former farmworkers or are children of Latino migrant workers serve as role models for younger students, supporting those who wish to stay in school and pursue an education.

Steady Success for Migrant Students

Vidal A. Rivera, Jr., director of the Federal Office of Migrant Education for its first sixteen years, had a succinct phrase for capturing the essential biases in Migrant Education. He said, "This is our country—we do things differently here." In effect, this is exactly the attitude migrant children encounter each time they enroll in a new school. This is why Rivera spoke of the nation's school districts as being sixteen thousand little kingdoms with their own laws, customs, and rituals, some of which are invariably unfamiliar to the newcomer. State and local operation of schools is sometimes touted as one of the United States' greatest values, the cornerstone of democracy. Even if this were true, it would be hard to deny that the independence of each state's school system and the relative independence of many districts in many states can result in obstacles for children who move from school to school.

Yet despite the myriad challenges educators and students face, we must take heart from the growing success attributable to Migrant Education Programs. In the face of many barriers to education, graduation rates for migrant students continue to improve steadily. The National Program for Secondary Credit Exchange and Accrual reported that 50.7 percent of migrant students nationally graduated from high school in 1992, compared to the graduation rate in 1974 of less than 11 percent (U.S. Department of Education 1994).

Despite enormous difficulties, many migrant students do advance to college or vocational training and eventually on to careers of their choice. Strong family ties and supportive communities greatly add to their success. Education and farmworker advocates must work together with migrant students and families to achieve and maintain further successes.

I Don't Think People Give Up

Sheila Payne, farmworker organizer

Interview by Melinda Steele, 1998 SAF intern

To me it's the most basic right, all the other organizing I do around peace, justice, and poverty issues, other activists I've worked with don't see labor as the most basic thing to fight for, but I do. That advocacy stuff that I do always comes back mostly to what power that [people] have economically, and whether they have power, whether they have rights where they work. To me, it doesn't make sense to not care about these issues. And farmworkers just don't have any power, it's really hard to organize them, and because a lot of it is transient, and people come and go. Like right now, the H-2C program, I just wrote my letters, everyone knows there's too many workers and it's just a way to keep people from being able to organize.

I don't see the workers being empowered anymore, every time I'm involved in a new campaign, and I actually meet the workers, I don't get a sense of anything but starting back at the beginning. You know, you just have to start over each time. It doesn't build on itself, like other labor campaigns. The workforce keeps changing and once they leave, nothing that's happened to them applies anywhere else. There's new people that come in.

The farmers are going to try to get rid of any people who have any kind of union ideals, we'll never see those workers again in that community. And, yeah I guess I'm basically recycling. I mean there's so many tricks to it, to be able to close down farms or fields, and not even have to honor any of the negotiated contracts. I mean even if it's without a union contract, just to have negotiated with the workers that you work with, when workers go to growers and say we want this, this, and this, I mean, even if that does work, it's never binding, and it never lasts very long. I just think you have to fight the fight all the time, I don't think people give up.

CHAPTER 9

From Slavery to Cesar Chavez and Beyond

Farmworker Organizing in the United States

Paul Ortiz

If there is no struggle, there is no progress. Those who profess to favor freedom, and yet depreciate agitation, are men who want crops without plowing up the ground. They want rain without thunder and lightning. They want the ocean without the awful roar of its many waters.

FREDERICK DOUGLASS,

FORMER SLAVE AND FARMWORKER (1857)

Reconstruction and Farm Labor

Students of history know that the Civil War ended slavery in the South. Fewer are aware that for agricultural workers in the South, slavery was replaced by institutions and laws such as debt peonage, sharecropping, and convict labor that kept millions of African Americans and many poor whites segregated from economic, social, and political power for generations after the Confederate surrender at Appomattox (Daniel 1972).

W. E. B. Du Bois noted that the southern elite was determined to maintain a low-wage labor force. Du Bois cites the case of Judge Humphrey of Alabama, who stated:

I believe, in case of a return to the Union, we would receive political co-operation so as to secure the management of that labor by those who were slaves. There is really no difference in my opinion, whether we hold them as absolute slaves or obtain their labor by some other method (Du Bois 1935, 140).

One hundred thirty years later, Farm Labor Organizing Committee (FLOC) organizers in North Carolina reported a grower near New Bern who boasted, "The North won the War on paper but we Confederates actually won because we kept our slaves. First we had sharecroppers, then tenant farmers and now we have Mexicans" (Farm Labor Organizing Committee 2000).

During the early stages of Reconstruction, however, the power of planters to control society and politics seemed to be coming to an end. For a few critical years, newly freed slaves enjoyed the support of the radical wing of the Republican Party as well as the aid of sympathetic missionaries who came South to teach literacy skills to African Americans. Exercising the right to vote for the first time in their lives, plantation workers in the late 1860s and early 1870s demanded a wide range of reforms in the United States. Newly enfranchised African American farm laborers agitated for land redistribution, free schools, state-mandated minimum wages, and a ceiling on interest rates. According to Du Bois, "They tried to secure laws to prevent the discharge of laborers before they were paid, or the removal of crops before satisfactory settlement. They objected to the working of plantations by gangs, and wished to lease farms" (Du Bois 1935, 416–417).

African Americans demanded a stake in their society. Above all, former slaves struggled for land and the ballot. In 1867, a correspondent from Florida reported hopefully: "They are all seeking lands for themselves and building houses to live in. Some have been fortunate enough to make five or ten bales of cotton and many bushels of corn . . . We are all looking for the day when we shall vote, to sustain the great Republican Party" ("Letter from Jax" 1867). "It has been said that the Negro here will not work, that they are becoming indolent and vicious," wrote an African American minister in Florida. "The facts are," he continued, "they have become tired of working without pay . . . Those who have considered it their God-given right to swindle the Negro out of the hard earned money due him are left without help" ("Land and Labor" 1877).

Many growers believed that they must achieve complete domination over their workers before they would be able to institute a profitable system of agriculture. This process of disenfranchisement was especially transparent in Florida, a state that would become notorious for its harsh agricultural labor relations in the twentieth century (Wilkins 1990). Employers used two tools to erase democracy in Florida: violence and "the black list." African Americans testified that plantation owners in Florida used the Ku Klux Klan to target small black landowning farmers as well as laborers who demanded higher wages (*Testimony Taken by the Joint Selection Committee* 1872, 54–59). In Leon County, white supremacists targeted 10 percent of the plantation workforce for reprisals as a penalty for engaging in politics. The employers formed a "club" to institute this list: "Let every member of this club bind himself to refrain from rent[ing] land or a house to, or to employ as a labourer for any consideration however small, any one whose name appears on the Black List—Refuse shelter & employment to every one—Let them drift away silently from the neighbourhood by the *force of circumstances* . . ." ("Hints for the Consideration of White Men" n.d., emphasis in the original).

Speaking at a political rally in 1884, R. C. Long, a spokesman for Florida plantation-owner interests, articulated a strategy for white employers to slash wages: call a constitutional convention that would effectively take the vote away from African American agricultural workers. Long shouted from the podium:

We are going to have a Constitutional Convention in less than eight months; that convention will be controlled by white men; no one but white men will be allowed a vote there; the angel Gabriel himself will not be allowed a vote; and don't you forget that the status of the nigger as a factor in the politics of this State will then be fixed. Then we want them to come [to Florida]. There are thousands of niggers in Georgia and Alabama who are working from 25 to 50 cents per day, while, in South Florida especially, we are being compelled to pay from one dollar and a quarter to two dollars a day ("Democratic Doctrine" 1884).

Long promised that when African Americans lost their political rights and any hope of attaining land, employers would be able to slash their wages and lynch them if they complained. The construction of white supremacy in the United States rested upon the subjugation of African American agricultural workers. These long-forgotten events provide vital clues regarding the contemporary powerlessness of farmworkers in U.S. society. Chicano historian Ernesto Galarza argued that farmworkers were discriminated against in large part because their ancestors did not own land (Galarza 1977). Because most farmworkers live on growers' land, they lose the ability to speak freely or communicate openly with the outside world and seek assistance. Farmworker advocates should question the unequal distribution of land that characterizes the rural United States and facilitate independent living situations for farmworkers. Initiatives such as the Housing Development Corporation of the North Carolina Council of Churches, which assists farmworkers to become homeowners, should be replicated throughout the country.

Florida's plantation owners discovered that the most effective tool for maintaining slavery and peonage was to bar laborers' access to citizenship. Today, this means that farmworker advocates must continue to push for immigration reforms, a general amnesty, and a streamlined process of gaining legal permanent residency and citizenship. Union organizers have long understood the importance of voting to attain the goal of creating an empowered working-class citizenry. Without the franchise, farmworkers today are as powerless as African Americans were during the period of legal segregation.

"A Scarcity of Labor"

Despite losing the franchise and seeing their aspirations for democracy crushed after Reconstruction, African American farmworkers in Florida did not give up the struggle to improve their lives. When World War I erupted, industrial employers in the North sent out a call for more workers to help fill wartime orders from Europe. Many African Americans in the Deep South, including Florida, migrated North in search of higher wages and political freedom.

Black agricultural workers who stayed in Florida took advantage of the more favorable labor market and began organizing. At the end of October 1919, Crescent City "Negro orange pickers connected with the Sawyer & Godfrey packing house went on strike . . . , demanding 10 cents per box for picking" ("Orange Pickers May Strike" 1919). African American laborers in the potato region around Palatka began organizing a similar campaign for higher wages. A black newspaper enthusiastically noted, "Everywhere we hear the cry for labor almost at its own price. Minors are paid $2.00 per day in the potato fields while skilled labor is being offered 80 cents per hour and more" (*New York Age* 1920).

African American farmworkers in Florida fought to increase the hourly wage rate as high as they could. Beating a tactical retreat, some growers' associations began offering $3.50 a day for field labor, a major increase over the wages current just two years earlier but still lower than what Florida turpentine and timber workers were demanding, according to the U.S. Employment Service ("Skilled Labor in Jacksonville" 1919). African American farmworkers seized on this new wage scale and held onto it with every ounce of bargaining power they possessed.

A writer for *The Florida Grower* dramatized the battle between black workers and white employers over the wage scale, stating that he advised newly arrived white farmers from the North to beware of farm laborers' demands. "I had just passed through a grove section where I had been told that there was a scarcity of labor and where they were paying negroes $3.50 a day for common labor" (Whitman 1920). Hamilton County employers complained, "Farm labor has become plutocratic, causing thousands of fertile acres to remain idle, and with only a few small 'patches' planted to corn, cotton, etc." ("Farmers Backward" 1920).

Black workers trying to organize for better wages in Florida confronted severe obstacles including police repression. "The Hastings potato section is not going to sit idly by and witness agitators entering its confines to encourage laborers to strike, just because the agitator thinks that they should strike," thundered the *Palatka Morning Post*. Subsequently, farmworker activists in the region were arrested and removed from the fields ("Labor in the Potato Section" 1920). When African American workers in Florida began registering to vote in 1919, white supremacists struck back with a vengeance. The Ku Klux Klan reorganized and began to assassinate black activists in rural areas, while state authorities ensured that black Floridians would not be able to vote on election day (Ortiz 2000). The postwar downturn of the economy ended the state's relative labor shortage, and growers regained the upper hand.

The Southern Tenant Farmers' Union

Working people forged new social movements during the Great Depression. The Southern Tenant Farmers' Union (STFU), which organized union locals in Arkansas, Oklahoma, Mississippi, Missouri, and Tennessee, was one of the most important new movement organizations. The STFU was an interracial union that at its peak had twenty-five thousand members (Kester 1969; Naison 1996, 106). The STFU owed its remarkable growth to cooperative networks of activist farmworkers, veteran political organizers, clergy, Socialists, and student supporters who raised funds and spread awareness of the union's struggles through events such as National Sharecroppers Week ("New York Hears Sharecroppers" 1937).

The Southern Tenant Farmers' Union grew because it helped to restore the dignity of impoverished farm laborers in the South. The STFU fought against the eviction of members from their homes, agitated for higher wages, and sought to end the tyrannical power that large land-owners exercised over southern counties. Members discovered that collective action often brought improvements in their communities. In 1935 an Arkansas STFU local reported that plantation owners began paying for much-needed repairs on tenants' houses. "Until the Southern Tenant Farmers' Union began organizing," The *Sharecroppers' Voice* reported, "the Arkansas planters rarely made any effort to repair a house . . . Moral: JOIN THE UNION AND WE WILL MAKE THEM ALL PROVIDE HOUSES DECENT TO LIVE IN" ("Improved Conditions Result" 1935).

Seeking to gain self-respect, higher wages, and a measure of democracy, sharecroppers joined the STFU in large numbers. An African American woman in Arkansas explained why she wanted to join the union:

Dear Sirs, I am a widow . . . also a share-cropper. I have two children with me. We have worked half-hungry to make this crop with no clothing. The house we live in has never been finished and now it is old . . . Every time any one on this plantation . . . tries to get another place we are made to move or whipped . . . I am sick, no way to get a Doctor . . . I saw the Demands of the Union for share-croppers. Honest, when can we get it! ("People's Column" 1935).

While the STFU was cofounded by a group of Socialist Party members, local chapters enjoyed considerable autonomy. The blending of Socialist ideas about workers' control and land redistribution meshed quite well with the intense Christianity of black and white farmers. A kind of liberation theology emerged from the STFU's meetings. "Jesus of Nazareth was an Agitator," became a popular refrain among STFU members, "a very dangerous one too." The union members asserted:

The rich men of His day had Him crucified—Nailed to the Cross. It was charged "That He Stirreth up the people." Should He return to earth . . . in Arkansas if the night riders didn't string Him up or throw Him in the St. Francis River, the lawyers and the preachers would frame Him up for Anarchy. In Georgia He would face a sentence of twenty years on a chain gang ("Agitators for a Better Life" 1935).

The STFU also became popular among the poor because the union argued that landless farmers, sharecroppers, and tenants alike should share in New Deal relief programs ("S.T.F.U. Members Get W.P.A. Jobs" 1938). In an era when the federal government began heavily subsidizing agriculture and delivering checks directly to large growers, STFU leaders kept up a constant lobbying presence in Washington, D.C., in an attempt to ensure that non-landowning farmers shared in the new federal benefit programs ("Government to Crack Down on Unfair Planters" 1938). The union did not enjoy great success in this area. Franklin Delano Roosevelt needed the support of southern plantation owners who controlled the Democratic Party in the one-party South.

Another social force that crippled the STFU was the mechanization of agriculture. Southern growers used cash payments received directly from the federal government to purchase tractors and other farming implements such as cotton harvesters, which sped up the substitution of machinery for human labor. To its credit, the STFU sought to counter the devastating impacts of farm mechanization on its membership by establishing what it called "migratory locals" ("STFU Starts Migratory Organization" 1940). However, there is little evidence that these locals took root in an increasingly hostile environment in which STFU leaders were being whipped, driven off of their land, and assassinated ("Another Killing" 1935).

Agricultural workers in the United States were very active in the "Silent '50s" and early 1960s. In the Mississippi and Arkansas delta region, veteran African American STFU activists formed the bulwark of an underground community of activists; the resulting wave of rural movements culminated in the formation of the Mississippi Farm Labor Union (MFLU) in 1965 (Woodruff 1993, 33–51). Black plantation workers like Fannie Lou Hamer understood the connection between their lack of civil rights and their crushing poverty. Given the risks involved, a surprising number of African American small farmers joined the National Association for the Advancement of Colored People (NAACP) in the years after World War II. An even larger number "voted with their feet" and moved to urban areas in the South as well as the North in search of economic opportunity and political equality. In California, Cesar Chavez, Dolores Huerta, and other Mexican American Community Service Organization (CSO) activists encouraged farmworkers to register to vote as a first step to reforming a political system that was under the control of agribusiness and other anti-labor forces. Rural protest in the Deep South as well as the West Coast during this era involved farmworkers' efforts to regain the citizenship rights they viewed as being integral to their ability to sustain themselves and their families.

Organizing a Social Movement

In 1993 the farmworker movement suffered a terrible blow. The cofounder of the United Farm Workers of America (UFW), Cesar Estrada Chavez, died. Born in 1927, Chavez, a son of farmers and migrant parents, sacrificed his health and ultimately his life to help build and lead the most successful farm labor union in U.S. history. Chavez had engaged in a series of water-only fasts ranging from twenty-four to thirty-six days to dramatize the greater deprivation suffered by hundreds of thousands of farmworkers in the United States. Battling to the end, the UFW leader died in Yuma, Arizona, where he had been fighting a lawsuit by the Bruce Church Lettuce Company that threatened to destroy the union.

Chavez had asked his brother Richard to bury him in a plain, unvarnished pine casket. In death as in life, the president of the UFW was careful to place himself no higher than the people he had helped to organize. "Ninety-five percent of the strikers lost their homes and their cars," Chavez stated after the first grape boycott ended successfully in 1970. "But I think," he continued, "that in losing those worldly possessions they found themselves, and they found that only through dedication, through serving mankind, and, in this case, serving the poor and those who were struggling for justice, only in that way could they really find themselves" (Levy 1975, 325). Cesar Chavez never owned a house or a car. "He didn't believe you could organize the poor unless you were willing to share in their plight," recalled Chavez's son-in-law Arturo S. Rodriguez (Rodriguez 1993).

In the early 1960s Chavez and his family arrived in Delano, California, and, with Dolores Huerta, founded the organization that would later become the National Farm Workers Association (NFWA) and ultimately the UFW. Chavez and a small but ever-growing cadre of activists that included fellow CSO veteran Gilbert Padilla and the young director of Migrant Ministry, Chris Hartmire, began canvassing farmworkers in labor camps, at pool halls, and in homes throughout the San Joaquin Valley. The NFWA concentrated its early energies on building support within the year-round or "settled out" farm labor force. Dorothy Healey, a veteran of the bitter Depression-era strikes in California agriculture, wrote, "I was very impressed with Cesar Chavez's grasp of organizing strategy. He started organizing around small fruit to begin with, where there was a semi-permanent work force. That gave the union continuity. These workers didn't move around to follow the different crops. You didn't start fresh every time there was a strike" (Healey and Isserman 1990, 52).

In 1962, however, strikes were a losing proposition for farmworkers. Excluded from the country's labor laws and denied protections to organize by the federal government's exclusionary National Labor Relations Act (NLRA), agricultural workers in the United States were virtually powerless. Carey McWilliams, who published his classic text on California farm labor around the same time that John Steinbeck wrote *The Grapes of Wrath*, found that growers routinely used vigilante violence and terror to prevent the "unionization of farm labor on any basis." McWilliams uncovered the existence of a concentration camp near Salinas that was built to imprison farmworker union activists. One grower claimed that the camp was constructed "to hold strikers, but of course we won't put white men in it, just Filipinos" (McWilliams 1929). McWilliams characterized the authority that agribusiness exerted in California as "Farm Fascism." Growers' federations, backed by the banking interests that controlled much of California agriculture, exerted enormous control over the state legislature and raked in tens of millions of dollars each year in federal subsidies (Galarza 1977, 363). In contrast, farmworkers received no federal benefits and had no voice in Sacramento or in Washington, D.C.

As a result, working conditions in the fields were brutal. Most growers refused to furnish clean drinking water in the sweltering fields. Clara Eliosa, a lettuce picker who worked near Salinas, recalled working in fields "where up to 150 workers toiled from sunrise to sundown and shared one bucket of drinking water" ("Rally for Cesar Chavez Street Brings Out 5,000 in Fresno" 1993). Few employers provided sanitary outhouses. Women and men were crippled after years of stooping to work over row crops with short-handled hoes, relics of slavery that were referred to by field hands as *el brazo del diablo*, "the devil's arm." While they were working, farmworkers frequently were sprayed in the fields with toxic pesticides like DDT. At the time, no regulations required employers to apply such insecticides safely.

"We can't afford to lose our jobs, so we keep quiet and don't complain and the farmers think we are happy," lamented Ernesto Loredo, a California farmworker. Loredo explained: "You whistle in the fields and you go out and get drunk on Saturday night because you can't face the truth—that you are so damned poor, that the kids are sick and that your life is depression" (Meister and Loftis 1977). Like many others who labored in the agricultural industry, Jessie de la Cruz lost a child to these abysmal conditions. "The cause was the way we were living," Jessie de la Cruz remembered, "under the tree, with only chicken wire to separate us from the cows and horses. There were thousands of flies. I didn't have a refrigerator, no place to refrigerate the milk. She got sick. I couldn't stop the diarrhea and my little girl died. We were so poor and I felt so helpless—there was nothing I could do" (Cantarow 1980, 118).

The primary topic of discussion between NFWA activists and stressed-out farmworkers boiled down to the dismal living conditions. Cesar Chavez believed from the outset that farmworkers needed to build a labor union to improve their lives. However, Chavez's training and experience as an activist in the CSO had taught him that the top-down models of leadership used in traditional service agencies or mainstream labor unions would not work with migrant workers. Instead, the young activist worked with local communities to tackle social problems that the people could work together to solve.

The organizing philosophy of the NFWA was simple. Give people a reason to attend the meetings and share the leadership. Ask new members to contribute whatever they have—dues, food, time, and so forth—to keep the organization running. Encourage men and women to develop their own solutions to problems instead of dictating the solutions as if one was presenting a classroom lecture. Show new members that they can begin to change their lives for the better. NFWA organizers and farmworkers began tackling job discrimination, police harassment, and difficulties securing loans. "We'd take the big problems that they [farmworkers] had," Chavez noted, "some of the police problems, labor problems like nonpayment of wages, and [workers'] compensation cases. We'd service problems at county hospitals, anything that affected them. This was a community Union" (Levy 1975, 171).

In the process of challenging longstanding patterns of racism, farmworkers discovered that they had the ability to initiate social change. When an action failed, and many did, members regrouped to talk to each other about what went wrong and how to do better the next time. Fred Ross, the founder of CSO and Chavez's mentor in the pre-NFWA days, recalled that Chavez was adept at forming relationships of trust and encouraging people to develop their own leadership abilities:

[T]he Service Center, with Cesar in command, was much more than your routine problem clinic; it was a sovereign restorative of human dignity and a means of drawing the people, whose lifestyle had been one of being pushed around by the authorities without a peep, soon learned to stand their ground, speak out, and get what they came after. In the agony of forcing themselves to do this, they suffered a sea change: they got organized (Ross 1989, 24).

Restoring human dignity. Regaining self-respect. This is what organizing is all about. In the process of leading a number of highly successful campaigns for Mexican American citizenship and voter registration, initiated by the CSO in the 1950s, Cesar Chavez, Dolores Huerta, Gilbert Padilla, and other activists had learned to listen carefully to the ideas of workers themselves rather than trying to solve everything for them. This patient perseverance likewise was employed by Myles Horton, the founder of the Highlander Center in Tennessee. As a young activist during the Depression, Horton grew angry with the many low-income people he tried to organize who were "apathetic" about their situations. Horton discovered that he was making an error. "I said to myself," Horton recalled, "I've got to find a way to work with people who should be angry but aren't. And, if I turn them off by saying, 'We've got to do this now, I can't stand it any longer,' and make it too much of a personal thing, then I'm not going to be able to make a contribution to any change" (Horton, Kohl, and Kohl 1990, 80; Matthiessen 1971, 284).

Successful community organizing takes time, great amounts of it. People do not rebel against oppressive situations or initiate social movements because times are hard. For farmworkers, times had always been hard. Yet beyond wildcat strikes and a series of failed organizing drives dating back to the turn of the century, no successful mass movement had emerged to permanently improve conditions in California agriculture (Daniel 1981). Most *campesinos* understandably feared the power that agribusiness exerted over their lives and their communities. Farmworkers did not need to read *The Grapes of Wrath* to understand that the entire power structure of California—from local law enforcement to the governor's office—was arrayed on the side of agribusiness.

Acutely aware of this painful history, NFWA organizers issued no manifestos or dramatic press releases that would draw the ire of employers or the police. Instead, NFWA activists engaged in intimate discussions with farm laborers who talked in turn about the common problems they faced in California's fruit orchards and vegetable fields. "There are some very simple things that have to be done in organizing," Chavez believed, "certain key things that nobody could get away without doing, like talking to people. If you talk to people, you're going to organize them. But people aren't going to come to you. You have to go to them. It takes a lot of work" (Levy 1975, 161). Chavez and the other NFWA members learned by experience that successful organizing begins by building relationships of trust with other people. It happens no other way (Greider 1992, 223–224; Burtman 1995).

Chavez believed that one way to break through the fear that many farmworkers felt was to talk to them in a religious language that they understood and respected. Thus, Chavez frequently invoked the teachings of the Catholic Church and Pope John XXIII on economic justice and the rights of the world's agricultural workers to live lives of dignity. Lofty papal pronouncements on social justice did not always have much of an impact on local parishes. Farmworkers in California had experiences with priests and churches who sided with the growers who in turn funded many churches. Chavez understood this level of collusion between churches and employers and turned it upside down: God, Cesar Chavez emphasized, was really on the side of the poor. "Those who oppose our cause are rich and powerful," Chavez duly noted, "and they have many allies in high places. We are poor. Our allies are few. But we have something the rich do not own. We have our own bodies and spirits and the justice of our cause as our weapons . . . To be a man is to suffer for others. God help us to be men!" (Levy 1975, 286).

Sexism within Latino communities and the larger culture was a major obstacle faced by NFWA organizers. They understood that the fledgling union would fail if it excluded female farmworkers. One of the most revealing stories about the way that Chavez helped to challenge male-centered patterns of authority within Latino communities was told by Jessie de la Cruz, who noted that women had very little authority in their families. "Your husband would say, 'Go here,' you'd do it. You didn't dare go out without your husband saying you could." She recalled,

One night in 1962 there was a knock at the door and there were three men. One of them was Cesar Chavez. And the next thing I knew, they were sitting around our table talking about a union. I made coffee. Arnold [her husband] had already told me about a union for the farm workers. He was attending their meetings in Fresno, but I didn't. I'd either stay home or stay outside in the car. But then Cesar said, "The women have to be involved. They're the ones working out in the fields with their husbands. If you can take the women out to the fields, you can certainly take them to meetings." So I sat up straight and said to myself, "That's what I want" (de la Cruz 1987, 409–411).

The NFWA's grassroots organizing style took months of house meetings, countless conversations, and arguments to unfold. The payoffs were slow. One month, the group would sign up dozens of new members. The next month, the new members would stop coming to meetings. Still, Chavez and the NFWA never lost faith in its mission. He recalled, "Of every hundred workers I talked to, one would say, 'It's time.' Everybody said no one could organize farmworkers, that it couldn't be done. But we got a group of forty or fifty, and one by one, that's how we started" (Ferriss and Sandoval 1997, 11–12). After three years of intensive face-to-face meetings the NFWA grew to twelve hundred members.

While the NFWA was slowly building its membership base, hundreds of Filipino farmworkers, members of the Agricultural Workers Organizing Committee (AWOC), called a grape strike in Coachella Valley in the first week of September 1965. Picking grapes several miles away from the strike's epicenter, Philip Vera Cruz, a Filipino farmworker, was electrified by the news (Sengupta 1992). Vera Cruz came to the United States in 1926 hoping to become a lawyer. Instead, he joined the rest of the *Manong* generation of male Filipino migrants who worked in low-wage occupations and who were forbidden by U.S. immigration laws to bring their wives with them from the Philippines. Filipino farmworkers in California were subjected to harsh racism. As Pete Velasco, another Filipino farmworker, recalled: "When we walked the sidewalks in those early days, they shouted at us, 'Hey monkey, go home!'" (Bacon 1995). Four decades after his arrival in the United States, Philip Vera Cruz saw his opportunity to build an organization dedicated to justice and equality. "That's when I stopped picking grapes for the first time in over 20 years," Vera Cruz remembered. "And I never went back" (Sengupta 1992). The sixty-year-old farmworker became a strike leader. So did Pete Velasco.

The NFWA was faced with a momentous decision: join their Filipino brothers and sisters on strike or watch from the sidelines. After Dolores Huerta, the secretary-treasurer of AWOC, rushed to the picket line, the NFWA called a meeting to deliberate on the situation. By design, Chavez and the leadership of the organization decided to hold the strike vote on September 16, Mexican Independence Day. At the meeting, hundreds of NFWA members unanimously voted to support AWOC's strike against the Coachella grape growers. The die was cast for the most important farm labor struggle in modern U.S. history.

Workers, Students, and the Grape Boycott

To win this strike, farmworkers resurrected a venerable tool of the labor movement: the consumer boycott. Cesar

FIGURE 9.1. *SAF intern Lori with farmworker Vicente in a tobacco field, 1999. Photograph by Mendi Drayton.*

Chavez, Dolores Huerta, and others argued that a boycott of the California table-grape industry was the only way to achieve a major victory in the campaign. Conventional strikes, while inspiring and headline-generating, were not getting the job done. Agribusiness was so powerful that it was quickly able to pressure the courts to issue crippling injunctions against many of the local grape strikes. To compound the problem, since agricultural workers were not covered by the NLRA, growers fired farm labor union activists with impunity. The California Ku Klux Klan began burning crosses at ranches where workers were on strike. Governor Ronald Reagan dedicated state resources to fund convict laborers to replace striking workers. Once again, farmworkers discovered that the entire society was being used to stifle their efforts to improve their lives. Disheartened workers began drifting away from the picket lines, and employers recruited workers from Texas and Mexico to break the strikes. Two years into the struggle to organize the grape fields, *La Causa* was in serious trouble.

Chavez conceived of the boycott as a nonviolent tool of social change that would end the decades of isolation that farmworkers had suffered

in the United States ("Plática con Chavez" 1973). Strategically, the boycott of California table grapes would link farmworkers and consumers
in an alliance that could challenge the enormous power of agribusiness.
Chavez reasoned that Mahatma "Gandhi taught that the boycott is the
most nearly perfect instrument of non-violent change, allowing masses
of people to participate actively in a cause . . . Even if people cannot
picket with us or contribute money or food, they can take part in our
struggle by not buying certain products. It is such a simple sacrifice to
make" (Meister and Loftis 1977, 140).

Boycotts remind the larger public that issues such as exposure to toxic
pesticides affects everyone—consumers and *campesinos* alike. Trained
from an early age to avoid conflict, people in the United States sometimes forget that their nation was born from a famous boycott called the
Boston Tea Party. The survival of this democratic tool is a reminder that
while corporations may control politicians and markets, an organized
and energized citizenry can redeem social justice. During the grape boycott farmworkers expressed this idea by creating a new slogan on the
picket lines: "*Los rancheros son pocos, nosotros somos muchos*—The
ranchers are few, we are many."

To win the grape boycott, Chavez and the union had to educate U.S.
consumers. If consumers did not understand who was responsible for
tending and harvesting the bountiful crops that made U.S. agriculture
the envy of the world, then someone had to teach them. Chavez was
blunt: "We need the help of all to add power to the poor" ("Huelga Wins
One" 1970). Soon students joined workers, clergy, and other supporters
in boycott committees who were responsible for bringing the boycott
to the attention of the United States and eventually the world. Student activists, including members of the Student Non-Violent Coordinating Committee (SNCC), as well as members of the Congress of Racial
Equality (CORE) who had worked with the civil rights movement in
the South, played integral roles in the grape boycott. While Chavez welcomed student support, he urged the young volunteers, whether black,
white, Asian, or Chicano, not to overidealize the people they were working with:

In the beginning there was a lot of nonsense about the poor farm worker:
"Gee, the farm worker is poor and disadvantaged and on strike, he must be
a super human being!" And I said, "Cut that nonsense out, all right!" That
was my opening speech: "Look, you're here working with a group of men;
the farm worker is only a human being. You take the poorest of these guys

and give him that ranch over there, he could be just as much of a bastard as the guy sitting there right now. Or if you think that all growers are bastards, you're no good to us, either. Remember that both are men. *In order to help the farm workers, look at them as human beings and not as something extra special, or else you are kidding yourself and are going to be mighty, mighty disappointed. Don't pity them either. Treat them as human beings, because they have just as many faults as you have; that way you'll never be in trouble, because you'll never be disappointed"* (Matthiessen 1971, 115).

Teams of *campesinos*, students, and other supporters organized grape boycott committees across the United States. These committees set up informational leaflets and pickets at grocery stores, sought boycott endorsements, and exhorted unionized transportation workers to honor the boycott. Eventually, longshoremen in Oakland, sympathetic truck drivers on the West Coast, and European dock workers refused to load, unload, or deliver California table grapes. Such breakthroughs were critical. However, the real success of the boycott was in squeezing or closing off new markets to the profit-minded grape growers. Boycott committee members spent long hours in front of supermarkets explaining to consumers why they should support farmworkers.

On many occasions shoppers would greet student activists at storefronts with hostile remarks or unkind words. ("Get a job!" was a staple insult.) Over time, however, an increasing number of newly enlightened consumers took the UFW leaflets and marched right in to chastise store managers for siding with the exploitative growers. The persistent consumer-outreach work of the boycott committees gained momentum. Grape sales in urban markets like New York plummeted (Jenkins 1985, 171). Pressured by the now-constant leafleting and picketing, many supermarkets dropped California table grapes from their produce departments. College students pressured university administrators to purge grapes from campus menus. An executive order issued by President Richard Nixon to the Defense Department to increase its orders of table grapes only highlighted the fact that the boycott had placed the grape industry on the defensive.

The union, by now known as the United Farm Workers' Organizing Committee (UFWOC), had one overarching goal: to pressure agribusiness to sign contracts with farm laborers that would bring immediate improvements in working conditions. Collectively bargained union contracts give farmworkers the ability to negotiate for a greater voice in the terms of their employment. For Chavez, collective bargaining was the linchpin of his philosophy that farmworkers did not need charity—they needed the power to change their lives and the system altogether. Many other civil rights leaders including Rev. Martin Luther King, Jr., also recognized this need for structural change.

Most growers fought unionization with every tool at their disposal. Mack Lyons, a UFW organizer, recalled: "They [the growers] didn't see why they should be required to put ice in the water in the summertime, or to buy cups, so we would have individual drinking cups. Just some of the smallest things" (Ferriss and Sandoval 1997, 133). Lyons and his fellow workers were struggling for medical benefits, rest breaks, pensions, and an end to being sprayed by chemical pesticides. Local "ranch committees" of farmworkers were responsible for ensuring that contracts were enforced fairly and consistently.

The rank-and-file UFWOC organizers who entered the growers' fields —which were often guarded by armed men—to encourage and at times cajole workers to join the cause are the unsung heroes of the 1965–1970 struggle. Philip Vera Cruz moved relentlessly through the vineyards organizing Filipino and Mexican American workers. One worker whom Vera Cruz recruited, Eliseo Medina, recalled later that Vera Cruz "had a real deep concern for people and real anger at the way people were mistreated." To the nineteen-year-old Medina, the elder farmworker was "someone who had fire in his heart" (Sengupta 1992).

Jessie de la Cruz spread the idea of organization as a way to restore the battered sense of dignity that farmworkers felt after years of abuse. "I knew people were scared," de la Cruz noted, "but I told them I was scared too and that unless we unify, things were not going to change" (Sengupta 1992). Jessie de la Cruz became one of UFWOC's most effective organizers:

Wherever I went to speak to [farmworkers] they listened. I told them how we were excluded from the NLR[A] in 1935, how we had no benefits, no minimum wage, nothing out in the fields—no restrooms, nothing. I would talk about how we were paid what the grower wanted to pay us, and how we couldn't set a price on our work. I explained that we could do something about these things by joining a union, by working together (Cantarow 1980, 135).

UFWOC and its supporters relied heavily on expressive culture— songs, dances, and poetry, among other art forms—to spread their message and improve morale on the picket lines. No rally was complete without an invocation given by a priest who gave God's blessing to *La Causa*. At the same time, union members used the revolutionary iconography of Mexican American history to demonstrate the continuities between past struggles of *La Raza* and the grape boycott. During an informational session at a church in San Antonio, Texas, UFWOC organizers set up a table about the boycott that included bumper stickers, buttons, and posters of Mexican revolutionary heroes such as Emiliano Zapata and Pancho Villa ("S.A. Archbishop Gives Support to UFW" 1972). Union supporters used the past to build the movement. In turn, activists helped to teach a more egalitarian brand of U.S. history.

Luis Valdez, a young Chicano actor, approached Chavez early on in the grape boycott and proposed an audacious idea: use theater as a tool in the struggle. *El Teatro Campesino* was born. Valdez used *El Teatro* to create performances that explained union contracts, lampooned strike breakers, and celebrated Mexican American culture. Significantly, *El Teatro* cast farmworkers as actors in these performances, thus contributing to the growing sense of dignity that formerly isolated workers were building through their participation in the grape boycott and the larger *movimiento* (Benavidez 1997, 130).

Careful observers of the grape boycott understood what was at stake. In March 1968 another freedom fighter who frequently wielded the boycott as a weapon of social justice, Dr. Martin Luther King, Jr., sent a telegram to Chavez. He said, "My colleagues and I commend you for your bravery, salute you for your indefatigable work against poverty and injustice, and pray for your health and continuing service as one of the outstanding men of America. The plight of your people and ours is so grave that we all desperately need the inspiring example and effective leadership you have given" (Kushner 1975, 164). Dr. King supported the grape boycott because he believed that it represented a two-pronged assault on racism and poverty (King 1964, 24).

After five years, the grape growers finally admitted defeat. By 1970 the boycott had cut deeply into their profits and had turned popular opinion against their industry—at one point, it was estimated that 17 percent of the U.S. public supported the boycott (Harrington 1973). In addition, the constant strikes, marches, and organizing in their fields undermined the growers' claims that they knew what was best for "their" workers. On July 29, 1970, the United Farm Workers of America signed more than 130 contracts with agribusiness covering approximately thirty thousand workers in the grape industry. As historian Robert Gordon notes, "All of the newly signed contracts insured substantial wage increases, created a union hiring hall, and established strict regulations regarding the use of pesticides" (Gordon 1999, 51). DDT was banned, and soon thereafter, the crippling short-handled hoe was retired to agricultural history, where it belonged. Equally important, farmworkers, through their local ranch committees, were creating democracy, challenging racism, and negotiating directly with employers.

A Movement in Crisis

After 1970 the UFW had to fend off Teamster raids on the union's membership, a powerful agribusiness counteroffensive, and a succession of anti-labor governors in California. In 1973 two UFW members were killed in anti-union violence (Ferriss and Sandoval 1997, 187–188). Membership in the UFW along with that of most unions in the U.S. private sector declined precipitously. Chavez adopted a defensive posture and exercised tighter control over union operations. As the UFW became more bureaucratic, the local ranch committees lost their autonomy and strength (Acuna 1988, 327). Several key longtime union staffers resigned in protest over what they felt were autocratic practices as well as a crisis of purpose affecting the UFW (Bardacke 1993).

Perhaps the most telling blow came when several Filipino pioneers of the struggle, including Larry Itliong and Philip Vera Cruz, left the UFW. Approaching his eighties, Vera Cruz protested that Chavez was not allowing younger farmworkers to exercise any leadership in union business. "The way I see it, you've got to train young people to replace the old ones," Vera Cruz noted. "That's not the way they saw it" (Sengupta 1992). When Chavez accepted an invitation from dictator Ferdinand Marcos to visit the Philippines in 1977, Philip Vera Cruz resigned in disgust. The courageous veteran of four decades of farm work and two decades of union organizing called for the United Farm Workers of America to return to its democratic roots.

"Leadership is incidental to the movement," Vera Cruz stated shortly before his death. "You don't have a (Martin Luther) King if you don't have years of oppression of black people. You don't have a Gandhi if the British Empire was fair in ruling India" (Sengupta 1992). The veteran strike leader was trying to explain that the UFW owed its greatest victories to thousands of active farmworkers—not to charismatic leadership. Insurgent movements grow and sustain themselves insofar as they can generate democratic social relations. Any time a single individual or even a small group begins to exercise exclusive control over an organization, the incentive for ordinary people to participate disappears.

On the day of Chavez's funeral, thirty-five thousand people came to honor the memory of the fallen union leader. Sandra Canez, who grew up working in the fields, eulogized: "When farmworkers stand up from their labors in the field now, they should look in the sky and say: 'Thank you, God, for bringing us Cesar Chavez'" ("For the Final Time They March for Chavez" 1993). Many other union leaders, including Cipriano Ferrel of Pineros y Campesinos Unidos del Noroeste (PCUN), felt that Chavez's death, while a great loss, also challenged activists to expand their efforts and continue the struggle.

"We Want the Union"

Within a few months of Chavez's funeral, farmworker organizations had stopped mourning and had started organizing. In California, thousands of farmworkers struck the vegetable fields and fruit orchards. Subsequently, the UFW won fifteen straight union representation elections. In 1995 vineyard workers at Chateau Ste. Michelle in Washington signed the first agricultural union contract in that state's history after waging an eight-year international boycott. Farmworkers and their advocates in Florida, Texas, Oregon, and other states built viable, community-based organizations in which *campesinos* could meet and discuss common problems and solutions. In 1999 FLOC launched a national boycott of Mt. Olive Pickles to gain union recognition for cucumber workers in North Carolina, a state long known for its fierce anti-unionism (Seewere 1999). The same year, more than four hundred mushroom workers in Quincy, Florida, won a three-year boycott campaign that led to a UFW contract with their employer (Maxwell 1999).

Critics continue to ask farmworkers and their supporters why they bother to struggle to improve their working conditions. After all, many in the United States are taught from an early age, "If you don't like it, quit." While quitting is a relatively easy way out of a difficult predicament, it is not the only option. As Lucas Benitez, a farmworker and an organizer with the Coalition of Immokalee Workers in Florida observes, "I could leave and get a better job, but someone else would come and replace me. And he would be stuck in the same place. It is far better for me to stay and try to change it" (O'Hara 2000).

Students and farmworker advocates have played a key role in the resurgence of agricultural laborers' hopes for lives of dignity and respect. Scores of high school and college students have volunteered as interns with migrant legal service centers, health clinics, and housing assistance programs. Interns and advocates alike are serving as interpreters who help new immigrants collect unpaid wages, expose corrupt employers, learn English, and better understand their rights. Student activists have logged hours at farmworker rallies and union picket lines and registered workers to vote, while also agitating for immigration law reform.

Dolores Huerta asserts, "We've got to appeal to the public. We can't go through the legal system because the legal system is stacked" ("Migrant Workers Protest for Change" 1992). Following in the tradition of the UFW's grape boycott, farmworker-based unions across the country stress their need to build links of solidarity with consumers in order to call attention to the deplorable conditions that continue in U.S. agriculture. As the UFW and FLOC stepped up their presence in the South, they began to work harder to garner the support and solidarity of Mexican labor organizations as well (Velasquez and Blackwell 1992, 8–9). Indeed, the only way to successfully organize migrant farmworkers in the modern era is to create transnational unions that can match the transnational nature of global capital.

Students can be especially helpful in bringing farm laborers' concerns to the broader public to support new organizing campaigns. The boycott of Chateau Ste. Michelle (CSM) called by the United Farm Workers of Washington State (UFWWS) is an excellent example. In 1987 vineyard workers began organizing to improve their working conditions, citing an especially abusive foreman. After ten employees were summarily fired, remaining workers contacted the UFWWS and "describe[d] deplorable conditions in the fields, including blatant racism, poor field sanitation and incidents of serious pesticide exposure" ("History of Farmworkers Struggle for Workplace Democracy" 1992, 135). The company, according to vineyard employee Roberto Corrasco, had "always treated us as something less than human." The UFWWS called a boycott of the corporation when it refused to collectively bargain with the union and, according to the workers, resorted to a campaign of intimidation.

At the outset of the boycott in 1987 the company vowed, "We cannot and will not recognize any agricultural union" and boasted, "We are the best agricultural employer in the state" (Chateau Ste. Michelle 1987). The vineyard workers were equally adamant. Pastor Mejia, a longtime employee of CSM, insisted, "We want the union, because mere words are like dust in the wind. Right now they may promise us this, that and the other, but if it's not signed and in writing, what good is it?" (Lobet 1995).

The UFWWS approached student, social justice, church, and labor organizations for help. As the boycott progressed, student activists and interns served as vital conduits of information between the isolated eastern Washington grape vineyards and the urban markets where most of the boycotted wines were served and sold. Students wrote articles alerting the public to the boycott, organized leafleting at stores and restaurants, and vigorously participated in the UFWWS's boisterous demonstrations at the CSM winery's popular concert series.

Five years into the campaign, boycott committees in major cities in western Washington had successfully pressured more than one hundred restaurants to drop the offending wines. Working with progressive religious and labor groups, the boycott committees kept in close touch with the UFFWS, which frequently sent vineyard workers to participate and testify at rallies and marches in Seattle, Olympia, Bellingham, and other cities. The testimony of vineyard workers, who were risking their livelihoods by participating in these events, deeply inspired and energized student activists, who signed up in droves to volunteer for the boycott. Lidia Romero, a CSM worker, told supporters: "I am going to struggle until I receive my citizenship as soon as possible and struggle, if it is possible, to the end of the world to win this first collective bargaining agreement . . . My life will never be the same because I know now that I cannot stop struggling until we are equal" ("Notes from the Vineyard" 1993, 4).

As the consumer boycott gained momentum, the vineyard workers in turn became more assertive in defending their rights and calling for a union election. After one boycott rally, a CSM employee stated, "I have never seen such a demonstration. I will remain in this struggle until we have a contract" ("No More Business as Usual" 1994, 1). Speaking on the role of student activists in the union's efforts, the UFWWS wrote in a memo on the eve of winning the boycott: "We are very fortunate to have these talented and dedicated individuals working with us. In the end, they will surely enhance the already effective support committees" (United Farm Workers of Washington State 1994, 3). *Campesinos* reported to the boycott committees that working conditions in the vineyards began to improve due to the spotlight that the boycott was shining on the company. Six years into the struggle, UFWWS activists from the vineyards traveled with a group of supporters to give testimony at the company's annual shareholders' meeting in New Haven, Connecticut. Eight years after the beginning of the boycott, the UFWWS and CSM assented to the creation of a five-member commission of arbitration, headed by former U.S. House Speaker Tom Foley, that would oversee the first binding agricultural union election in the state's history. *The Wall Street Journal* reported, "Labor experts are incredulous that the winery's field workers got to vote at all" (Zachary 1995). The "experts" did not understand the power of people working together for social justice. A boycott and an alliance among farm laborers, students, and other supporters had brought a major corporation to the bargaining table. The UFWWS won the election, and the vineyard workers continue to enjoy the benefits of union representation ("Winery Workers Vote to Unionize" 1995). One important lesson of the breakthrough at Chateau Ste. Michelle is that community organizing between rural farmworkers and their urban supporters takes enormous energy. This is where students and advocates can make a difference.

Teamster Local 890, a union composed primarily of Latino agricultural workers in Salinas, California, is explicit about the pivotal role that students have been playing in aiding the union's boycott of Basic Vegetables. The local called the boycott after the company "permanently replaced [the workers] because they are defending their rights and their jobs." The union states:

We believe that University campuses are among Basic Vegetable's principal customers. Students who care about the exploitation of workers anywhere in the world have shown their solidarity by passing Boycott Basic Resolutions through their student government, residence hall associations and by approaching their campus administrators and requesting that these products be removed from campus cafeterias and dormitories (Teamster Local 890).

America's Newest Abolitionists

An increasing number of students and other farmworker advocates understand that they have a role to play in challenging the oppression that agricultural workers face in the United

States. Sarah Betson, a student at Guilford College and an intern with Student Action with Farmworkers (SAF), served as a health outreach worker in North Carolina during the summer of 2000. After discovering that "[s]ometimes the workers refuse help for fear of losing work or angering the grower," Betson vowed to become a farmworker advocate:

I now consider myself a farmworker advocate because I have begun to see that the struggle for the rights of the workers reflects upon my own rights in our society. We cannot live in a free and just society until those rights are shared by everyone. Advocates must play the role of an "ally" in a movement—meaning that the advocate must take her cue from the people themselves to foster true revolution rather than some type of surface change. The farmworkers are already fighting for their own rights through organizations such as FLOC—we at SAF have a responsibility to follow their lead and assist in any way that we can (Student Action with Farmworkers 2000).

Sarah Betson and her counterparts stand in a long tradition of American abolitionism. The original abolitionists were activists who sought an immediate end to slavery. Inspired by the humanitarian ideals of the Enlightenment as well as the rise of large-scale slave revolts in the age of the American and French revolutions, abolitionists, slave and free, black and white, created an international movement for justice that produced leaders like Frederick Douglass, Harriet Tubman, and William Lloyd Garrison. Abolitionists used moral persuasion, political agitation, and direct action—most memorably in the form of the Underground Railroad—in an effort to break the chains of slavery.

While plantation workers in the South were increasingly revolting against their masters, abolitionists were agitating for an end to America's "Peculiar Institution." Abolitionists hailed from a broad spectrum of society and included church members, workers, and seminary students. Frederick Douglass, a former Maryland farmworker and self-emancipated slave, became perhaps the most noted abolitionist in the final years of slavery. The fact that Douglass had physically fought his way out of slavery gave him great moral standing in the abolitionist movement. Douglass also became a champion for women's rights, Irish liberation, and anticolonialism. Douglass believed that all forms of oppression were connected with each other. As long as one group in society is oppressed, Douglass reasoned, this posed a threat to all (McFeely

FIGURE 9.2. *March from Mount Olive to Raleigh, North Carolina, in support of the Farm Labor Organizing Committee's efforts to organize cucumber workers, 1998. Photograph by Jason Hicks.*

1991). Today, farmworker advocates continue to echo Frederick Douglass's sentiments.

The Future in the Past

The struggle of farmworkers to organize in the United States is far from over. Indeed, even many sympathetic observers of agricultural labor today argue that there are too many obstacles to overcome. For the pessimist, the evidence seems overwhelming. The federal government is indifferent to the rights of farmworkers, many of whom are not citizens. Anti-union growers exert too much power in local communities and state legislatures. Workers are too scared to fight back. And critics point out how "complex" the issues surrounding agriculture are. During slavery, "objective" observers in the media and colleges never tired of pointing out that there "were good masters as well as bad ones." The "good master" philosophy, while perhaps comforting to some, ignores the need for fundamental changes in a larger system that dooms so many people to poor health, low wages, and bad treatment.

Frederick Douglass, Cesar Chavez, Dolores Huerta, and other farmworker advocates throughout U.S. history did not let pessimism squelch their hopes for a just society. If farm laborers and their advocates have learned one lesson over the years, it is that progress is never achieved without a struggle. Two years into the Prime Mushroom boycott in Quincy, Florida, the company adamantly refused to sign a union contract with farmworkers. The president of the Quincy Chamber of Commerce referred to United Farm Workers' organizers and other supporters of the workers' cause as "outside agitators" and "liars" who "keep lying and lying" (Maxwell 1999). A year later, Quincy mushroom workers signed a union contract with their employer that included paid vacations, a 401(k) savings plan, and health insurance. A man who had worked as a mushroom picker with the company for eight years described how the boycott campaign had brought a greater sense of dignity to the workers: "We're going to be normal people now," he said. "We'll be just like the people who work at Wal-Mart, Federal Express and the bank" (Maxwell 1999).

To organize successfully, farmworkers need allies in the larger society. From slavery to freedom, farmworkers have been excluded from many of the nation's protective laws. Despite the pivotal role their labor plays in the larger society, farmworkers have been denied citizenship and landownership. The greatest gains that agricultural workers have made—whether during Reconstruction or in the 1960s—have come about through alliances between farm laborers and supporters or advocates. It is impossible to imagine the grape boycott of the 1960s or FLOC's more recent boycott of Mt. Olive Pickle products succeeding without the participation of high school and college students along with sympathetic clergy, progressive labor unions, and other such activists.

Democratic alliances that cross lines of race, nationality, sex, and class have something important to teach all of us. The lesson might be something like this: in this era of globalization, no individual intent on progressive change can afford to stand alone. Like farmworkers, we all need to draw on the cooperative energies of everyone in the larger society to survive with a modicum of dignity and respect.

**Sowing Seeds
for Change
symposium
address,
Gainesville,
Florida**

Lucas Benitez,
farmworker
and organizer

The workers must be the real actors in making
. . . change. The good news is that [it] is already happening. Our example—our campaign
for dialogue and a living wage—is one of the
many examples from across the country where
workers are demanding a voice in the industry
and their supporters—students, clergy and lay
people, union leaders and everyday citizens—
are standing with them in their fight . . . Our
experience in 1995 left us more determined than
ever to not just fight for higher wages, but for a
new voice in the industry, for a new role where
we are no longer only two hands to work but a
mind and soul—a whole person to be respected
and to be compensated as a person and not a
beast of burden. And to do so, we knew that we
would have to not only keep organizing in our
own community but to enlist the support of the
"outside community," people unfamiliar with the
fields who, given the opportunity to learn of our
situation would lend their support, lend their
voice, to our fight.

An Invocation to Act

Melinda F. Wiggins

As we began this book with Lucas Benitez's reminder that "farmworkers are in desperate need of . . . [a] decent wage, the right to organize without fear of retaliation, [and] the right to earn overtime wages for overtime worked," it is fitting that we conclude with his invocation to students, clergy, lay people, and everyday citizens to stand with farmworkers as they fight for change (Benitez 1998). As contributors and editors, we encourage you to continue to think critically about social and economic injustices facing farmworkers and to raise awareness of these injustices with others. We challenge you to reflect on your personal connections to those who harvest the food you eat.

In addition to working to change the immediate problems faced by farmworkers, we also challenge you to support long-term efforts for systemic change, such as labor organization and legislative improvements for workers. In doing so, you will join a movement of farmworker advocates who have made connections between their own lives and those of farmworkers. By combining personal narratives with the theoretical analysis of our agricultural system, we hope to "engage listeners who might otherwise feel estranged, alienated" (hooks 1989, 77). I will include some personal narratives of these advocates below. But first, I will begin with my own story, claiming my working-class and agricultural roots as my connection with immigrant farmworkers.

Claiming My Connection

Despite being the daughter and granddaughter of sharecroppers and growing up on a cotton farm in rural Leflore County, Mississippi, I have only recently begun to connect my story with farmworkers in my community. Though I grew up in a place where there is more land than people and am aware of how human lives depend on the land and those who tend the land, I was estranged from the local African American workers who hoed cotton in fields surrounding my home. When I finally began making the connection, I was years and thousands of miles away from my Delta roots. After finishing college and leaving the Delta in 1992, I began to think critically about social injustices in the rural South. Having worked with migrant and seasonal farmworkers in the Carolinas since 1993, I now realize just how strongly my life is connected to those who harvest field crops in the southeastern United States.

I grew up hearing my mom's stories of working with her siblings and a half-dozen African American hired hands picking cotton during the harvest, and stories of my father's family migrating from the hills to the Delta to work as sharecroppers. My mother's parents started farming as sharecroppers in 1933. After nearly a decade of working on other people's land, they were able to purchase eighty-four acres of their own for five thousand dollars through the Farmer's Home Administration (FmHA). This New Deal outgrowth of the Farm Security Administration (FSA) enabled sharecroppers to buy small farms, thus reclassifying people like my grandparents as farmers.

Corporate farms of today hardly resemble such small-acreage farms. For corporate "farms" perhaps we should revive the antebellum South's nomenclature of "planter." For example, companies like the Mt. Olive Pickle Company, which contracts with more than twelve hundred growers to raise cucumbers on more than twenty-eight thousand acres each year (Mt. Olive Pickle Company, Inc. n.d.), or Weyerhaeuser, which owns and grows timber on six hundred thousand acres in North Carolina alone, should be called plantations, not farms.

Although my mom and her four siblings inherited the land my grandparents owned, none of them today are farmers. When farmers receive less than seventeen cents of every dollar paid for crops, and their net profit is much less than that, farming households such as those I am from must seek off-farm income or specialize in niche crops or livestock such as catfish. Even while cotton farming provided full-time work for my mom's entire family, it did not bring in a living wage. My grandmother tailored clothing and upholstered furniture part-time to earn needed income for the family.

The Delta of my childhood lacked the significant numbers of fieldworkers that created the plantation dynasty of the nineteenth and early twentieth centuries. The introduction of machines, especially the cotton picker, left little need for a transient workforce, and thus local African Americans were the only workforce needed to hoe the fields and work in local cotton gins. And though these fieldworkers were present in my community, I did not know them. My ignorance of the seasonal workforce in that small rural community is typical of the disconnect between consumers and farmworkers, and surprisingly even between rural farm families and seasonal workers. Even farmers who employ farmworkers distance themselves from laborers, some by hiring crew leaders to recruit and manage workers.

Although I did not know farmworkers, I did learn where my food comes from firsthand in my family's acre garden. Each year my family raised a lush garden of corn, watermelons, cantaloupes, okra, tomatoes, peppers, potatoes, cabbage, lettuce, peas, butter beans, and radishes adjacent to my house. Childhood hardly rescued me from working the garden, much less shelling, shucking, freezing, and canning vegetables after the harvest. At the time, I did not link my experiences harvesting our food with large-scale food-crop production or with those who performed the same tasks on a much larger scale just down the road. Now I understand the skill that is involved in producing food, and I disagree with the notion that farmworkers are "unskilled" laborers, a belief often fostered by employment services, government departments, and even many farmers.

The other important connection that I now see between my family and farmworkers is a class connection. Though I began questioning the assumed hierarchy among owners, managers, and workers in our economic system while studying political science as an undergraduate in the late 1980s at Millsaps College in Jackson, Mississippi, I did not begin to identify with my own family's working-class status until late in my college years. As a child I was ashamed that my mother worked in a meter factory and my dad was a mechanic. Now as an adult I have a new appreciation for the values I learned in a working-class family.

As the first person in my extended family to receive a graduate education, I feel an obligation to connect academics with my working-class experiences. I am now in a place in which, as Zandy says, I can "cross the borders of class difference and make [my own place] in the world" (Zandy 1995, 9). By combining my class consciousness and education, I can be a strong advocate for working-class people. As bell hooks reminds us, it is important to claim connections we have with our kin, especially those of us who crossed the boundaries from materially underprivileged to privileged yet who want to maintain our class allegiance. She tells "students from poor and working-class backgrounds that if you believe what you have learned and are learning in schools and universities separates you from your past, this is precisely what will happen. It is important to stand firm in the conviction that nothing can truly separate us from our pasts when we nurture and cherish that connection" (hooks 1989, 80). I believe that claiming the connection to my kin also means claiming relations to others in similar socioeconomic places.

After graduating from Millsaps College in 1992 I moved to Durham, North Carolina, to study theology at Duke Divinity School. During the summer of 1993, between my two years of graduate studies, I participated in a summer internship with Student Action with Farmworkers (SAF). SAF's mission is to bring students and farmworkers together to learn about each other's lives, share resources and skills, improve conditions for farmworkers, and build diverse coalitions working for social change. As an intern, I worked at the Episcopal Farmworker Ministry in Newton Grove, North Carolina, assisting farmworkers with immigration applications, locating land for a farmworker homeownership project, and identifying religious communities that supported farmworkers.

The internship allowed me to work directly with farmworkers and encouraged me to reflect on their role in agriculture and society. It provided the setting I needed to link my own family's history in the Delta with current difficulties faced by agricultural workers. Though I grew up in a segregated community, I began to comprehend the similarities between my white parents' and grandparents' lives and many poor African Americans and Latinos. Almost all poor people in rural agricultural areas have suffered from the shift toward corporate agriculture. And almost all working-class communities, particularly rural communities, have suffered from the injustices of our economic system.

During my summer with SAF I also reflected on the fact that agricultural workers suffer not only because they are poor; they also face discrimination based on geography and race. People of color, especially those living in rural areas, are much more likely to be poor than their white urban neighbors. This, in part, stems from the fact that "the richest one percent of U.S. households have 40 percent of all wealth— more than the bottom 95 percent of households" (Collins, Leondon-Wright, and Slelan 1999). Often wealthy landowners or managers use race and ethnicity to create competition between low-wage workers in order to prevent them from building solidarity. For instance, often farmworkers from different countries are housed in separate labor camps, isolating them from their fellow workers.

Following my internship with SAF I began searching for a job that would allow me to build on what I had learned and to continue to work for change with poor people in the rural South. Upon graduating from Duke in 1994 I was hired by SAF, first as the program director coordinating the Into the Fields internship program, and in 1996 I took my current position as SAF's executive director. Through SAF, I have endeavored to build a movement of students and community members educated about the complexities of agribusiness who will speak out about the abuses farmworkers endure and who will form coalitions with others involved in social and economic justice work.

Today when I drive down Highway 82 from the hills of Winona to the flatlands of the Mississippi Delta, I still feel the overwhelming strength of the dark soil that stretches as far as the eye can see. And now as never before I feel the connection to the land and farmworkers who work on it. But few of my peers have had the experience I did growing up on a farm or working in a large family garden or even participating in an internship that provides a structure for thinking critically about agricultural inequalities. Although I had a direct link in my family to sharecropping and spent eighteen years surrounded by cotton fields, soybean fields, crop dusters, and cotton gins, I still had to make a conscious effort to connect my story with that of the predominantly Latino, young, male agricultural labor force of today. Thus, even from my familiar perspective, understanding farm work, reflecting on how one's life is connected to food, land, and workers, and committing oneself to social and economic change within agriculture is a difficult task. Nevertheless, I believe students, faculty, and consumers are a vital and consciously connected part of the farmworker movement.

The Complexities of Farm Work

In the southeastern United States today, nearly 140 years after slavery was abolished, we occasionally still hear grievous cases of farmworkers living in indentured servitude. For instance, in 1999 two Florida farmers were convicted and charged with peonage, or holding migrant farmworkers against their will in order to collect a debt. The farmers forced more than twenty tomato pickers to work off a smuggling-fee debt of $800 per person before they could leave the farm. The employers threatened workers who attempted to escape with violence. For this heinous crime, the perpetrators were sentenced to only a maximum of five years in prison and fined $250,000 (Associated Press 1999b).

While such cases invoke community concern and public outrage, as well they should, many community members only respond to farmworker causes in the context of sensationalist media stories of extreme farmworker abuses. However, these egregious cases can eclipse the everyday facts of farmworker abuse, such as 61 percent of farmworkers living in poverty and earning only half the average national wage. And the extreme overcrowding of three-fourths of farmworkers' housing rarely makes the news. Horrible stories of workers dying in the fields, while true, may obscure the fact that farmworkers suffer the highest rate of toxic chemical injuries of any workers in the United States on a daily basis. It is easy to forget, too, the stark reality that it takes roughly three years for a migrant child to advance one grade level because of the family's constant mobility.

These sensational cases of employer abuses and farmworker conditions do not inform us of the daily harshness of agricultural labor and do not encourage sustained public interest and involvement in making change. The media's reliance on spectacular cases robs us of the opportunity to hear the voices of farmworkers who may not be victims of tragedy in the fields but who nonetheless face a daily regimen of dangerous work in exchange for too little pay, benefits, or respect.

Below are excerpts from interviews by Student Action with Farmworkers' interns with agricultural workers in the Carolinas regarding these more mundane problems.

Interview with Brenda Garcia by Erica Lian, 1998 SAF intern

Erica: What do you do during the months where there is no work?
Brenda: Well, we stay here without working, thinking, "What are we going to do to eat?"
Erica: Do you like your work?
Brenda: Even if I don't like it, what else am I going to do? We can't find anything else to work in.
Erica: What would you like to work in?
Brenda: In something easier. In anything as long as it's not that tobacco.
Erica: Which one would you like to do more, stay here or return to Mexico?
Brenda: No, return to Mexico, to my country. I like it here also but one has to return back. Staying here is difficult. In both places. In Mexico and here.

Interview with Vanessa by Kris Adams, 1997 SAF intern

Although Vanessa says she can't consider what she makes in the field "good money," she did get $150 a week or $7 a bin for picking oranges. She [got] paid by the hour for tobacco and everything else [was] piece rate. "When you get paid 'piece rate' you take your full bucket to be dumped at the truck. There the crew leader will empty your bucket and give you a ticket which is usually worth forty or fifty cents. At the end of the day the bookkeeper will take up your tickets, count them, and write down how many tickets you collected. At the end of the week the crew leader pays the farmworker according to the amount of tickets you collected throughout the week."

Interview with Miguel by Luis Mendoza, 1997 SAF intern

Luis: Do you think it was worth it to come here to the United States?
Miguel: There are a lot of people who come and are lucky to find a stable job. But going from here to there doesn't do anything for you. One leaves the family to suffer to come to make money here in the United States and it is not true, how one imagines it will be . . . It has been almost a year and I have only been able to make money to support my family. I have not made money to say, "I have already sent three or four thousand dollars to my land" (the way us Mexicans talk) . . . I have not found a stable job. I have only been from here to there and from there to here.

Interview with Guadalupe by Kris Adams, 1997 SAF intern

"When we picked camote [sweet potatoes] we get paid by the bucket. In an hour when it is really good you can make like fifty buckets, but when it is not you can only make about ten . . . It is also hard when they cheat you and you don't get paid. When you give [the crew leader a full] bucket they pour it out and put a chip in your bucket. Sometimes they cheat you and don't put [in a] chip. You say, 'You didn't give me a chip!' And they say, 'You [must've] dropped it or something.'"

Such stories show that within the agricultural system, farmworkers represent the lowest-paid, least protected, and most endangered workers. Farmworkers symbolize the antithesis of the "American Dream": they work hard and remain poor. As Charlie Thompson mentions in his chapter, "Layers of Loss: Migrants, Small Farmers, and Agribusiness,"

FIGURE 10.1. *SAF student interns march in support of the Mt. Olive boycott in Charlotte, North Carolina, 1999. Photograph by Lori Fernald Khamala.*

farmworkers rarely climb the social ladder in agriculture from worker to owner. As did slaves, sharecroppers, and tenant farmers, modern-day farmworkers labor on someone else's land and often are dependent on off-farm jobs to supplement their farm income. The unstable and temporary nature of farm work, coupled with the lack of a living wage and benefits, creates a job that leads to nowhere better. Instead of earning enough money to remain in farm work for their lifetimes or perhaps eventually to buy a farm, most farmworkers eventually attempt to leave farm work for more stable and better-paid permanent work.

Most farmworker organizing campaigns and advocacy are about improving these everyday problems and not just the extreme cases. They are about farmworkers gaining basic respect in the workplace, earning a daily wage, and working in a safe environment.

Sustaining long-term efforts to establish farmworker justice is perhaps our greatest challenge as advocates. Farmworkers face major obstacles when organizing due to race, immigration status, poverty, and lack of public support. Yet at the same time, in every historical era since slavery, U.S. agricultural workers have fought to end below-poverty wages, poor living conditions, and inhumane treatment. Because farmworkers face countless obstacles to organizing, they also rely on supporters to help end the abuses. Successful campaigns often hinge on farmworkers uniting with other workers and advocates.

Long-Term Challenges and Successes

Winning wage, legislative, or union victories can take decades or longer. Mobility and high turnover rates of farmworkers complicate the chances of finding a group of workers who can commit to a long-term campaign. The task becomes even harder considering that most agricultural employers and legislators cannot communicate with the Spanish-speaking farmworker population. The high number of undocumented farmworkers creates a highly vulnerable workforce, afraid to speak out or complain about problems on farms because of threats and intimidation by growers. Often workers lose their jobs while organizing for changes in agricultural labor practices, becoming martyrs for the next generation of workers. Rarely do farmworkers who organize for long-term change reap the benefits of their own sacrifices.

As Greg Schell mentions in this volume, many otherwise progressive federal legislative initiatives throughout the past century excluded farmworkers, beginning with the significant labor laws passed during the New Deal in the 1930s. For instance, the exemption of farmworkers in 1935 from the National Labor Relations Act (NLRA), which affords wage earners in other industries protection while organizing and bargaining collectively, virtually ensures job loss for farmworkers who stand up to the agricultural industry. NLRA exemption effectively debilitates efforts of some farmworker organizations.

The H-2A guestworker program poses another obstacle to fieldworkers' organizing efforts, as contributor Garry Geffert explains in detail. Beginning in the 1930s, farmers convinced the federal government to import foreign workers to fill their perceived labor shortage. In *The Fruits of Their Labor*, Cindy Hahamovitch contends that the federal government began importing labor to weaken farmworker organizations. Hahamovitch writes:

Yet the same agencies that imported foreign workers freely admitted that the nation's problem was not a labor shortage but a maldistribution of labor. If domestic workers had been carefully directed to labor-scarce regions, their numbers would have been adequate to meet the demands of agricultural war production . . .

Thus the state entered the affairs of farm labor relations in order to compensate for growers' Achilles' heel—their vulnerability to farm labor strikes—and native-born farmworkers lost their opportunity to transform the conditions of East Coast agriculture by organizational resolve and collective will (Hahamovitch 1997, 181).

Grower associations and cooperatives continue to use guestworker programs endorsed by the federal government, thereby stripping local workers of organizing power. Guestworkers, whose work contracts only allow them to stay in an area on a temporary basis, are unlikely to participate in campaigns that challenge the industry that applied for their visas and pays their wages. To do so is to risk deportation, job loss, and the possibility of not returning on a guestworker visa in the future.

Despite their exemption from the NLRA and the presence of other barriers not shared by most workers, farmworkers have organized three nationally recognized labor unions. The domestic unions that represent fieldworkers are the United Farm Workers (UFW), Farm Labor Organizing Committee (FLOC), and Pineros y Campesinos Unidos del Noroeste (PCUN, Northwest Treeplanters and Farmworkers United). These unions, as well as smaller community-based organizing groups, use consumer boycotts, leafleting, hunger strikes, protests, and lobbying to call for the end of systems that oppress farmworkers. Farmworkers also join forces with other labor, religious, and civil rights groups to pursue common goals of better wages and conditions and to demand respect as full human beings (Mooney and Majka 1995, 223). Particularly because of the extraordinary risks to farmworkers who organize, all of these campaigns require the support of advocates from "outside communities."

The California-based United Farm Workers (UFW), founded in 1962 by Cesar Chavez and Dolores Huerta, mobilized tens of thousands of individuals in the 1960s, 1970s, and 1980s on behalf of farmworkers to support consumer boycotts of grapes and lettuce. The first two grape boycotts succeeded because of the overwhelming response from consumers who used their economic power to pressure the industry to negotiate better working conditions for farmworkers. In 1984 the UFW called the third boycott of California table grapes in response to the discovery that pesticides were still being sprayed on crops in a manner that endangered workers.

After Chavez's death in 1993 the UFW focused its efforts on improvements in mushrooms and strawberry fields. In 1999, after eighty-four mushroom workers were fired by Quincy Farms for protesting low wages, unsafe conditions, poor medical treatment, and the company's refusal to respond to workers' grievances, the UFW called for a consumer boycott of Quincy Farms mushrooms. The UFW successfully aligned with other unions to build their base of support. One machinist union member who supported the Quincy workers said, "I hope this shows the company that you can't treat employees the way *they* treat employees. We can't stand by while farmworkers work in deplorable conditions" (Ash 1996). Quincy Farms agreed to negotiate with workers when, as a result of consumer pressure, it lost one of its largest contracts—Pizza Hut.

Faced with employers plowing under ready-to-harvest strawberry fields instead of negotiating with organized workers, the UFW now calls on consumers to pay five cents more per pint of strawberries, consequently increasing farmworker wages. "People who buy strawberries, people who consider themselves allies with working families, and industry players must raise and answer the question: Is five cents for fairness too much to ask?" (Strawberry Workers Campaign 1996, 27). The "Five Cents for Fairness" campaign demonstrates how consumers' choices at grocery stores can directly affect farmworkers' economic situation and how little their grocery bills would change if increases in food prices were passed on directly to workers as wage increases.

The Farm Labor Organizing Committee (FLOC) enlists advocate support by educating consumers about how food processors determine farmworkers' wages. Consumer pressure on companies such as Campbell's allowed FLOC to win successful contracts with pickle and tomato processors in Ohio and Michigan. FLOC recently expanded its efforts to include the cucumber industry in North Carolina. Since the mid-1990s almost three thousand of the seven thousand cucumber workers in North Carolina have signed cards indicating they want FLOC to represent them. FLOC's three-way bargaining agreements remind supporters and opponents alike that farmworkers' poor wages are a problem larger than a single "bad" grower. By bringing workers, farmers, and food processing companies together, FLOC gives workers opportunities to negotiate with their employers and processors for improved living and working conditions. FLOC holds large and wealthy companies such as Heinz and Vlasic accountable to the needs of workers by forcing them to negotiate contracts with growers who supply their raw produce that in turn will benefit workers. During the spring of 1999, FLOC called a national boycott of Mt. Olive Pickle Company products because of the company's repeated refusal to negotiate with cucumber workers in eastern North Carolina.

Pineros y Campesinos Unidos del Noroeste (PCUN), an Oregon-based farmworker union that represents tree planters and farmworkers in the Northwest, credits its 1999 Gardenburger victory to the support of college students. Faced with poverty wages and health concerns, Oregon farmworkers asked consumers to boycott North Pacific Canners and Packers, or NORPAC Foods, Inc., a large grower cooperative that employs farmworkers and distributes food. Since NORPAC distributed Gardenburger, PCUN called a secondary boycott of Gardenburger. PCUN used a smart and simple strategy: since Gardenburger is popular on college campuses, PCUN mobilized students to get their universities to honor the boycott. In the midst of PCUN's East Coast tour of college campuses during the spring of 1999, Gardenburger announced that it would find another distributor. A mobilized student effort contributed to this farmworker victory.

Never has a non-union, grassroots farmworker organization gained so much community support as did the Coalition of Immokalee Workers (CIW) during three members' hunger strike in 1998. Farmworkers Samuel Mar, Abundio Rios, and Antonio Ramos fasted for thirty days in Florida, calling for open dialogue and discussion between workers and tomato growers about wages. The Coalition of Immokalee Workers, a diverse group of Latino, Haitian, Mayan, and African American workers in southwestern Florida, has successfully formed a strong united front with religious, student, and community members throughout the United States. According to Greg Asbed, an organizer with the coalition,

A broad front of support formed almost overnight, as thousands of Floridians told industry leaders with one voice their industry is part of a larger community and the continued poverty of their workers is an issue that concerns us all. Suddenly, [the tomato industry's] secret was on the front page, and their only response was silence, hoping the pressure for reform would eventually wane as it always had in the past. But one thing is clear: change will come. It may not be today, it may not be tomorrow, but change will come (Asbed 1998).

As Lucas Benitez has pointed out, workers must be their own agents for change while also relying on the support of advocates. Consumers, students, and labor and religious activists can join workers to dialogue with the agricultural industry and change farmworker conditions. Consumers can support farmworker organizing efforts by honoring boycotts, educating others about union campaigns, and urging agricultural giants to negotiate contracts that guarantee farmworkers better wages, benefits, and improved living conditions. First, though, consumers must reflect critically on what connection they have with farmworkers. Choosing to listen to farmworkers' voices and identifying ways to honor their work are essential steps in claiming a connection with farmworkers.

Community Responses to Immigrant Farmworkers

The help of United States Citizens is requested to inform the U.S. Department of Immigration to locate and deport illegal aliens that have been a problem in Alamance County. They may be found in groups in MO-BILE HOME PARKS playing loud Mexican music that is disturbing the neighborhood, consuming beer and trespassing.

This quote is from an anonymous flier that was circulated in 1996 around Alamance County, North Carolina. This anti-immigrant stereotyping creates fear among Latino farmworkers of deportation and vigilante violence. Propaganda of this nature could easily incite residents to take matters into their own hands and attempt to eradicate immigrants from their communities.

Fortunately, hostile expressions such as this are uncommon. Yet assumptions that all farmworkers are undocumented, Spanish-speaking immigrants from Mexico do help create an environment of distrust and segregation. The lack of acceptance in the communities in which they live and work compounds the already harsh conditions of farm work. Community members' prejudices often prevent farmworkers from fully integrating into their communities or receiving needed services, as happened in western North Carolina in 1996. A Yadkin County commissioner issued a directive to the county health department to ban foreign-language signs in the department's offices. The commissioner said the signs in Spanish might be "anti-American or anti-government since it was in a language he cannot understand" (Davis 1996). Even though other Yadkin County commissioners expressed disdain at this commissioner's decree, the county did not allow the health department to accept funds to translate a prenatal health care workbook into Spanish.

This action to prevent the Latino community from receiving prenatal information implies a sense of disregard and even scorn toward new immigrants. Most residents know little about immigrant farmworkers who stay near their communities for two to eight months each year harvesting fresh fruits and vegetables. Many assume the workers do not want to integrate with the local community or because workers will be migrating soon that it is not worth community members' time to get to know them. The distancing of farmworkers from their neighbors is tragic and raises questions about class barriers, values, and patterns that reinforce a white-supremacist, exploitative patriarchy (hooks 1989).

To begin combating these problems, we must reflect on the following questions: Are farmworkers ignored because they are minorities, immigrants, and/or Spanish-speakers? Are agricultural workers' poor working conditions accepted because we believe that things are better here than in their home countries? Do we really believe in the myth that farmworkers can simply pull themselves up by their bootstraps? And finally, if we disagree with these stereotypes, what is our role in changing them?

Many people make wrong assumptions about farmworkers. Most are removed from the everyday struggles of farmworkers or feel immobilized to act. Too few know what is needed to make the structural changes that can prevent the next generation of immigrant farmworkers from facing some of the same problems that workers face today. Yet we must begin.

We must notice connections with farmworkers, welcoming them into our communities and responding to their daily struggles. Fortunately, we have examples of community members who stand in solidarity with farmworkers. Below are stories about the lives and experiences of farmworker advocates.

Advocates Lend Their Voices

Through my work with SAF, I have had the opportunity to witness and participate in an amazing student movement supporting agricultural workers. By pressuring universities to endorse boycotts called by farmworkers, mentoring migrant children, leafleting consumers about farmworker campaigns, and initiating courses on farmworker issues, students make substantial contributions to the movement for farmworker justice. Each summer through SAF's Into the Fields Internship and Leadership Development Program, thirty student interns work with a variety of community-based farmworker organizations focusing on issues such as labor rights, immigration, wage abuses, health, and education. The interns write guided journal entries to reflect on the connections between their lives and the workers they support. Each summer SAF asks interns to respond to the following questions in a journal entry: "What is an advocate? Do you consider yourself a farmworker advocate? What role do students play in social change movements? Do you feel that you are part of the farmworker movement?" Below are excerpts from interns' responses in 1999:

Advocates are generally thought of as working to change circumstances concerning a particular matter, but most of the time one does not hear of that person being changed by the circumstances surrounding the cause. I began the summer thinking that I would work FOR the farmworkers, and I used to call the organization Student Action FOR Farmworkers. But I have found that the WITH is much more appropriate.

DANIELLE DAVIS, UNIVERSITY OF SOUTH CAROLINA-COLUMBIA

An advocate [is a person] who takes up for someone who oftentimes doesn't have the opportunity to speak up for themselves. The role of an advocate is not to act for the people they advocate for or to tell them what to do. An advocate should empower people to act for themselves or work for change that will provide others with opportunities to act for themselves.

ANGELINE ECHEVERRÍA, UNIVERSITY OF SOUTH CAROLINA-COLUMBIA

To me an advocate is a person who supports a specific cause by actively participating in activities that motivate the people involved, that draw attention to the problems at hand, and that promote or propose alternatives to solve problems. I have trouble labeling myself as an advocate, because I still feel like I have a lot to learn about farmworker issues and also that I need to have more experience working with farmworkers before I can really be called an advocate. I think I'm more like an advocate-in-training. Working with SAF and with all the interns makes me feel like collectively we are really having an effect on the strength of the farmworker movement, and I am very proud of that.

ANA HOLMES, DUKE UNIVERSITY

These students understand that they must go beyond a mentality of charity and helping the needy to advocating for workers through empowerment, collective action, and mutual learning. In addition, contributors to this book provide inspiring examples of how advocates from the "outside community" can connect with farmworkers and lend their voices to the farmworker movement.

Sister Evelyn Mattern got involved with farmworkers through her work with the Peace and Justice Office of the Roman Catholic Diocese of Raleigh, North Carolina. Sister Evelyn learned about the large number of farmworkers in the state after attending hearings held by the Advisory Committee to the U.S. Committee on Civil Rights in the mid-1970s. She spoke with North Carolina church members about their involvement in the lives of farmworkers, and many responded that no farmworkers lived in their county. Despite the church members' reports, data from the North Carolina Department of Labor revealed that farmworkers were in fact living in these counties. Sister Evelyn realized the invisibility of farmworkers and found ways to introduce church members to farmworker issues.

Colin Austin came in contact with Latino farmworkers for the first time as a teenager while picking strawberries in upstate New York. His hard work in the fields alongside Puerto Rican harvesters encouraged him to learn more about this isolated and segregated workforce. As a result, Colin became an outreach worker with Farmworkers Legal Services in North Carolina during the summer of 1990, visiting farmworkers in their homes and at their workplaces. After that summer, Colin continued supporting farmworkers through work with a migrant health clinic, research projects, and a workforce development program.

Christopher Holden, a native of rural New Hampshire, also worked on farms as a teenager. He picked apples, blueberries, and worked on Christmas tree farms to help improve his family's poor economic situation. Chris's friendships with migrant workers enabled him to witness their living conditions firsthand. His appreciation for the difficulty of farm work and special interest in safe housing led him to work to improve farmworkers' housing and standard of living.

Former SAF intern David Cruz provides an inspiring example of support for Latino farmworkers' children in public schools with his testimony of the difficulties he experienced growing up in a farmworker family. His desire to mentor migrant students arose from his own experiences in school of being ridiculed by fellow students for being Mexican, poor, and Spanish-speaking. He currently works with a New Jersey hotline for migrant families.

Through connections to agriculture, Latino communities, and social justice issues, these advocates found positive ways to support farmworkers. Many individuals cannot support farmworkers through their

FIGURE 10.2. *The Coalition of Immokalee Workers protests low wages for tomato pickers in Florida, 1995. Photograph by Kim Weimer.* © Naples Daily News.

occupations, but they can be vital advocates within the farmworker movement by volunteering their time and giving money to support the struggle.

How Can You Connect with Farmworkers?

Without understanding the complexities of agribusiness today, it is easy to pit farmworkers against farmers in a simplistic fashion. The media, for example, often contrast a bad crew leader or farmer against farmworkers, thereby implying that changing practices on one individual farm is the solution to solving agricultural injustices. Yet, the systemic problems facing farmworkers cannot be addressed merely by changing individual farmers or requiring a single crew leader to pay a living wage, provide decent housing, or treat workers with respect and dignity.

Rather, the agricultural system needs systemic change. Farmworkers must be included in the federal labor laws that protect workers who participate in labor organizing. Farmworker organizations must build new collaborations, especially with groups focusing on economic, racial, social, and environmental justice. In our policies, our actions, and our eating habits, we must treat farmworkers as whole persons, as human beings who deserve respect and honor for their work in the fields. This respect for farmworkers must come in the form of good pay and benefits, the right to organize, and a voice in our legislative system. Farmworkers must be seen as vital components of our local communities instead of as outsiders simply passing through.

I hope that this book empowers you to make connections between your life and farmworkers' lives, fostering a deeper understanding of food production and rural, agricultural communities, and encourages you to support social and economic justice movements for all oppressed people, not only for farmworkers. I hope you will begin by asking some hard questions about how you can connect with a working-class community that is predominantly Spanish-speaking, undocumented, and exploited. Do you feel or imagine these largely immigrant, sometimes transient, workers to be a part of your community? How can you help farm laborers settle into communities like yours, even if temporarily? And most important, how will we work both individually and collectively with farmworkers to end the long period of abuse?

Here is a list of concrete actions you can take to claim connections with farmworkers:

- Stay informed about farmworkers and other agricultural issues by subscribing to farmworker advocacy newsletters, reading books about the history of farmworkers, and taking classes related to migration, immigration, farm work, slavery, or agribusiness. Once you have educated yourself, educate others about farmworker issues by sharing information at local religious organizations, agencies, and community groups, writing articles and letters to the editor of your newspaper, and promoting and teaching college courses related to farmworkers. Pass this book along to others.

- Support farmworker organizing campaigns. Endorse food boycotts called by farmworkers,

leaflet consumers at grocery stores about current farmworker campaigns, and write letters to
growers, food processors, and distributors who
refuse to negotiate with farmworkers.

- Stay informed of current immigration and agricultural legislation that affects farmworkers.
Write letters to your congressional representatives in support of legislation benefiting farmworkers.

- Work in a profession that supports farmworkers
(outreach worker, clinic staff, English as a Second
Language teacher, community organizer, labor
or immigration attorney, documentary photogra-
pher, or writer). If you are not able to work with
a farmworker organization, volunteer with organizations supporting farmworkers, Latinos, or
other immigrants in your community or support
them by making a financial contribution.

- Avoid foods produced with harmful pesticides.
Support sustainably grown foods by planting
your own pesticide-free garden or purchasing
locally grown organic produce at food cooperatives, farmers markets, and organic grower
associations. Promote those groups that have
commitments to fair labor practices.

- Develop your connection with farmworkers,
farmers, and the rural United States by inter-
viewing a worker or grower about working on
a farm, the problems facing rural communities,
and that person's ideas about how to improve the
situation.

We want this text to be a resource for farmworker advocates and consumers. We also want this book to encourage the important task of
introducing the farmworker movement and working-class consciousness into an arena where it has been marginal—academic institutions.
If class consciousness permeates academia, students will learn to be political activists, perhaps challenging academia's own neglect of univer-

FIGURE 10.3. *Florida farmworkers at a community-wide labor stoppage, 1995. Photograph by Kim Weimer.* © Naples Daily News.

sity workers' struggles (Zandy 1995). Solidarity between academic institutions, community-based farmworker organizations, and consumers could advance farmworker advocacy significantly. The farmworker movement can become a formidable front, providing models for resistance that can be used by other oppressed communities. Above all, farmworkers' resistance to oppression, supported from members of the "outside community," symbolizes a revolt against a long history of discrimination toward poor and working-class minorities in the rural South. As we challenge the dominant culture's ignorance of the daily struggles of farmworkers, we hope to learn what 1996 SAF intern Mendi Drayton has learned about farmworker advocacy: "What I have learned most about being an advocate is there is not a switch to turn it on or off. It permeates every facet of your life. Being an advocate for something is who you are, not just what you do."

Developing a Syllabus on Farmworker Advocacy

Below are topics, suggested readings, and films for a fourteen-week semester seminar. Note that this syllabus was developed prior to the release of this book, and therefore this volume does not appear in this sample. This work is very much intended for course use, and we hope that courses will be organized around the themes of the book, with a week devoted to each chapter's theme.

See the recommended reading list and works cited in this volume for further suggestions and full citations to supplemental materials. SAF houses readings and films related to farmworkers that can be checked out through SAF's lending library.

Basic elements for a course on farmworkers and advocacy:

- History of farm work particular to the region where the course is offered. In the Southeast, any discussion of farm work must discuss links between current farmworker conditions and slavery, sharecropping, and tenant farming.
- Contextualization of farm work with region's agricultural crops. How did the crops that farmworkers prune, plant, and harvest in this region become popular here? Why grow these crops and not others? How are these crops transported to markets? How have these cropping patterns and crop selections changed over time?
- Changes in farmworker populations over time. Discuss the shifts of farmworker population ethnicities and countries of origin. Why do whites and African Americans make up only a small percentage of the farmworker population today, while Latinos make up the overwhelming majority?
- Push/pull factors that encourage or force farmworkers to enter farm work today. In the Southeast, discuss the vacuum created by the out-migration of the descendants of slaves and sharecroppers from agricultural communities. Also review the economic and social aspects of communities in Mexico, Central America, and elsewhere that create a climate where inhabitants must leave in order to survive. Discussions about NAFTA and other federal trade programs and how U.S. policy has helped create poverty in Latin America are also important.

- Patterns of farmworker travel and labor in the present. Where do farmworkers who work in the region being studied stay in the winter? What months are they in your community? How long do they stay? Where do they come from and where do they go when they leave? Are there year-round workers in the area?
- Farmworker advocacy. What were the antecedents to present-day farmworker advocacy? How do farmworker advocates of the past resemble those of the present? Familiarize the students with various areas of advocacy including education, legislation, housing, health, and immigration.
- Direct experience with farmworkers and advocates. While it may be difficult to work with farmworker communities during the academic year, students should have some contact with farmworkers and farmworker advocates. This can come in the form of a field trip to a labor camp and farm, inviting farmworkers and advocates as guest speakers, or requiring students to volunteer with local farmworker organizations.
- Volunteer experience with farmworker advocacy organizations. Service-learning requirements can be a useful tool to involve students in the farmworking community. In lieu of writing academic papers, students can document their volunteer experiences as a means of conveying what they have learned through oral histories, photography, video, and/or ethnographies of the agency personnel/community members/farmworkers with whom they have worked. A journal is an effective means of documenting experiences, and required presentations encourage students to convert journal writings into effective communication.
- Special reports by the students to expand upon topics only slightly covered by required readings. Depending upon the level of student experience and interest, students may have their own topics of interest to explore and present to the class.

Suggested class topics

Abbreviated citations (last name and page numbers) from the particular texts listed below appear in the syllabus as readings for each week. Additional readings are listed for individual weeks.

- Brandt, Deborah, ed. 1999. *Women Working the NAFTA Food Chain: Women, Food, and Globalization.* Toronto: Second Story Press.
- Flowers, Linda. 1990. *Throwed Away.* Knoxville: University of Tennessee Press.
- Hahamovitch, Cindy. 1999. *The Fruits of Their Labor: Atlantic Coast Farmworkers and the Making of Migrant Poverty, 1870–1945.* Chapel Hill: University of North Carolina Press.
- Hellman, Judith Adler. 1994. *Mexican Lives.* New York: New Press.
- Manly, Libby, Alejandra Okie, and Melinda Wiggins, eds. 1998. *Campos sin Fronteras/Fields without Borders.* Durham, N.C.: Student Action with Farmworkers.

- Rothenberg, Daniel. 1998. *With These Hands: The Hidden World of Migrant Farmworkers Today.* New York: Harcourt Brace and Co.
- Steinbeck, John. 1939. *The Grapes of Wrath.* Reprint, New York: Penguin Books, 1992.
- Buss, Fran Leeper (ed). 1993. *Forjada bajo el sol/Forged under the Sun: The Life of Maria Elena Lucas.* Ann Arbor: University of Michigan Press.

Week 1: Introductions to the Course and Participants

Begin with students' experiences with farmworkers, agriculture, and advocacy and elicit the questions they want to explore in the course. By having students share these prior experiences during the first week, class members begin learning from one another from the outset, and the instructor can design the course accordingly.

ACTIVITIES

Introductions, including the professor's interest in the class; service-learning site descriptions; course requirements; journal guidelines

FILM

"Harvest of Shame," CBS documentary on farmworkers, first televised on Thanksgiving Day 1960

READINGS

Short clipping from local newspaper that can be read in class and discussed

Week 2: Slavery and Its Recollections— The Origins of American Farm Poverty

READINGS

- Hahamovitch pp. 3–112
- Cohen, William. 1991. *At Freedom's Edge: Black Mobility and the Southern White Quest for Racial Control.* Baton Rouge: Louisiana State University Press.
- Daniel, Pete. 1972/1990. *The Shadow of Slavery: Peonage in the South 1901–1969.* New York: Oxford University Press.
- Federal Writers Project Life Histories. Southern Historical Collection. Wilson Library of the University of North Carolina at Chapel Hill.
- Hurston, Zora Neale. 1978. *Their Eyes Were Watching God.* Chicago: University of Illinois Press.

- Litwack, Leon F. 1981. *Been in the Storm So Long: The Aftermath of Slavery.* New York: Knopf.
- Rosengarten, Theodore. 1974. *All God's Dangers: The Life of Nate Shaw.* New York: Knopf.
- Wesley, Charles H. 1927. *Negro Labor in the United States.* New York: Vanguard.
- Woodward, C. Van. 1995. *Strange Career of Jim Crow.* New York: Oxford University Press.

SPECIAL ASSIGNMENT FOR
EVERY CLASS MEMBER

Research an aspect of slavery and its aftermath, particularly as forced labor relates to agriculture in the South.

SPECIAL REPORT

Jim Crow South and Migrant Labor

Week 3: Agrarianism, World War II, and the State

READINGS

- Hahamovitch pp. 113–181
- Conway, Mimi. 1979. *Rise Gonna Rise: A Portrait of Southern Textile Workers.* Photographs by Earl Dotter. Garden City, N.J.: Anchor Press.
- Hall, Jacquelyn, et al. 1987. *Like a Family: The Making of a Southern Cotton Mill World.* Chapel Hill: University of North Carolina Press.

SPECIAL REPORT

Rise of textiles manufacturing and the shift from small farming to small town manufacturing in the South

Week 4: Farm Labor and the Great Depression

READINGS

- Steinbeck chapters 1–10
- Mitchell, H. L. 1979. *Mean Things Happening in This Land: The Life and Times of H. L. Mitchell, Cofounder of the Southern Tenant Farmers Union.* Montclair, N.J.: Allenheld, Osmun.
- Grubbs, Donald H. 1971. *Cry from the Cotton: The Southern Tenant Farmers Union and the New Deal.* Chapel Hill: University of North Carolina Press.
- Kester, Howard. 1997. *Revolt among Sharecroppers.* Knoxville: University of Tennessee Press.

SPECIAL REPORT

Southern Tenant Farmers Union

Week 5: Federal Policy and Farm Labor to World War II

READINGS

- Steinbeck, especially chapters 10–19
- Hahamovitch pp. 182–204

SPECIAL REPORT

Early federal relief in farm labor camps during the Great Depression

Week 6: "Throwed Away": North Carolina Tenants and Agricultural Changes

READINGS

- Flowers preface, introduction, parts 1 and 2
- Daniel, Pete. 1985. *Breaking the Land: The Transformation of Cotton, Tobacco, and Rice Cultures since 1880.* Urbana and Chicago: University of Illinois Press.

SPECIAL REPORT

Tobacco: The program, the industry, and mechanization

Week 7: Working and Living and Getting By

READINGS

- Flowers part 3, endnotes to chapter 9, and epilogue
- Hellman introduction and chapter 5
- Statistics and studies pertinent to your region and state

SPECIAL REPORT

Two U.S. economies: rural and urban comparisons

Week 8: Mexican Lives—Reasons Mexicans Work on Farms in the United States

READINGS

- Hellman pp. 113–232
- Buss introduction and pp. 1–44

FILM

"Milagritos"

Week 9: Farmworker Lives

READINGS

- Rothenberg chapters 1–3 (pp. 1–90)
- Buss part 1 (pp. 45–104)

SPEAKER

Farmworker/advocate

Week 10: Contracts and Borders

READINGS

- Rothenberg chapters 4–6 (pp. 91–180)
- Buss part 1 (pp. 105–150)

Week 11: Farmworker Lives Today

READINGS

- Rothenberg chapter 7 (pp. 181–204)
- SAF's *Fields without Borders* all
- Buss part 2 (pp. 151–260)

FILM

"Cruceros y Caminos," available through Student Action with Farmworkers

Week 12: Farmworker Politics and Unions

READINGS

- Rothenberg chapters 8 and 9 (pp. 205–271)
- Buss part 3 (pp. 261–302)
- Article on Mt. Olive Pickle boycott and the Farm Labor Organizing Committee

GUEST SPEAKER

Union organizer

Week 13: NAFTA, the Food Chain, and Our Place in It

READINGS

- Rothenberg pp. 323–326
- Brandt pp. 36–58, 62–76, 238–247, 250–259

Week 14: Class Presentations of Documentary Projects and Journals

READING

Steinbeck remainder, especially chapters 28–30

Farmworker-Related Organizations and Agencies

Advocacy Sites

Association of Farm Worker Opportunity Programs (AFOP)
703-528-4141
703-528-4145 (fax)
http://www.afop.org

Campaign for Labor Rights
541-344-5410
541-431-0523 (fax)
http://www.summersault.com/~agj/clr

Catholic Migrant Farm Worker Network
208-384-1778
http://www.cmfn.org

Center for Campus Organizing
617-725-2886
617-725-2873 (fax)
http://www.cco.org

Farmworker Justice Fund
202-776-1757
202-776-1792 (fax)
http://www.fwjustice.org

National Council of La Raza
202-785-1670
http://www.nclr.org

National Farm Worker Ministry
314-726-6470
314-726-6427 (fax)
http://www.nfwm.org

National Interfaith Committee for Worker Justice
773-728-8400
773-728-8409 (fax)
http://www.nicwj.org/index.html

Sin Fronteras
915-532-0921
915-532-4822 (fax)
http://www.farmworkers.org

Student Action with Farmworkers
919-660-3652
919-681-7600 (fax)
www.saf-unite.org
Student Action with Farmworkers provides information on current farmworker issues in weekly alerts by email listserve. To receive the alerts, type "subscribe" in the subject line of an email to farmworkers-request@duke.edu. SAF's mailing address is 1317 W. Pettigrew St., Durham, NC 27705.

United Students Against Sweatshops
202-NO-SWEAT
202-393-5886 (fax)
http://www.usasnet.org

Education Sites

East Coast Migrant Head Start Project
703-243-7522
703-243-1259 (fax)
http://www.ecmhsp.org

Eastern Stream Center on Resources and Training (ESCORT)
800-451-8058
607-432-7102
http://www.oneonta.edu/~thomasrl

ERIC Clearinghouse on Rural Education and Small Schools
Appalachia Educational Laboratory
304-347-0448
304-347-0467 (fax)
http://www.ael.org/eric

Migrant Education Even Start Program
202-260-2815

Government Sites

U.S. Census Bureau
http://www.census.gov

U.S. Department of Agriculture
http://www.usda.gov

Rural Development
http://www.rurdev.usda.gov

U.S. Department of Education
http://www.ed.gov
Office of Migrant Education
202-260-1164
http://www.ed.gov/offices/OESE/MEP
Disabled Migratory Agricultural Workers-
Seasonal Vocational Rehabilitation Services Projects
202-205-8435

U.S. Department of Health and Human Services
http://www.bphc.hrsa.gov
Migrant Health Program
301-594-4303
301-594-4997 (fax)
http://bphc.hrsa.gov/migrant/dcfault.htm

U.S. Department of Justice
Immigration and Naturalization Service
http://www.ins.usdoj.gov

U.S. Department of Labor
http://www.dol.gov
Migrant and Seasonal Agricultural Worker Protection Act
202-219-7605
Migrant and Seasonal Farmworker Services
202-219-5174 ext. 167
Division of Seasonal Farmworker Programs
202-219-5500 ext. 121

U.S. Environmental Protection Agency
http://www.epa.gov

U.S. General Accounting Office
http://www.gao.gov/main.html

Health and Housing Sites

Farmworker Health Services
202-347-7377
202-347-6385 (fax)
http://www.farmworkerhealth.org

Housing Assistance Council
202-842-8600
202-347-3441 (fax)
http://www.ruralhome.org

Migrant Clinicians Network
512-327-2017
512-327-0719 (fax)
http://www.migrantclinician.org

National Center for Farm Worker Health
512-312-2700
512-312-2600 (fax)
http://www.ncfh.org

National Rural Health Association
816-756-3140
816-756-3144 (fax)
http://www.nrharural.org

National Rural Housing Coalition
202-393-5229
http://www.nrhcweb.org

Labor Sites

AFL-CIO
202-637-5000
202-637-5058 (fax)
http://www.aflcio.org

Coalition of Immokalee Workers
941-657-8311
941-657-5055 (fax)
http://www.ciw-online.org

Farm Labor Organizing Committee (FLOC)
419-243-3456
http://www.floc.com

Labor Net
http://www.labornet.org

Pineros y Campesinos Unidos del Noroeste (PCUN)
503-982-0243
503-982-1031 (fax)
http://www.pcun.org

United Farm Workers
661-823-6252
661-823-6177 (fax)
http://www.ufw.org

Law and Immigration Sites

Legal Services Corporation
202-336-8800
202-336-8959 (fax)
http://www.lsc.gov

Migrant Legal Action Program
202-462-7744
202-462-7914 (fax)

National Network for Immigrant and Refugee Rights
510-465-1984
510-465-1885 (fax)
http://www.nnirr.org

The Mexican American Legal Defense and Educational Fund (MALDEF)
213-629-2512
213-629-0266 (fax)
http://www.maldef.org

The National Immigration Forum
202-544-0004
202-544-1905 (fax)
http://www.immigrationforum.org

Recommended Readings

Anzaldua, Gloria. 1987. *Borderlands: La Frontera.* San Francisco: Aunt Lute Books.

Association of Farmworker Opportunity Programs (AFOP). 1997. *ESL for Farm Safety: Teacher's Manual.* Arlington, Va.: AFOP.

Atkin, S. Beth. 1993. *Voices From the Fields: Children of Migrant Farmworkers Tell Their Stories.* New York: Little, Brown, and Co.

Barger, W. K. and Reza M. Ernesto. 1994. *The Farm Labor Movement in the Midwest: Social Change and Adaption among Migrant Farmworkers.* Austin: University of Texas Press.

Barndt, Deborah, ed. 1999. *Women Working the NAFTA Food Chain: Women, Food and Globalization.* Toronto, Canada: Second Story Press.

Buss, Ran Leeper, ed. 1993. *Forged Under The Sun: The Life of Maria Elena Lucas.* East Lansing: University of Michigan Press.

Cobb, James. 1984. *Industrialization and Southern Society.* Lexington: University of Tennessee Press.

———. 1982. *The Selling of the South.* Baton Rouge: Louisiana State University Press.

Coles, Robert. 1967. *Migrants, Sharecroppers, Mountaineers.* Boston: Little, Brown and Co.

Collier, George. 1994. *Basta! Land and the Zapatista Rebellion in Chiapas.* Oakland, Calif.: Institute for Food and Development Policy.

Collins, David R. 1996. *Farmworker's Friend: The Story of Cesar Chavez.* Minneapolis: Carolrhoda Books, Inc.

Craig, Richard B. 1971. *The Bracero Program: Interest Groups and Foreign Policy.* Austin: University of Texas Press.

Dusinberre, William. 1996. *Them Dark Days: Slavery in the American Rice Swamps.* Cary, N.C.: Oxford University Press.

Ferriss, Susan, Ricardo Sandoval, and Diana Hembree, eds. 1998. *The Fight in the Fields: Cesar Chavez and the Farmworkers' Movement.* New York: Harcourt Brace.

Fite, Gilbert. 1984. *Cotton Fields No More: Southern Agriculture, 1865–1980.* Lexington: University of Kentucky Press.

Galarza, Ernesto. 1964. *Merchants of Labor: The Mexican Bracero Story.* Charlotte and Santa Barbara: McNally and Loftin.

————. 1970. *Spiders in the House and Workers in the Field.* Notre Dame, Ind.: University of Notre Dame Press.

Gilmore, Glenda Elizabeth. 1996. *Gender and Jim Crow: Women and the Politics of White Supremacy in North Carolina, 1896–1920.* Chapel Hill: University of North Carolina Press.

Goodwyn, Lawrence. 1978. *The Populist Moment: A Short History of the Agrarian Revolt in America.* Cary, N.C.: Oxford University Press.

Grubbs, Donald. 1971. *Cry from the Cotton: the Southern Tenant Farmers Association.* Chapel Hill: University of North Carolina Press.

Hellman, Judith Adler. 1994. *Mexican Lives.* New York: New Press.

Jamieson, Stuart. 1946. *Labor Unionism in American Agriculture.* Bulletin No. 836. Washington, D.C.: U.S. Government Printing Office.

Krebs, A. V. 1992. *Corporate Reapers: The Book of Agribusiness.* Washington, D.C.: Essential Books.

Kulikoff, Allan. 1992. *The Agrarian Origins of American Capitalism.* Charlottesville: University Press of Virginia.

————. 1998. *Tobacco and Slaves: The Development of Southern Cultures in the Chesapeake, 1680–1800.* Chapel Hill: University of North Carolina Press.

Levy, Jacques. 1975. *Cesar Chavez: Autobiography of La Causa.* New York: Norton.

Light, Ken. 1998. *To the Promised Land.* New York: Aperture Foundation, Inc.

Massey, Douglas, Rafael Alarcón, Jorge Durand, and Humberto González. 1987. *Return to Atzlán: The Social Process of International Migration from Western Mexico.* Berkeley: University of California Press.

McWilliams, Carey. 1939. *Factories in the Field: The Story of Migratory Farm Labor in California.* Boston: Little, Brown, and Co.

Meister, Dick, and Ann Loftis. 1977. *A Long Time Coming: The Struggle to Unionize America's Farm Workers.* New York: MacMillan.

Mines, Richard, Susan Gabbard, and Ruth Samardick. 1991. *National Agricultural Worker Survey.* Washington, D.C.: U.S. Government Printing Office.

Mintz, Sidney. 1985. *Sweetness and Power: The Place of Sugar in Modern History.* New York: Viking Press.

Perez, Ramon. 1991. *Diary of an Undocumented Immigrant.* Houston: Arte Publico Press.

Pineros y Campesinos Unidos del Noroeste (PCUN). 1997. *Testimonies from the Fields: Clergy, Community Activists, Students and Members of Labor Unions Report on the Oregon Farmworkers' Struggle for Justice.* Portland, Ore.: PCUN.

Rivera, Tomas. 1987. *This Migrant Earth.* Houston: Arte Publico Press.

————. 1992. *Tomas Rivera: The Complete Works.* Houston: Arte Publico Press.

Rosales, Arturo F. 1997. *Chicano: The History of the Mexican American Civil Rights Movement.* Houston: Arte Publico Press.

Stull, Donald, Michael Broadway, and David Griffith. 1995. *Any Way They Cut It: Meat Packing and Small Town America.* Lawrence: University Press of Kansas.

Taylor, Ronald B. 1975. *Sweatshops in the Sun.* Boston: Beacon Press.

Thomas, Robert. 1985. *Citizenship, Gender, and Work*. Berkeley: University of California Press.

Traub-Werner, Marion and Lynda Yanz, eds. 2000. *Women behind the Labels: Worker Testimonies from Central America*. Chicago: Stitch and The Maquila Solidarity Network (September).

Valle, Isabel. 1994. *Fields of Toil: A Migrant Family's Journey*. Pullman, Washington: Washington State University Press.

Wilkinson, Alec. 1989. *Big Sugar: Seasons in the Cane Fields of Florida*. New York: Random House.

Videos

"Cesar Chavez: Celebration of Life." 1994. United Farm Workers of America, Inc. (UFW), AFL-CIO.

"Children of the Harvest." December 1998. NBC *Dateline*. Andy Court and Victor Anrango (producers), Dennis Murphy (reporter).

"From the Mountains to the Maquiladoras." 1991. Tennessee Industrial Renewal Network (TIRN).

"H2 Worker." 1990. Stephanie Black. New York: Icarus Films.

"Harvest of Shame." 1960. CBS News, with Edward R. Murrow.

"Legacy of Shame." 1995. CBS News, with Dan Rather. Fox Video.

"Listening to Children: A Moral Journey with Robert Coles." 1995. Social Media Productions.

"Milagritos . . . Little Miracles: When Communities Create Farmworker Housing." 1998. National Center for Farmworker Health (NCFH), Austin, Tex.

"PCUN Boycott for Justice in the Fields." 1993. Pineros y Campesinos Unidos del Noroeste (PCUN) and Nuvistamedia. Portland, Ore., cable access.

"Strawberries: The Fruit of Injustice." 1997. United Farm Workers of America, Inc. (UFW), AFL-CIO.

Works Cited

Acuna, Rodolfo. 1988. *Occupied America: A History of Chicanos.* New York: Harper and Row.

"Agitators for a Better Life." 1935. *Sharecroppers' Voice,* August.

Allegood, Jerry. 1999. "Farmers Look at Price, Not Package." Raleigh (N.C.) *News and Observer,* August 5.

Alvarez, Rodolfo. 1973. "The Psycho-historical and Socioeconomic Development of the Chicano Community in the U.S." *Social Science Quarterly* 53 (March): 920–942.

"Another Killing." 1935. *Sharecroppers' Voice,* June.

Arceo, Ramiro. 1999. Personal communication with Joy Kusserow.

Arcury, Thomas A., Colin K. Austin, Sara A. Quandt, and Rosa M. Saavedra. 1999a. "Enhancing Community Participation in Intervention Research: Farmworkers and Agricultural Chemicals in North Carolina." *Health Education and Behavior* 26, no. 4: 563–578.

Arcury, Thomas A., Sara A. Quandt, Colin K. Austin, John Preisser, and Luis F. Cabrera. 1999b. "Implementation of EPA's Worker Protection Standard Training for Agricultural Laborers: An Evaluation Using North Carolina Data." *Public Health Reports* 114, no. 5: 459–468.

Arrieta, Martha I., Frances J. Walker, and Thomas J. Mason. 1998. *A Profile of Demographic, Occupational, and Health-Related Characteristics of the Migrant and Settled (Seasonal) Hired Farmworker Population of Florida.*

Asbed, Greg. 1998. "What Have We Learned from the Hunger Strike?" *Fort Myers (Fla.) News Press,* February 25.

———. 1999. Interview by Alejandra Okie Holt, March 1.

Ash, Barbara. 1996. "Workers and Unions Boycott Mushrooms." *Tallahassee (Fla.) Democrat,* March 28.

Associated Press. 1999a. "Two Men Plead Guilty in Southwest Florida Slavery Ring." May 26.

———. 1999b. "Thirteen Die in Labor Van Crash in California." August 9.

Austin, Colin K., Thomas A. Arcury, Sara A. Quandt, John S. Preisser, Rosa M. Saavedra, and Luis F. Cabrera. 2001. "Training Farmworkers about Pesticide Safety: Issues of Control." *Journal of Health Care for the Poor and Underserved* 12: 236–249.

Avery, Rachel. 1998. "Wells Farms." In *Fields Without Borders/Campos Sin Fronteras: An Anthology of Documentary Writing and Photography by Student*

Action with Farmworkers' Interns, edited by Libby Manly, Alejandra Okie, and Melinda Wiggins, 37–39. Raleigh, N.C.: ADS Printing Co.

Bacon, David. 1995. "The Death of Pete Velasco." *San Francisco Examiner,* December 9.

Baer, Roberta D., and Marta Bustillo. 1993. "Susto and Mal de Ojo among Florida Farmworkers: Emic and Etic Perspectives." *Medical Anthropology Quarterly* 7, no. 1: 90–100.

Bagby, Joe. 2000. "Rancheros and Románticas." In *Recollections of Home/Recuerdos de mi tierra: A Compilation of Folklife Documentaries by Student Action with Farmworkers' Interns,* edited by Stacey Van Vleet, 18–19. Raleigh, N.C.: Grass Roots Press.

Bardacke, Frank. 1993. "Cesar's Ghost: Decline and Fall of the U.F.W." *Nation,* July 26.

Barry, Tom. 1995. *Zapata's Revenge: Free Trade and the Farm Crisis in Mexico.* Boston: South End Press.

Belden, Joseph N. 1986. *Dirt Rich, Dirt Poor: America's Food and Farm Crisis.* London: Routledge and Kegan Paul.

Bell, David, Patricia Roach, and Glenn Sheets. 1994. "The Nation's Invisible Families—Living in the Stream." *Migrant Education Messages and Outlook (MEMO)* 12, no. 4 (September/October): 18–21.

Benavidez, Max. 1997. "Chavez and El Teatro Campesino." In *The Fight in the Fields: Cesar Chavez and the Farmworkers Movement* by Susan Ferriss and Ricardo Sandoval; Diane Henbree, ed. New York: Harcourt, Brace and Co.

Benitez, Lucas. 1998. "Sowing Seeds for Change." Address presented at the Student Action with Farmworkers symposium. Gainesville, Fla. November.

Berger, John. 1979. *Pig Earth.* New York: Vintage International.

Berry, Wendell. 1996. *Another Turn of the Crank.* Washington, D.C.: Counterpoint.

———. 1986. *The Unsettling of America: Culture and Agriculture.* San Francisco: Sierra Club Books.

Blank, Susan, and Ramon S. Torrecilha. 1998. "Understanding the Living Arrangements of Latino Immigrants: A Life Course Approach." *International Migration Review* 32 (spring): 3–19.

Burns, Allan F. 1993. *Maya in Exile: Guatemalans in Florida.* Philadelphia: Temple University Press.

Burtman, Bob. 1995. "Working For The UFW: Interview with Dolores Huerta." *Works in Progress,* May.

Byrd, F. A. n.d. "Hints for the Consideration of White Men," Dr. F. A. Byrd Collection, Special Collections Library, Florida State University.

Cantarow, Ellen, ed. 1980. *Moving the Mountain: Women Working for Social Change.* New York: McGraw-Hill.

Carter, Sally A., with Roger C. Rosenthal. 1996. "Migrant Farmworker Housing: An American Tragedy, an American Challenge." *Clearinghouse Review: Journal of Poverty Law,* December.

Chateau Ste. Michelle. 1987. "To Our Customers." Letter in possession of Paul Ortiz. May 2.

Cavenaugh, David. 1980. *Final Report: National Farmworker Housing Survey.*

InterAmerica Research Associates, for the Farmers Home Administration, U.S. Department of Agriculture, Washington, D.C. Photocopy.

Chávez, Leo R. 1998. *Shadowed Lives: Undocumented Immigrants in American Society*. New York: Holt, Rinehart, and Winston.

Chavkin, Nancy Feyl, and Dora Lara Gonzalez. 1995. "Forging Partnerships Between Mexican American Parents and the Schools." *ERIC Digest* (Appalachia Educational Laboratories, Arlington, Va.). Bulletin EDO-RC-95-8 (October).

Ciesielski, Steven, Dana P. Loomis, Susan Rupp Mims, and Annella Auer. 1994. "Pesticide Exposures, Depresssion, and Symptoms among North Carolina Migrant Farmworkers." *American Journal of Public Health* 84: 446–451.

Coles, Robert. 1967. *Migrants, Sharecroppers, Mountaineers*. Boston: Little, Brown and Co.

Collier, George. 1994. *Basta! Land and the Zapatista Rebellion in Chiapas*. Oakland, Calif.: Institute for Food and Development Policy.

Collins, Chuck, Betsy Leondon-Wright, and Holly Slelan. 1999. *Shifting Fortunes: The Perils of the Growing American Wealth Gap*. Boston: United for a Fair Economy.

Commission on Agricultural Workers. 1992. *Report of the Commission on Agricultural Workers* (November). Washington, D.C.: U.S. Government Printing Office.

Commission for Labor Cooperation. 2000. "Legal Background Paper: Protection of Migrant Agricultural Workers in Canada, Mexico, and the United States" (February). Secretariat for the Tri-National Cooperative Activity on Migrant Agricultural Work.

Congressional Globe. 1886.

Cornwall, A., and R. Jewkes. 1995. "What is participatory research?" *Social Science and Medicine* 41:1667–1676.

Cruz, David. 1999. Letter to Student Action with Farmworkers, May 26.

Daniel, Cletus E. 1981. *Bitter Harvest: A History of California Farmworkers, 1870–1941*. Ithaca, N.Y.: Cornell University Press.

Daniel, Pete. 1972, 1990. *The Shadow of Slavery: Peonage in the South, 1901–1969*. Chicago: University of Illinois Press.

Davis, Jay R. 1996. "Commissioner Orders Ban on Spanish Signs." *Tribune*, July 3.

Davis, Shelley. 1997. "Child Labor in Agriculture." *ERIC Digest* (Appalachia Educational Laboratories, Arlington, Va.). Bulletin EDO-RC-96-10 (February).

"Day Care Feud Splits Town." 1999. *Tennessean*, August 30.

de la Cruz, Jessie Lopez. 1987. "The First Woman Farmworker Organizer Out In The Fields." In *Women's America: Refocusing the Past*, edited by Linda K. Kerber and Jane De Hart-Mathews. New York: Oxford University Press.

de la Fuente v. Stokely-Van Camp, Inc., 514 F. Supplement 68 (C.D. Ill. 1981).

de la Rosa, Denise, and Carlyle E. Maw. 1990. *Hispanic Education: A Statistical Report 1990*. Policy Analysis Center, Office of Research, Advocacy and Legislation, National Council of La Raza (NCLR). Washington, D.C.: NCLR.

de la Torre, Adela. 1993. "Hard Choices and Changing Roles among Mexican Migrant Campesinas." In *Building with Our Hands: New Directions in Chicana Studies*, edited by Adela de la Torre and Beatríz M. Pesquera. Berkeley: University of California Press.

"Democratic Doctrine." 1884. *New York Globe,* September 20.

DeWind, Josh, Tom Seidl, and Janet Shenk. 1979. "Contract Labor in U.S. Agriculture: The West Indian Cane Cutters in Florida." In *Peasants and Proletarians: The Struggles of Third World Workers,* edited by Robin Cohen, Peter C. W. Gutkind, and Phyllis Brazier. New York: Monthly Review Press.

Diamond, Jeff. 1998. "African American Attitudes towards U.S. Immigration Policy." *International Migration Review* 32 (summer): 451–470.

Diaz-Stevens, Ana Maria, and Anthony M. Stevens-Arroyo. 1998. *Recognizing the Latino Resurgence in U.S. Religion: The Emmaus Paradigm.* Boulder: Westview Press.

Du Bois, W. E. B. 1935. *Black Reconstruction in America: An Essay toward a History of the Part Which Black Folk Played in the Attempt to Reconstruct Democracy in America, 1860–1880.* Reprint, New York: Meridian Books, 1965.

Duchon, D. A. 1997. "Home Is Where You Make It: Hmong Refugees in Georgia." *Urban Anthropology* 26, no. 1: 71–92.

Edwards, Gina. 1998. "Immokalee, My Home." *Naples (Fla.) Daily News,* March 15.

Elton Orchards v. Brennan. 508 F. 2d 500 (1974).

Espinoza v. Stokely-Van Camp, Inc. 641 F. 2d 535 (7th Circuit 1981).

"Breaking the Silence: Women Learning Their Rights." 1997. *The Exchange* 1: 3.

Farm Labor Organizing Committee (FLOC). "Why Is FLOC Organizing in North Carolina?" Online at http://www.iupui.edu/~floc/nc.htm.

"Farmers Backward with Their Work." 1920. *Jasper News,* February 20.

Ferriss, Susan, and Ricardo Sandoval. 1997. Edited by Diana Hembree. *The Fight in the Fields: Cesar Chavez and the Farmworkers Movement.* New York: Harcourt, Brace and Co.

Fesperman, Dan, and Kate Schatzkin. 1999. "Ten Ways to Show Who's Boss." *Baltimore Sun,* February 28.

Finnegan, William. 1996. "The New Americans." *New Yorker,* March 25, 52–71.

Flowers, Linda. 1990. *Throwed Away: Failures of Progress in Eastern North Carolina.* Knoxville: University of Tennessee Press.

Foner, Nancy. 1997. "The Immigrant Family: Cultural Legacies and Cultural Changes." *International Migration Review* 31 (summer): 961–974.

"For the Final Time, They March for Chavez." 1993. *Los Angeles Times,* April 30.

Galarza, Ernesto. 1977. *Farm Workers and Agri-Business in California, 1947–1960.* Notre Dame, Ind.: University of Notre Dame Press.

Garcia, Brenda. 1998. "Interview with Brenda Garcia" by Erica Lian. In *Living the American Dream: Economic Justice for Farmworkers, A Compilation of Documentary Works by 1998 Student Action with Farmworkers' Interns.* Durham, N.C.: Student Action with Farmworkers, 41–47.

Geffert, Garry G. 1993. "The Bias of a Majority of the Commission on Agricultural Workers Led to Recommendations Which Ignore the Factual Findings." In *In Defense of the Alien.* New York: Center for Migration Studies.

GEMS: Graduation Enhancement for Migrant Students. 1997. STAR Center. San Antonio, Tex.: Intercultural Development Research Association.

Goldschmidt, Walter. 1978. *As You Sow: Three Studies in the Social Consequences of Agribusiness.* Montclair, N.J.: Allanheld, Osmun, and Co.

Gordon, Robert. 1999. "Poisons in the Fields: The United Farm Workers, Pesticides, and Environmental Politics." *Pacific Historical Review* 68 (February): 51.

"Government to Crack Down on Unfair Planters." 1938. *STFU News,* May.

Greenhouse, Steven. 1998. "As Economy Booms, Migrant Workers Housing Worsens." *New York Times,* May 31.

Greider, William. 1992. *Who Will Tell the People.* New York: Simon and Schuster.

Griffith, David. 1986. "Peasants in Reserve: Temporary West Indian Labor in the U.S. Farm Labor Market." *International Migration Review* 20 (winter): 875–898.

———. 1995. "Hay trabajo: Poultry Processing, Rural Industrialization, and the Latinization of Low-Wage Labor." In *Any Way They Cut It: Meat Packing and Small Town America,* edited by D. Stull, M. Broadway, and D. Griffith. Lawrence: University Press of Kansas.

Griffith, David, and Ed Kissam. 1995. *Working Poor: Farmworkers in the United States.* Philadelphia: Temple University Press.

Grimes, Sister Gail. 1998. "The Farmworker Health and Safety Institute." *Journal of Agromedicine* 5, no. 2: 33–37.

Griswold del Castillo, Richard, and Arnoldo De Leon. 1996. *North to Aztlán: A History of Mexican Americans in the U.S.* New York: Twayne Publishers.

Griswold del Castillo, Richard, and Richard A. Garcia. 1995. *César Chávez: A Triumph of Spirit.* Norman: University of Oklahoma Press.

Guarnaccia, Peter J., Jacqueline Lowe Angel, and Ronald Angel. 1992. "The Impacts of Farm Work on Health: Analysis of the Hispanic Health and Nutrition Examination Survey." *International Migration Review* 26, no. 1: 111–132.

Hahamovitch, Cindy. 1997. *The Fruits of Their Labor: Atlantic Coast Farmworkers and the Making of Migrant Poverty, 1870–1945.* Chapel Hill: University of North Carolina Press.

———. 1999. "The Politics of Labor Scarcity" (December). Washington, D.C.: Center for Immigration Studies.

Hanson, Pat. 1997. "The Arts: The Incomparable Luis Valdez; Leader of a Teledramatic Revolution." *Hispanic Outlook in Higher Education* 7 (May 30): 9.

Harrington, Jim. 1973. "Filosofia del Boicoteo." (San Juan, Tex.) *El Campesino,* November 5.

Healey, Dorothy, and Maurice Isserman. 1990. *Dorothy Healey Remembers: A Life in the American Communist Party.* New York: Oxford University Press.

Hemming, Jill. 1996. "Health and Healing." Interview notes and tape index. Raleigh: North Carolina Museum of History.

Hernandez, Diego. 1994. Interview by Gerardo Martinez. Morganton, N.C.

Hernandez-Flecha v. Quiros. 567 F. 2d 1156 (1978).

Hightower, Jim. 1978. *Hard Tomatoes, Hard Times.* Cambridge, Mass.: Schenkman Publishing Co.

"History of Farmworkers Struggle for Workplace Democracy at U.S. Tobacco-Owned Vineyards." n.d. Flyer in Paul Ortiz's possession.

hooks, bell. 1989. *Talking Back.* Boston: South End Press.

Horton, Myles, with Judith Kohl and Herbert Kohl. 1990. *Myles Horton: The Long Haul, An Autobiography.* New York: Doubleday.

Housing Assistance Council. 1996. *Fitting the Pieces Together: An Examination of Data Sources Related to Farmworker Housing* (February). Washington, D.C.: Housing Assistance Council.

Housing Assistance Council. 1997a. *HOME, CDBG, and Farmworker Housing Development.* Washington, D.C.: Housing Assistance Council.

Housing Assistance Council. 1997b. *Survey of Demand for the RHS Farm Labor Housing Program* (October). Washington, D.C.: Housing Assistance Council.

Housing Assistance Council. 1998a. *Leveraging Funds for Section 514/516 Farmworker Housing Development* (July). Washington, D.C.: Housing Assistance Council.

Housing Assistance Council. 1998b. *Fair Housing, the Zoning Process, and Land Use Politics in Rural Areas* (December). Washington, D.C.: Housing Assistance Council.

Housing Assistance Council. 2000. *Abundant Fields, Meager Shelter: Findings from a Survey of Farmworker Housing in the Eastern Migrant Stream* (October). Washington, D.C.: Housing Assistance Council.

"Huelga Wins One." 1970. *Basta Ya!* (San Francisco), August.

Hurtado Gomez, Marcella. 1998. "That Summer." In *Campos sin fronteras/Fields without Borders: An Anthology of Documentary Writing and Photography by Student Action with Farmworkers' Interns,* edited by Libby Manly, Alejandra Okie, and Melinda Wiggins, 46–50. Raleigh, N.C.: ADS Printing Co.

"Improved Conditions Result From Organization of Croppers." 1935. *Sharecroppers' Voice,* July.

Inciardi, J. A., H. L. Surratt, H. M. Colon, D. D. Chitwood, and J. E. Rivers. 1999. "Drug use and HIV risks among migrant farmworkers on the DelMarVa Peninsula." *Substance Use and Misuse* 34, no. 4–5: 653–666.

Jenkins, J. Craig. 1985. *The Politics of Insurgency: The Farm Worker Movement in the 1960s.* New York: Columbia University Press.

Kester, Howard. 1969. *Revolt among the Sharecroppers.* New York: Arno Press.

King, Martin Luther, Jr. 1964. *Why We Can't Wait.* New York: Mentor.

Kushner, Sam. 1975. *Long Road to Delano.* New York: International Publishers.

"Labor in the Potato Section." 1920. *Palatka (Fla.) Morning Post,* April 12.

Lacy, Elaine C. 1988. "Mexican Immigrant Workers in the Southwest: The 1920s and the 1980s." *Review of Latin American Studies* 1, no. 2: 103–120.

LaCour, Rachel. 1999. "Life on Easy Street." In *Farmworker Folklife: A Compilation of Documentary Works by 1999 Student Action with Farmworkers' into the Fields Interns,* 63–64. Durham, N.C.: Student Action with Farmworkers.

"Land and Labor." 1877. *Christian Recorder,* May 31.

LeBlanc, Judith, ed. 1996. *Children of La Frontera: Binational Efforts to Serve Mexican Migrant and Immigrant Students.* Charleston, W.V.: ERIC Clearinghouse on Rural Education and Small Schools.

Leon, Edgar. 1996. "Challenges and Solutions for Educating Migrant Students." *Julian Samora Research Institute Research Report* 28. East Lansing: Michigan State University.

"Letter from Jax." 1867. *Christian Recorder*, September 28.

Levy, Jacques. 1975. *Cesar Chavez: Autobiography of La Causa.* New York: W. W. Norton and Co.

Linder, Marc. 1992. *Migrant Workers and Minimum Wages: Regulating the Exploitation of Agricultural Labor in the U.S.* Boulder, Colo.: Westview Press.

Lobet, Ingrid. 1995. "Ste. Michelle/UFW" (March). Radio documentary transcript. Seattle: KPLU-FM.

Marshall v. Coastal Growers Association, 598 F. 2d 521 (9th Circuit 1979).

Martin, Phillip L., and David A. Martin. 1994. *The Endless Quest: Helping America's Farm Workers.* Boulder, Colo.: Westview Press.

Martínez, Rubén. 1997. "Beyond Borders: Culture, Movement and Bedlam on Both Sides of the Rio Grande." *NACLA: Report on the Americas* 30 (January/February): 36–39.

Matthiessen, Peter. 1971. *Sal Si Puedes: Cesar Chavez and the New American Revolution.* New York: Dell Publishing Co.

Maxwell, Bill. 1999. "Farm Workers Make Progress." *(Vero Beach, Fla.) Press Journal,* July 31.

McElroy, Ann. 1982. "Intra-Cultural Diversity and Change among Migrant Farm Workers in Northern California." *Anthropology and Humanism Quarterly* 7 (June-September): 35–38.

McFeely, William S. 1991. *Frederick Douglass.* New York: W. W. Norton and Co.

McVea, K. L. 1997. "Lay injection practices among migrant farmworkers in the age of AIDS: Evolution of a biomedical folk practice." *Social Science and Medicine* 45, no. 1: 91–98.

McWilliams, Carey. 1939. *Factories in the Field: The Story of Migratory Farm Labor in California.* Boston: Little, Brown, and Co.

Mehta, Kala, Susan M. Gabbard, Vanessa Barrat, Melissa Lewis, Daniel Carroll, and Richard Mines. 2000. *Findings from the National Agricultural Workers Survey (NAWS) 1997–1998: A Demographic and Employment Profile of United States Farmworkers.* Research Report No. 8. (March). Office of the U.S. Department of Labor, Office of Program Economics. Washington, D.C.: U.S. Department of Labor.

Meister, Dick, and Ann Loftis. 1977. *A Long Time Coming: The Struggle to Unionize America's Farm Workers.* New York: MacMillan.

Meister, Joel S. 1991. "The Health of Migrant Farm Workers." *Occupational Medicine: State of the Art Reviews* 6, no. 3: 503–518.

"Mexican Farm Laborers Face 'Slave Labor' Conditions in both Mexico and the U.S." 1998. *Mexican Labor News and Analysis* 3, no. 13 (July 16).

Migrant Clinicians Network (MCN). 1996. *Domestic Violence and Migrant Farmworker Women.* Austin, Tex.: Migrant Clinicians Network.

———. 1997. "Tuberculosis among Agricultural Workers." *MCN Streamline* 3, no. 1: 1–2. Austin, Tex.: Migrant Clinicians Network.

———. 1998. *The TBNet System.* Monograph Series. Austin, Tex.: Migrant Clinicians Network.

———. 1999. *MCN Monthly Report* 3, no. 11. Austin, Tex.: Migrant Clinicians Network.

"Migrant Workers Protest for Change." 1992. *Bellingham (Wash.) Herald,* May 4.

Miller, Randall M. 1994. "Roman Catholic Church." In *Encyclopedia of Religion in the South,* edited by Samuel S. Hill. Macon, Ga.: Mercer University Press.

Mines, Richard. n.d. "Ethnic Shift in Eastern Crop Agriculture: Replacement or Displacement?" n.p.

Mines, Richard, Beatriz Boccalandro, and Susan Gabbard. 1992. "The Latinization of U.S. Farm Labor." *NACLA: Report on the Americas* 27 (July): 42–46.

Mines, Richard, Susan Gabbard, and Anne Steirman. 1997. *A Profile of U.S. Farm Workers: Demographics, Household Composition, Income and Use of Services.* Research Report No. 6, based on data from the National Agricultural Workers Survey (NAWS). U.S. Department of Labor, Office of Program Economics. Washington, D.C.: U.S. Government Printing Office.

Moberg, Mark, and J. Stephen Thomas. 1993. "Class Segmentation and Divided Labor: Asian Workers in the Gulf of Mexico Seafood Industry (Bayou La Batre, Alabama)." *Ethnology* 32 (winter): 87–99.

Mooney, Patrick, and Theo Majka. 1995. *Farmers' and Farmworkers' Movements: Social Protest in American Agriculture.* New York: Twayne Publishers.

Moore, Truman. 1962. *The Slaves We Rent.* New York: Random House.

Morse, Susan C. 1997. "Unschooled Migrant Youth: Characteristics and Strategies to Serve Them." *ERIC Digest* (Appalachia Educational Laboratories, Arlington, Va.). Bulletin EDO-RC-97-2 (March).

Mt. Olive Pickle Company, Inc. n.d. Mount Olive, N.C. Flyer.

Naison, Mark. 1996. "The Southern Tenant Farmers' Union and the CIO." In *We Are All Leaders: The Alternative Unionism of the Early 1930s,* edited by Staughton Lynd. Urbana: University of Illinois Press.

National Interfaith Committee for Worker Justice (NICWJ). 1998. "Human Cost of Poultry." Chicago: NICWJ.

National Migrant Resource Program, Inc. (NMRP, subsequently National Center for Farmworker Health). 1990. *Migrant and Seasonal Farmworker Health Objectives for the Year 2000.* Austin, Tex.: National Migrant Resource Program, Inc.

National Program for Secondary Credit Exchange and Accrual. 1994. *Options and Resources for Achieving Credit Accrual for Secondary-aged Migrant Youth.* Texas: U.S. Department of Education, Office of Migrant Education, Texas Education Agency.

New York Age. 1920. May 29.

"New York Hears Sharecroppers." 1937. *Sharecroppers' Voice,* June.

Nixon, Ron. 1995. "Working in Harm's Way." *Southern Exposure* (fall/winter): 15.

"No More Business as Usual." 1994. *Si Se Puede,* Newsletter of the United Farm Workers of Washington (fall): 1.

North Carolina Department of Labor. 1997. "Grower Registrations 1992–1997 and Current Housing Inspections." N.C. Department of Labor Report (July 1). Raleigh, N.C.: N.C. Department of Labor.

North Carolina State Government Statistics Abstract. 1973. 2nd Edition. Raleigh, N.C.: Statistical Services Section of the Office of State of the Department of Administration.

"Notes from the Vineyard." 1993. *Si Se Puede,* Newsletter of the United Farm Workers of Washington (summer): 4.

O'Hara, Timothy. 2000. "Migrants on the March." *Sarasota (Fla.) Herald-Tribune*, February 25.

"Orange Pickers May Strike for More Pay." 1919. *Palatka (Fla.) Daily News*, November 15.

Ortiz, Paul. 2000. "'Like Water Covered the Sea': The African American Freedom Struggle in Florida, 1877–1920." Ph.D. diss., Duke University.

Payne, Sheila. 1998. "Oral History of Sheila Payne." Interview by Melinda Steele. In *Living the American Dream: Economic Justice for Farmworkers, A Compilation of Documentary Works by 1998 Student Action with Farmworkers Interns*, 138–151. Durham, N.C.: Student Action with Farmworkers.

"People's Column." 1935. *Sharecroppers' Voice*, August.

Pfeffer, Max J. 1994. "Low-wage Employment and Ghetto Poverty: A Comparison of African American and Cambodian Day-haul Farm Workers in Philadelphia." *Social Problems* 41 (February): 9–29.

"Plática con Chavez: Entrevista con El Macriado." 1973. *(San Juan, Tex.) El Campesino*, May 15.

Prieto, Norma Iglesias. 1997. *Beautiful Flowers of the Maquiladora: Life Histories of Women Workers in Tijuana*, translated by Michael Stone with Gabrielle Winkler. Austin, Tex.: University of Texas Press.

Proctor, Samuel DeWitt. 1995. *The Substance of Things Hoped For*. New York: G. P. Putnam's Sons.

Quandt, Sara A., Thomas A. Arcury, Colin K. Austin, and Rosa M. Saavedra. 1998. "Farmworker and Farmer Perceptions of Farmworker Agricultural Chemical Exposure in North Carolina." *Human Organization* 57, no. 3: 359–368.

"Rally For Cesar Chavez Street Brings Out 5,000 in Fresno." 1993. *San Francisco Examiner*, November 22.

Report of the National Commission on State Workmen's Compensation Laws. 1972. Washington, D.C.

Risteen, Donna. 1998. "Domestic Violence." In *Living the American Dream: Economic Justice for Farmworkers, A Compilation of Documentary Works by 1998 Student Action with Farmworkers Interns*. Durham, N.C.: Student Action with Farmworkers.

Rivera, Tomás. 1996. *. . . Y no se lo tragó la tierra*. Houston: Piñata Books.

Robinson, Andrea. 1998. "Settled Out but Not Settled Down." In *Living the American Dream: Economic Justice for Farmworkers, A Compilation of Documentary Works by 1998 Student Action with Farmworkers Interns*, 30–38. Durham, N.C.: Student Action with Farmworkers.

Rochín, Refugio I. "Rural Latinos: Evolving Conditions and Issues." 1995. In *The Changing American Countryside: Rural People and Places*, edited by Emery N. Castle. Lawrence: University Press of Kansas.

Rodriguez, Arturo S. 1993. "The Resurrection of the UFW." *San Francisco Examiner*, December 7.

Rodriguez, Roman. 1991. Testimony before Commission on Agricultural Workers. *Hearings and Workshops before the Commission on Agricultural Workers 1989–1993 to Accompany the Report of the Commission, Appendix II*. West Palm Beach, Fla. (February 15): 651.

Ross, Fred. 1989. *Conquering Goliath: Cesar Chavez and the Beginning.* Keene, Calif.: El Taller Grafico Press.

Rothenberg, Daniel. 1998. *With These Hands: The Hidden World of Migrant Farmworkers Today.* New York: Harcourt, Brace and Co.

Ruley, Melinda. 1994. "Downeast: On Blackwater." *Independent Weekly,* June 29, 9–13.

Rumbaut, Ruben G. 1997. "Assimilation and its Discontents: Between Rhetoric and Reality." *International Migration Review* 31 (winter): 923–960.

Rust, George S. 1990. "Health Status of Migrant Farmworkers: A Literature Review and Commentary." *American Journal of Public Health* 80, no. 10: 1213–1217.

"S.A. Archbishop Gives Support to UFW." 1972. *Barrio* (Corpus Christi, Tex.), September.

Saragoza, Alex M. 1994. *Mexican Immigrant Children in American Schools: An Update.* San Francisco: Many Cultures Publishing.

Schwartz, Harry. 1945. *Seasonal Farm Labor in the U.S.* New York: Columbia University Press.

Seewere, John. 1999. "Farm Workers Union Takes Its Fight to the South." Associated Press, March 24.

Semler, Michael. 1983. "Aliens in the Orchards." *Yale Law and Policy Review* 1: 187.

Sengupta, Somini. 1992. "A Duty to Fight." *Los Angeles Times,* August 4.

Shorris, Earl. 1992. *Latinos: A Biography of the People.* New York: W. W. Norton and Co., Avon Books.

Shover, John L. 1976. *First Majority—Last Minority: The Transforming of Rural Life in America.* Dekalb: Northern Illinois University Press.

"Skilled Labor in Jacksonville Exceeds Demand." 1919. *Florida Metropolis.* Jacksonville, Fla. (January 17).

Smith, Harry, and Kate Poff, eds. 1997. *Farm Aid News and Views* 5, no. 3, online at http://periodicals.farmaid.faid.

Steinbeck, John. 1939. *Grapes of Wrath.* Reprint, New York: Viking Press, 1967.

———. 1988. *The Harvest Gypsies: On the Road to the Grapes of Wrath.* Berkeley: Heyday Books.

"S.T.F.U. Members Get W.P.A. Jobs." 1938. *STFU News,* May.

"STFU Starts Migratory Organization." 1940. *STFU News,* May.

The Strawberry Workers Campaign. 1996. *Five Cents for Fairness: The Case for Change in the Strawberry Fields.* California: United Farm Workers (November). Pamphlet.

Student Action with Farmworkers. 2000. "Journal by Into the Fields Intern Sarah Betson." Photocopy.

Teamster Local 890. Online at http://www.teamsters890.org.

Testimony Taken by the Joint Select Committee To Inquire into the Condition of Affairs in the Late Insurrectionary States: Miscellaneous and Florida. 1872. Washington, D.C.: U.S. Government Printing Office.

Tomás, Carmen. 1999. "The Virgin of Guadalupe." Interview by Wendy Daniels Ibarra. In *Farmworker Folklife: A Compilation of Documentary Works by*

1999 Student Action with Farmworkers' Into the Fields Interns, 40–51. Durham, N.C.: Student Action with Farmworkers.

United Farm Workers of Washington State (UFWWS). 1994. "To Support Committees." July 21. Letter in Paul Ortiz's possession.

U.S. Attorney General. 1959. *Opinion of the Attorney General on Migrant Farm Labor-Wagner Preyser Act, 41 Op. A.G. 406.* Washington, D.C.: U.S. Government Printing Office.

U.S. Bureau of Primary Health Care (BPHC). 1995. *Losing Ground: The Condition of Farmworkers in America, Recommendations of the National Advisory Council on Migrant Health.* Washington, D.C.: U.S. Government Printing Office.

U.S. Census Bureau. *Population Projections for States by Age, Sex, Race, and Hispanic Origin* PPL 47. Online at www.census.gov.

U.S. Congress. 1978. *The British West Indies Temporary Alien Labor Program.* 95th Congress, 2d Session. Washington, D.C.: U.S. Government Printing Office.

U.S. Congressional Research Service. 1980. *Temporary Worker Programs: Background and Issues* (February). Washington, D.C.: U.S. Government Printing Office.

U.S. Department of Agriculture (USDA). 2001. *Agricultural Statistics,* Washington, D.C.: U.S. Government Printing Office, NASS Environmental, Economics, and Demographics Branch.

U.S. Department of Agriculture (USDA). *Census of Agriculture.* Washington, D.C.: U.S. Government Printing Office.

U.S. Department of Commerce (DOC), Bureau of the Census. 1996. *Census of Agriculture.* Washington, D.C.: U.S. Department of Commerce.

U.S. Department of Education, Office of Migrant Education, National Program for Secondary Credit Exchange and Accrual. 1994. *Options and Resources for Achieving Credit Accrual for Secondary-aged Migrant Youth.* Edinburg, Tex.: Texas Education Agency.

U.S. Department of Health and Human Services (HHS), Health Resources and Services Administration, Bureau of Primary Health Care, Migrant Health Branch. 1999. *Proceedings for National Advisory Council on Migrant Health.* Coral Gables, Fla. (November 20).

U.S. Department of Housing and Urban Development (HUD), Office of Policy Development and Research. 2000. *Rental Housing Assistance—The Worsening Crisis* (March). Washington, D.C.: HUD.

U.S. Department of Labor (DOL), Wage and Hour Division. 1981. *Investigative narrative under the FLCRA with respect to Jack Simmons,* copy obtained by the author under the Freedom of Information Act. Washington, D.C.: U.S. Department of Labor.

U.S. Department of Labor (DOL). 1993. *U.S. Farmworkers in the Post-IRCA Period: Based on Data from the National Agricultural Workers Survey.* Report No. 3. Washington, D.C.: U.S. Department of Labor.

U.S. Department of Labor (DOL), Office of Inspector General. 1998. *Consolidation of Labor's Enforcement Responsibilities for the H-2A Program Could*

Better Protect U.S. Agricultural Workers. Report No. 04-98-004-03-321. Washington D.C.: U.S. Department of Labor.

U.S. Environmental Protection Agency (EPA). 1993. *A Guide to Heat Stress in Agriculture.* Washington, D.C.: U.S. Government Printing Office.

U.S. General Accounting Office (GAO). 1989. *Immigration Reform: Potential Impact on West Coast Farm Labor* (August). Washington, D.C.: U.S. Government Printing Office.

————. 1997. *H-2A Agricultural Guestworker Program: Changes Could Improve Services to Employers and Better Protect Workers* (December). Washington, D.C.: U.S. Government Printing Office.

U.S. House of Representatives Committee on Education and Labor. 1991. *Report on the Use of Temporary Foreign Workers in the Florida Sugar Cane Industry* (July). 102d Congress., 2d Session. Washington, D.C.: U.S. Government Printing Office.

U.S. House of Representatives. 1974. "Farm Labor Contractor Registration Act Amendments of 1974." Report 93-1493. 93rd Congress. Washington, D.C.: U.S. Government Printing Office.

U.S. Senate Committee on Labor and Public Welfare. 1969. *Migrant and Seasonal Farmworker Powerlessness, Part 4: Farmworker Legal Problems.* Washington, D.C.: U.S. Government Printing Office.

Velasquez, Baldemar, with Elise Blackwell. 1992. "Meeting the Transnational Corporate Challenge." *Beyond Borders* (winter): 8-9.

Velásquez, Gloria. 1994. *Bella Juventud/Wonderful Youth: I Used to Be a Superwoman.* Santa Monica, Calif.: Santa Monica College Press.

Vogeler, Ingolf. 1982. *The Myth of the Family Farm: Agribusiness Dominance of U.S. Agriculture.* Boulder, Colo.: Westview Press.

Watkins, Elizabeth L., Christina Harlan, Eugenia Eng, et al. 1994. "Assessing the Effectiveness of Lay Health Advisors with Migrant Farmworkers." *Family and Community Health* 16, no. 4: 72-87.

Weil, Simone. 1949. *The Need for Roots: Prelude to a Declaration of Duties towards Mankind.* London: Routledge.

Weiner, Tim. 1999. "The Nation; It's Raining Farm Subsidies." *New York Times,* August 8.

White, Heather Hiam. 1998. "Their Labor, Our Gifts, Your Choices." *Washington Post,* December 20.

Whitman, Frank. 1920. "The Onion and a Brick." *Florida Grower,* August 28.

Wilk, V.A. 1986. *The Occupational Health of Migrant and Seasonal Farmworkers in the United States.* Washington, D.C.: Farmworker Justice Fund.

Wilkinson, Alec. 1989. *Big Sugar: Seasons in the Cane Fields of Florida.* New York: Random House.

Williams, Bob. 1999. "Farms Fading Fast in North Carolina, Census Shows." Raleigh (N.C.) *News and Observer,* February 2.

"Winery Workers Vote to Unionize." 1995. *(Olympia, Wash.) Olympian,* June 3.

Wood, Charles H., and Terry L. McCoy. 1985. "Migration, Remittances and Development: A Study of Caribbean Cane Cutters in Florida." *International Migration Review* 19 (summer): 251-277.

Woodruff, Nan Elizabeth. 1993. "African-American Struggles for Citizenship in the Arkansas and Mississippi Deltas in the Age of Jim Crow." *Radical History Review* 55 (winter): 33–51.

Zachary, G. Pascal. 1995. "Winery's Field Workers Break New Ground in Union Election." *Wall Street Journal*, June 7.

Zahm, Shelia Hoar, Mary H. Ward, and Aaron Blair. 1997. "Pesticides and Cancer." *Occupational Medicine: State of the Art Reviews* 12, no. 2: 269–289.

Zandy, Janet, ed. 1995. *Liberating Memory: Our Work and Our Working-Class Consciousness*. New Brunswick: Rutgers University Press.

Contributors

Ramiro Arceo is the education director for Student Action with Farmworkers, where he coordinates a school success project for migrant students in North Carolina. He is a former College Assistance Migrant Program (CAMP) student at California State University in Sacramento. Ramiro is the son of farmworkers and a native of Colima, Mexico.

Colin Austin is a research associate at MDC, Inc., a nonprofit research and demonstration organization in Chapel Hill, North Carolina. He is a former outreach worker for legal aid and a rural health clinic, and has coordinated and published research on pesticide exposure. Colin chairs the board of directors of the Migrant Clinicians Network.

Garry Geffert splits his time between his position as staff attorney with the West Virginia Legal Services Plan, Inc., and a solo private practice. He has represented farmworkers, including temporary foreign workers, for more than twenty years.

Cindy Hahamovitch is a professor in the history department at the College of William and Mary in Williamsburg, Virginia. She is the author of *The Fruits of Their Labor: Atlantic Coast Farmworkers and the Making of Migrant Poverty, 1870–1945* and a founding member of the Tidewater Labor Support Committee.

Christopher Holden is a housing and community development specialist with Northwest Regional Facilitators in Washington State. His work supports local organizations developing affordable housing in the rural Northwest, with a focus on farmworker housing. Until July 2001 Christopher was a research associate with the Housing Assistance Council in Washington, D.C., and project manager for a national survey of farmworker housing conditions.

Joy Danielle Kusserow is the Australian representative for international recruiter with International Medical Corps based in Los Angeles, California. She is a former intern with Student Action with Farmworkers. Joy is a native of Australia and is interested in the effects of migration on health. She plans to study social work in 2002.

Sister Evelyn Mattern is on the staff of the North Carolina Council of Churches, where she works on issues of religious unity and social justice. She is the author of *Blessed Are You: The Beatitudes and Our Survival* and *Why Not Become Fire: Encounters with Women Mystics.*

Alejandra Okie Holt is the director of community education and a New Voices fellow at the Latino Community Credit Union in Durham, North Carolina. She is the cofounder of the SAF-North Carolina State University Migrant Scholarship Fund, former SAF program director, and a 1994 SAF intern.

Paul Ortiz is an assistant professor of community studies at the University of California-Santa Cruz. He is the former research coordinator for the Behind the Veil: Documenting the Jim Crow South Project at the Center for Documentary Studies. He is a recent member of the Farmworkers' Project, Institute for Southern Studies, and Triangle Friends of the United Farm Workers.

Greg Schell is an attorney with the Migrant Farmworker Justice Project in Florida, where he has advocated for farmworker rights for more than twenty years.

Charles D. Thompson, Jr., is the education director of the Center for Documentary Studies and an adjunct assistant professor of cultural anthropology and religion at Duke University. He is a member of the SAF advisory board and the author of *Maya Identities and the Violence of Place: Borders Bleed.*

Melinda F. Wiggins is the executive director of Student Action with Farmworkers. She is the former SAF program director and a 1993 SAF intern. She is a member of the Z. Smith Reynolds Foundation Advisory Panel and a 1999–2001 fellow in the William C. Friday Wildacres Initiative Program. Melinda is a native of the Mississippi Delta.

Al Wright is a consultant to the National Association of State Directors of Migrant Education. For eighteen years, he worked in the Louisiana Migrant Education Program and was involved in numerous interstate projects. He also edited *MEMO*, a nationally distributed newsmagazine covering the Migrant Education Program, for thirteen years.

Index